Praise for *Rivington Was Ours*

"Brendan Jay Sullivan is a writer's writer. Yes, he's that good."

— Gary Shteyngart, author of *Super Sad True Love Story*

"Sullivan delivers a delectable romp through Stefani Germanotta's early days—and offers a unique window into the process by which she became Lady Gaga."

— Zack O'Malley Greenburg, author of
Empire State of Mind: How Jay-Z Went from Street Corner to Corner Office

"I've long said New York City's greatest asset is its people, and Brendan Jay Sullivan is awesome proof. A great writer, an incredible dresser, and a proud slave to rock and roll, the man is firing on all cylinders like a motherf*cker."

— Dave Hill, comedian, contributor to *This American Life*

"Brendan Sullivan gives his love letter to the Lower East Side, where a big piece of my heart will always live, along with all of our friends and foes. This book perfectly sums up that last cusp of cool the LES had."

— Jake Bernstein, Bond Music Group

"Through charm and wit and sheer force of will, Brendan Jay Sullivan has insinuated himself into New York ᵢ ᵢₕtlife, and through his talent with words, he has brought ᵧ ₐₗₒₙ ₛ his plus-one."

Garden, writer for *The Onion*

"Richly detaile᷄   knew Lady Gaga's lower-Manhaᵢ   ᵢₑ 2000s needed a *Bright Lights, Big City*ᵢ

— Steve Knoppᵢ   ᵢtite for Self-Destruction: The Spectacular Crash of
the Record Industry in the Digital Age

"Brendan is an amazing talent, a gifted writer, and a wonderful spirit."

— Rob Principe, cofounder of Scratch DJ Academy

RIVINGTON
WAS OURS

LADY GAGA,
THE LOWER
EAST SIDE, AND
THE PRIME OF
OUR LIVES

BRENDAN JAY
SULLIVAN

*it***books**

HarperCollins books may be purchased for educational, business, or sales promotional use. For information please e-mail the Special Markets Department at SPsales@harpercollins.com.

FIRST EDITION

Designed by Paula Russell Szafranski

Library of Congress Cataloging-in-Publication Data

Sullivan, Brendan Jay.

　Rivington was ours : Lady Gaga, the Lower East Side, and the prime of our lives / Brendan Jay Sullivan. — First edition.

　　p. cm.

　ISBN 978-0-06-212558-3 (pbk.) — ISBN 978-0-06-212559-0 (ebook)
1. Lady Gaga. 2. Singers—United States—Biography. I. Title. II. Title: Lady Gaga, the Lower East Side, and the prime of our lives.

　ML420.L185.S85 2013

　782.42164092—dc23　　[B]　　　2013012598

13 14 15 16 17　OV/RRD　10 9 8 7 6 5 4 3 2 1

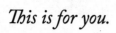

This is for you.

CAST OF CHARACTERS

Vh1 DJ, narrator, struggling writer.

Nikki Lingerie designer, part-time cocktail waitress at Stanton Social, Goddess, narrator's girlfriend.

Guy Former counter boy at latenight taco stand. Manager of a bar called St. Jerome's.

Gaga Singer, go-go dancer, girlfriend of Guy.

Conrad Former door guy, barstool poet, bartender at St. J's.

Jackie Daniels Go-go dancer at St. J's, Conrad's girlfriend.

Lady Starlight Performance artist, record collector, downtown big sister.

Dino Former guitarist for dozens of bands. Great guy, too many drugs.

St. Michael Former bassist, sober for fifteen years, barback at Pianos.

Joe Germanotta
Cynthia Germanotta
Natali Germanotta
Gaga's father, mother, and sister.

Leah Landon
Troy Carter
Rob Fusari
Pro Tools (more on that later)

NEW YORK

I can't explain all the feelings that you're making me feel

The upstairs lounge at Stanton Social looked like the inside of a silk lantern, everyone buzzing around in the dim light. They packed the upstairs banquettes and swarmed the bar with their graceless wealth. When Nikki came out in her little cocktail dress and apron, I couldn't help thinking of those myths where a goddess came down to earth in disguise. She never washed her thin black skirt. It hugged the contours of her thighs and glowed against her skin in the candlelight. She moved around the room, giving customers checks to sign with pens stolen from banks and restaurants.

They wanted drinks, they wanted to have a look at the bill, they wanted to have a little bit more of her in their lives.

I watched from the door.

She came up to the bar to pick up a drink order, double-checking her notepad. That's when I saw her laugh. One of the off-duty waiters sat on the end seat, drinking from a clandestine water glass filled with cheap champagne and laughing at an inside joke. I loved the people who worked here as much as she did.

The holiday crowd around her had skirted the coat check and

maneuvered around the room trailing scarves and undone winter jackets, their warm hats stuffed in puffed pockets. Nikki stood among them, stark as a nude in a museum. All legs and limbs, smooth skin that shimmered from the toe of her shoes to the hem of her skirt. Her scoop-necked top plunged below her collarbones, the contours of her shoulder blades as stark and visible in the candlelight as a pair of hidden angel wings. Her long blond hair tickled her bare shoulders.

When I got caught spying, she narrowed her gaze at me, piercing through the impossible gauntlet of the dancing crowd. I gave it right back. A standoff ensued. Then she blew me a kiss and took her tray on to the next adventure.

Tomorrow we would do and say all the things we didn't have time to do and say all week. Even sleep. We would have a date for lunch, a date for dinner, a date for dessert. Just the two of us. During the week we had no time. During the week bringing a coffee to the one who got the least sleep meant *I love you*. A work visit meant *I want to spend the rest of my life with you*. Waiting up all night to see the one who got out of work latest meant *I couldn't wait until tomorrow*. But tomorrow we wouldn't have to wait until tomorrow.

I knew from the lush crowd that she wouldn't finish for another few hours. I decided to head home.

Alone we were overworked and hopeless, delusional maybe. Over-extended for sure. There was never enough time, never enough coffee, never enough interest to justify the hours of our lives that passed through our fingers. But together we were the two luckiest people in New York City.

BEFORE I MADE IT OUT the door I got a text from her: "Did you go home?"

I couldn't keep my eyes open at the end of a double shift uptown. I came down on the highway, yawning into my cycle helmet and fogging up the glass on the chill winter night. I'd hoped I could sit around for a few and then give Nikki a ride home to her apartment, to steal an extra hour with her. I had worked since morning behind the gorgeous raw marble bar in the Museum of Modern Art. There were bartenders who spent all day behind the stick talking about varietals and classic cocktails and then went out after work to talk to other bartenders about mind-blowing garnishes, and I thought, there's nothing wrong with that. It was just not what I did.

"What do you do?" was that awful question people asked at parties. Difficult question if you didn't have a pie chart handy. I slept four to six hours a night, woke up and wrote stories that no one else would ever read, then I read them over. For my bread and butter I bartended in the most beautiful museum on earth and on my night off I DJ'd parties whenever I could.

On our first date I was so nervous that I blurted out, "So, Nikki, tell me, what are your hopes and dreams?" I had hoped to disqualify her, to hear she was boring or stupid or in graduate school. I had hoped to find just one reason that I could quit staring at her, to stop imagining how much of my life I'd change just to make room for more of her in my world.

She told me she was waiting tables ever since she quit designing lingerie for a bigger company. Now she wanted to start her own lingerie company with a partner who'd worked for Victoria's Secret. They would launch in February.

When she turned the question on me, I answered truthfully about my secret writings. Afterward we looked into each other's eyes like two lost sailors who first sighted land.

Outside the restaurant I got a text from her again: "??"

It would be hours before she could meet me. I plugged in the words to tell her I'd gone home. Then I imagined her there all alone with the noise and the people and their self-congratulatory drunkenness.

If she could only know what time she'd finish I would come right back for her. But at this time of night that might take an hour. She, as equally exhausted, might pass out if I didn't first. I decided to wait for her around the corner: "Let me know when you're off. I'll be at St. J's."

THE LOWER EAST SIDE BEGINS just south of where the numbered streets and avenues end. It's was where Manhattan stops making sense. Down Stanton Street, I hung a right at the next corner past Pianos, the keyboard store turned playhouse turned music venue. There would be no bands tonight because Saturday nights were just for dancing. A line of scenesters waited by the door doing their own little involuntary pre-dance—shivering and rubbing their hands together to fight off the chill. Lined neatly behind a retractable nylon belt on a metal stanchion pole, they looked like a bunch of people in line at the bank, itching to make their deposit into the night.

It was a left after that, down the tenement streets and past a few other venues where a lone guitar player shined out of the stage lights in the center of a chatty crowd. The people inside were always as vibrant and drunk as the herds outside. The neighborhood, much to the chagrin of the locals, had given itself to nightlife slowly over the past few years. The voices outside echoed up through the thin windows of the apartments directly above. Older residents had moved here when crime was up and the rent was down. Their new neighbors paid twice and even three times as much as they did in rent just for the privilege of living downtown. If the older residents—fed up and getting older—wanted to move, they wouldn't find an apartment that cheap without traveling an hour and a half north into the Bronx. I passed a few pricey lounges and hotel lobby bars where they served all the same kinds of drinks and beers, only the music was half as good and the prices were doubled. Two more blocks from there.

St. Jerome's was the bare-bones minimum of a bar and that's why I loved it so much. Loud music greeted you at the door, light from a tattered disco ball showed you to your table at the chummy, half-moon leather banquettes, their seats always torn and taped like the backseat of an old muscle-car. The array of drinks and bottled beers behind the bar (no taps) comprised the entire menu. Their idea of a classic cocktail was a bottle of Budweiser garnished with a shot of Jameson.

The only other light came from the flickering candles on the tables and a red spotlight beaming off a mirror at a low platform in the corner where a performance artist named Lady Starlight go-go danced to the hard-rock music in a leather bikini. The bar had a dozen black leather stools with metal pipe legs like the kind you see next to guitar amps on stage.

That's where I ran into someone we'll call Guy.

"VH1!" he shouted when I walked in the room that night.

If you stuck around here long enough, you ended up with a nickname. Thing was, you didn't get to pick your nickname. I was known for telling long stories and for knowing a little bit too much about bands in the scene, so I was named "VH1" after a show on the cable channel VH1 called *Storytellers*. When I first met Guy, he had long, ratty hair, teased out in an obscene heavy-metal style. Baby powdered and hair-sprayed. Everyone always asked him if it were a wig.

When I met Guy he was a humble guy in a bandana, serving tacos at a latenight storefront called San Loco up the street. He'd played drums in a band called the Fame. Now he worked at St. J's.

He had small eyes, perpetually on the verge of the kind of squint you see on drummers when they pull off a *killer* solo. His lips jutted out in the same way. He had a pair of mismatched mutton-chop sideburns and when customers made their drink orders he always listened with his mouth hanging open like a third ear. The hair, always teased out and sprayed in different directions—baby powder dusting the shoulders of his black T-shirts—managed to hide the fact that underneath it all he was a very fragile person with very delicate features.

At first glance you might find an emptiness to him, but in music, especially great music, emptiness isn't expressed as silence. It comes through in reverb.

Guy moved to New York City to become a rock star. He was a drummer. Or he had drums. He still played in bands but had an inherent disdain for any music that wasn't authentic, original hair metal. I didn't understand Guy. But I don't think there is that much about him to get.

He also had a five-year running crush on Nikki. I'd only known Nikki for about six months, but she wasn't into him.

Rumor was that Guy had met quite the catch. Someone new. I had seen her around the neighborhood before and I hadn't seen them together until this night. They made a cute couple, the little brunette girl, only twenty years old. When I walked into the bar I saw her with him.

Only he wouldn't let her speak to me.

"Where's Nikki?" he scoffed, as if I'd forgotten something he ordered.

"She's at Stanton Social. She'll be by."

"Who's Nikki?" The girl looked at him. She had an open curiosity of his world, always trying to piece together the names and faces from his stories.

His smile turned guilty, so he changed the subject. "I heard you're writing a book."

"I've written two." I looked down, knowing that failing twice isn't the same as success. "Haven't sold them yet."

"Two, really?" Guy said. "I think I've read maybe ten books in my life." He walked away. Guy took great care in putting me in my place in front of this new girlfriend. And she wasn't interested in being put in her place.

When he went out for a smoke she marched right up to me. "You're the DJ, right? I saw you spin at my friend's birthday party." Of all the things I did, DJ'ing I failed at the least. It made me smile. I looked up at the young girl. Behind her dark bangs she had the delicacy and eye makeup of the tiniest egg in a set of Russian dolls.

"Yep and you, uhm . . ." Oh, geez. Even I can't avoid another "What do you do?" so I said, "Where do you work?"

"Oh, I don't work anywhere. I'm a singer."

"What's the name of your band?"

"It's not really a band anymore . . ."

"Then send me your record. I like playing friends' music."

She started to answer and then let out a sheepish laugh. Her eyes fluttered back down to earth, heavy with makeup and impossibly thick lashes. She looked up, biting the corner of her lower lip. "I don't . . . uhm . . . I don't have a demo or anything. Not yet."

"Oh." I felt for the girl, actually. I'm the writer with too much to show for it. None of it good enough to share. "Well, when you get some shows together maybe you could book an after-party with me. Let me know, I'll give you my number."

I realized then that Guy never actually introduced us. I didn't even know her name. "How do you want me to put you in my phone?"

"Gaga." Her eyes sparkled like two disco balls. "Put me in your phone as Gaga."

"Gaga?"

"Gaga."

"Like Freddie Mercury?"

"Yes! Finally someone gets it."

"All we hear is radio Ga Ga . . ." I sang a bit of the Queen song. She came in on my harmonies.

She shrugged her shoulders when she smiled in a very adorable, surrendering way. "And I'll save you as—" Her screen lit up. So did her eyes. "I'm sorry. This is really important." She ran out the door to take a call.

I sent her a text: "Save my number and maybe we can work together. Good luck. —VH1."

WHEN GAGA RAN THROUGH THE door outside she found Guy scheming on a girl by the door. Nikki. Gaga shook her head and walked away as he cleared his throat and tried to wipe the smile off his delicate face. She pressed the phone hard to her ear.

"Hey!" Guy yelled after her, changing the subject. "Who's calling you this late?"

"Hang on one sec," she said as she shouldered the phone, enjoying the cat-and-mouse routine. She scowled right up at him. "It's my *producer* and I need to—" Just then her phone had another message from another man chiming in a little too late on a Saturday night. "Oh! And I got a text from *VH1*."

She turned her back to him and went back to her phone call.

I knew none of this yet. But seconds later the door of St. Jerome's burst open. Guy, now incensed, glared over at me. I couldn't tell if this were supposed to be a joke. Then again, it's hard to tell with this one. "Stop texting my *fucking girlfriend!*" he said with that faux machismo that just didn't work downtown. Too bridge-and-tunnel.

And that's when Nikki walked in the door, her bags heavy with her unwashed cocktail dress and work shoes. She was the object of all of his scheming, and that new girl caught them when she ran out to take her phone call. Only the Goddess who blew me a kiss just an hour before had disappeared. Nikki had turned cold.

"Are you finished here?" she said. "Because I'm going home." Guy hopped back behind the bar. He didn't want to miss this.

"Sure. Yeah. Work alright tonight? Looked busy."

"Fine. But I'm leaving now."

Guy intervened. "Nikki. You wanna stay for a Heineken? It's on me."

"No. I'm leaving."

"Okay. Let's go," I said. I stood up.

"Oh, now you're coming with me?"

"I've been waiting for you this whole time!" Tomorrow. We need to have tomorrow. Our entire relationship is Sundays. "Sunday Funday awaits."

When we stood up to leave I felt a tug at my sleeve. I turned around and saw the little singer again. "Guess what? Guess what?" Gaga bounced when she spoke, her hair jostling on top of those heavy lashes. "That was my producer! We're going to record! I'll make you a copy!"

Nikki dropped her purse back on the bar. "You know what?" She turned to Guy. "I'll take that beer. Stella." Now I'm on a double date with my girlfriend on a Saturday night. I take what I can get.

Guy delivered that beer to Nikki and then became distracted by a small coterie of drunk girls over by the corner. I started talking to Nikki again, the time between us blossoming inside of me like a winter flower. I kept an eye out for that underage girl, now all alone as I heard about Nikki's day and Guy laughed at the coterie's stories. Gaga couldn't be more than twenty. I remembered being her age and all I wanted was everything. From the corner of my eye I saw Guy in deep, charismatic laughter with the drunk girls. He had a certain charm to him.

The underage girl looked a little lost. Even her own boyfriend didn't have time for her. Her with the big news of the night. My heart went out to her and I asked if she'd like a drink.

She smiled. "Bud Light?"

"What's that, 'Bugbite'?" Guy interrupted every time we started talking. This time to accuse her of slurred speech. "Maybe you've had enough to drink tonight, there, Bugbite."

Funny. I hadn't noticed her acting drunk before. And she hadn't taken a drink since I got there.

Just then Nikki posted the bottle on her beer mat, white suds ringing the empty bottom. "Okay. Now I'm ready to go now."

"Are you leaving?" The underage girl smiled at Nikki and then turned to me. "I'll text you when I have some more info on the record."

WE RODE HOME IN A silence known only to boyfriends and those in solitary confinement. The silence was punishment for a crime I'd readily confess to, just to end it. Whether guilty or not.

"Look." I put her bags on the bed and sat down on the couch when we got to her apartment on East Twenty-First. Francois, her chubby pug, nuzzled up against my leg with his asthmatic sweetness. Frank always took my side. "He's just causing drama. And yes—I got that girl's number. But she's a singer and—ow!" Something sharp hit me in the chest. I looked down and saw a copper set of house keys.

The dog got up on all fours, growling.

"From now on you have a set of keys."

"Okay." This was good news. Right? That hurt a lot.

"I mean, what if I lost mine and I couldn't feed the dog? Or what if something happened to me?"

"That's fine." This should have been a moment. "Is this mutual? I can get you a set of my keys, but they all say 'Do Not Duplicate' so . . . so I might be looking at prison time if we pull this off. But I'll do it. For you."

She walked over and sat with me. "Don't leave me alone with him anymore." She poked my chest right where the keys hit.

"Oh, Guy? He's harmless. He's so protective of that girl." Frank looked up at me with his big brown marble eyes.

"When that girl went out to answer the phone she caught him hitting on me outside. He got all embarrassed and I thought he'd stop, but then apparently you got her number? You know when he shut the door after yelling at you? You know what he did? He leaned over while his girlfriend was on the phone and goes, 'Can you believe that? Your boyfriend is hitting on my girlfriend in there and she gave him her number right in front of us. You know what we should do? We should teach them a lesson right now, don't say a word to them. Let's go back to my place, just you and me. That'll show 'em.'"

You can't stop what you can't end

I'd like to say that was the only time he tried anything like that, but I also like to tell the truth.

GUY HAD CALLED ME JUST days before to come DJ his all-night, all-hard-rock New Years Eve party at St. Jerome's. Ten P.M. until a brutal, eyestrain-inducing eight A.M. St. Jerome's had a small DJ booth on a two-foot-tall stage in the blacked-out window by the door. A black velvet curtain hung from the waist-high mixing table to the platform. I'd been told to expect another DJ just before midnight, who would then take over. He arrived in a haze. His body and eyes rippled like a reflection of himself in a shallow puddle. He rubbed his temples as he crammed his swaying frame into the DJ booth with me. He squinted, wincing every time the disco ball shined in his nodding, bloodshot eyes. Originally he had canceled so he could go to an early party, but now he wanted to do at least a few hours. Namely, the best hours from midnight on. And now here he was.

I could tell he'd made it to that early party.

His big head bobbed around as if his feet were glued to the dashboard of a Chevy Nova. He faced the window with his back to the crowd. "I think I did the mix wrong."

I pulled my headphones off. "You haven't started yet."

"Can you take oxycodone and Ritalin together?"

"I really wouldn't." Drugs, you see, I did not do. Drugs were for losers and I was on my way to being a big famous novelist. I did, however, share a journalist's idle curiosity for the drug world. I thought it would have been really cool and really, like, *writerly* to have a big drug habit or some kind of encyclopedic, functional addiction. Especially considering my sleep habits and work schedule. All the really hardcore drug addicts I knew had big holes in their lives, chasms they shoveled pills and powders into like gravel into a pothole. Drugs didn't work on me like that.

Even then I wouldn't recommend mixing cancer surgery painkillers with children's attention deficit meds.

"How much would you give me just to do the whole night?" the DJ said. "Like I'll do an hour and we can split it." This former reporter noted that the drug user maintained a concern for money, which could be turned into more drugs.

"You want fifty percent of the money for doing ten percent of the night."

"No, I—" He looked as though he needed to pause and contemplate what God might be thinking right now. "I gotta go. Can you just do it?"

He grabbed his records and left a bag of white powder on the empty, spinning turntable. With five seconds' warning I grabbed the New York Dolls' "Personality Crisis" and threw the track on. I matched it with "Teenage Depression," Eddie Cochran's "C'mon Everybody," and, for the kids, "Summer of '69." The whole room was air guitars and sing-alongs and our collective triumph over the broken promises of 2006. We were over it, we were moving on. But tonight we were having breakup sex with the year.

Just then one of the dancers came behind the short velvet curtain between the turntables and the top of the stage. She nudged my calf. "Did he leave the bag?" I looked down and she rubbed her nose to illustrate. I handed her the bag.

At midnight Guy cut the music from behind the bar and called out, "Ten! . . . Nine! . . . Eight! . . ." I threw on Andrew W.K.'s "I Love NYC."

We were dancing and singing along, hugging strangers. Nikki came to the booth for a kiss. We were on a first date with the New Year, nervous and excited. Get ready for us, 2007!

Throughout the night I found that people on the way out to smoke delighted in powdering their nose at my feet. Bent over with the black velvet curtain draped over their necks and shoulders, they looked like old-timey camera operators.

At about 7:45 A.M., when none of us could fit another Jameson shot in our livers, Guy turned up the lights. I told Nikki I could meet her at her house. She decided to stay. While I cleaned up my records and needles and equipment, a go-go dancer we called Jackie Daniels came over to the DJ platform and stuck her head in the curtain. I really liked Jackie's fun-loving spirit, but after ten hours in the booth I really wanted to get home. Instead of feeling like a rock star at that moment after a great night, I felt more like a roadie. I had to coil up wires and clean up while everyone around me partied. "Hey," she said.

"I don't have any more."

"I wasn't coming in here for that. I just wanted to see that you're okay."

I crouched down to her level as she peered through the curtain beneath the turntables. "I'm fine. Very tired though."

"Everyone did a lot of drugs tonight and I just want to make sure you're okay."

"Yes. Thanks, I—" I then realized how wasted she was.

"What?"

Her eyes had emptied. Something kept her body awake but not her mind. "Hang on, hang on, hang on."

"Are *you* okay?"

"Am I okay?"

"Look. It's time to go home. I gotta pack up."

I stood up and put my records away.

WHAT I DIDN'T KNOW WAS that when Jackie came to check on me in the DJ booth that night, Guy leaned over the bar toward Nikki and pointed at the booth as the sequined bloomers on the hindquarters of a go-go dancer hung out the back of the curtain. At that moment, my head ducked beneath and did not resurface for minutes.

"Look at that." Guy shook his head at Nikki and then walked away to finish cleaning. "You gotta keep an eye on your man."

Coming out of my cage and now I'm doing just fine

Despite his best efforts, Guy and I became friends. My weeks had a new rhythm to them. Although I had a set of keys to Nikki's house, I would come downtown after work and wait for her somewhere in the Lower East Side. I even started to pick up regular Friday nights at St. J's. And when I didn't I came down anyway and loved getting lost in conversation with that Gaga girl, who turned out to be much brighter than I'd first assumed. With everyone else she acted a bit silly and young, like a girl in town from Long Island, but the more I knew her the more I realized she had an innate social intelligence that made her approachable to everyone from the fawning door guys to the idiot party kids I loved. Gaga's genius was in her ability to mirror those around her, like the disco ball glass she glued to her outfits. If you thought she was a bit dumb, it was probably because she thought you were not that bright and didn't try to say anything over your head. One night she came in with some of her friends from college. I was surprised to find out she had dropped out of NYU, because she used to act like she wasn't smart enough to get in. The only friends I'd made in college were Shakespeare, Dante, hooks, Joyce,

Proust, Freud, Lacan, Picasso, Tzara, and Warhol. Gaga wanted to talk about them all as if they were old buddies from the dormitory. Some days Nikki would get out of work and find Gaga and I up to our ankles in theory.

She was like the little sister I never had. Eager to play, happy to listen. Nikki was almost ten years older than her and the two of them never got on easy with each other. But for those lonesome hours before Nikki got out of work, I always had a friend downtown.

BY THAT TIME I WAS three years into my residency at Beauty Bar on Fourteenth Street. It was a marvelous and welcoming place in the same location as the old Thomas Beauty Salon—old-lady hairdryer chairs as banquettes and two red leather barber chairs right in the front window. During the afternoon you could listen to great music and get a martini and a manicure for ten dollars. When I first moved to New York City I DJ'd every joke club that would hire me. The dance clubs said I was too rock 'n' roll and the rock 'n' roll clubs (each of them territorial and disappearing every day) said I played too much disco. I just wanted to make the girls dance. Everywhere I called would say, "Where do you spin?" I knew that the best DJs in the city—the serious record collectors who were generous with their libraries—all played at Beauty Bar. And I wanted to be one of them. Mike Stewart, the owner, gave me that shot and I'll never forget it. He was patient with me when I first started out, always kind to the friends of mine who showed up. And he even didn't mind when I didn't have enough records to do a whole set and had to play songs twice.

No matter what kind of drama went on in the LES, I still always had a home on Fourteenth Street where I could sit and wait for an adventure to find me any night of the week.

But tonight would be our best.

Before a party, you get to a moment where you've texted everyone in your phone, worked and reworked your guest list, made all of the arrangements with the bar, made the set times for the DJs. The day of your party, you spend your time running around, getting things together, barely eating. If you're not answering emails, you are staring at the screen, willing it to just refresh one more goddamn time.

There comes a point where you cannot add anything to the flyer or call a single other person. That night I was extra nervous because of the deal I cut with the people downtown at Motor City, just below Rivington Street. I said they only had to pay if I broke the all-time ring at the cash register.

On the way to the party I crept through the squeaky door of Beauty Bar on Fourteenth Street to pick up a few records I had left there. One of the perks of being a resident DJ there was I could keep a crate of records in the booth. The bartender smiled at me as I came through the door. "Is it true?" she asked.

"Is what true?"

"Is it true you are throwing the Killers' after-party at Motor City?"

"Yes."

"How on earth did you get them?"

"They're really excited! Promised the party wouldn't be a big deal."

SECOND AVENUE BEARS DOWN ON the East Village with a running start for 128 numbered blocks, counting down from East Harlem until it T-bones Houston Street. Even Second Avenue doesn't want to go to the Lower East Side. At Fourteenth Street it begins a lifeless stretch of busy streets and half-empty cafés. I weaved through the side streets hoping that if I walked faster and zigzagged I would accomplish something. Then I could shake this feeling.

For backup tonight I had asked Jackie Daniels and Conrad, the go-go dancer and door guy from New Years, to team up with me. We had our eyes on doing a weekly party together. They were dating and had an apartment around the corner on Clinton Street inside of what used to be the lobby of an old Yiddish playhouse.

I didn't tell them about the gamble I'd made with the management.

We walked through the end of the numbered streets in the East Village to Houston Street. Even at night a line formed at Katz's Deli on the corner of Ludlow. This was the deli made famous by an eighties movie about fake orgasms and why men and women cannot be platonic friends. As I walked I peeked in on the Saturday night scene at Dark Room and tried to see whom we might recognize in the windows of Max Fish and Pink Pony. Many of the nicer shops and boutiques had lowered their graffitied shutters, their ulcerous mail slots rusting away, preserving the abandoned, lawless feel of the neighborhood. At the next block I peeked over at Stanton Social and hoped to catch a glimpse of Nikki inside. I crossed the street again at Pianos and everybody outside asked, "Are the Killers really coming to your party?"

Yes. We are really throwing the Killers' after-party as soon as they finish up at Madison Square Garden. No. We have no idea if they are coming.

I WALKED IN THE DOOR of Motor City, a Detroit-themed bar with muscle-car art on the walls and murals to the great American automakers. The bartender's bottle opener dangled from the ceiling on a black air-compressor coil. Just above the center of the room a disco ball hung still and malcontent, a bright light beaming off its stationary mirrors. The sphere budged with every gust of wind that came through the door when someone walked in. The bright, unmoving lights that were spread all over the room looked back at you as you entered, unimpressed: *What? What are you looking at?*

Nikki had to wait tables at Stanton Social and Gaga and Guy had tickets to the Killers. I wished Gaga were here just to have someone to talk to. In the early hours before a party gets going there's nothing to do except drink and try not to play all your best songs.

ALL ALONG LUDLOW STREET, A strange breed of haberdashers preyed on the drunk. Some guys sold flowers or drugs or empanadas. This one cute-in-a-dad-sorta-way Indian guy walked every night from Beauty Bar to Canal selling light-up crap like sunglasses and glow sticks. He always tried to entice young girls and then sell the toys to whatever boys they were with.

Conrad walked out. "When's Nikki coming?"

"She's pissed," I finally admitted. "She hates what we're doing."

"What?" Conrad said.

"I don't pretend to understand it. She just finds it annoying."

"I don't see how what she's doing is so virtuous. We're making do and having fun and throwing a party. She's fucking waiting tables. It's a job."

Another haberdasher made his way over. "Flowers for your sweetheart? Flowers for your sweetheart?"

Jackie took over in the DJ booth. I said, "If the Killers get here, just get them whatever they need. I've gotta take care of something."

A minute later I walked into the upstairs lounge of Stanton Social, where I saw her in full Saturday-night mode. The host and the other waitresses saw me with a flower and a three-piece suit and smiled. I walked up to her at the computer terminal, but she ignored me, thinking me a customer who wanted to get the check or ask about my tab. I waited patiently.

When she turned around I presented her with the single declawed rose.

"Tomorrow," I said. "I'll make it up to you tomorrow."

She shook her head and grabbed the flower, pressing it to her nose. "You'd better, mister."

WHEN I GOT BACK TO Motor City no one asked me when the Killers were coming. They had arrived. They blended in with the crowd in their jeans and flannel. They all had a week's growth of beard on their faces and if you noticed them at all they would just look back at you, shining like the malcontent disco ball: *What? What are you looking at?*

That's when Guy showed up. He had a bright smile on his face as he told everyone about the show. And next to him stood Gaga, the radiant little underage girl. The singer with no songs but who had a record deal with Island Def Jam.

She had a big smile on her face too. There's something about dressing up and getting excited and waiting to get picked up and waiting for the show to start and waiting to go out after that somehow becomes more exciting than just seeing a band play in a hockey rink. The excitement of the date—even before it happens—matters as much as whatever happens. Same thing here. Tonight was just another night of denim and rock 'n' roll in this glorious downtown shithole. Only it wasn't.

I didn't say anything then, but if Gaga were supposedly signed to the same record label as the Killers, shouldn't she have gotten backstage passes or something? Either she had a low position on the totem pole or she'd gotten dropped and didn't tell us. Turned out to be the latter.

But you wouldn't know it from her enthusiasm.

"Hey, *rock star*," she said when I walked back to the booth.

"Hey, gorgeous. How was the show?"

Her eyes grew starry like a pair of comets. *"Amazing."* She said it loud enough so Guy could hear before pulling me closer. The Killers had debuted just a few years earlier with a nerdy, dressed-up, indie rock attitude. Now they wanted more. The show was a success, stunning with their new stadium sound and arena vocals. She detailed every bit of the stagecraft as if she were already planning on topping them. Her eyes were glowing like bright factory windows, her mind inside chugging along, excited by the noise of production. I could see she was already full of ideas for her own show at Madison Square Garden. "How did you get them here in the flesh?"

"I'll tell you the story if you promise you'll believe me."

"Of course." We both glanced over at Guy, who had already disappeared into a welcoming nest of cigarettes, other women, and hair-care enthusiasts.

"When I was working for NASA my landing capsule was lost at sea. I eventually came to a remote island and waited for rescue." I watched her eyes as they patiently awaited my performance. "And one day I was working on a mixed-media found-object collage that would spell 'help' in all the languages I knew. And so I'm walking around this island and I pick up this vintage Jim Beam decanter, right? Only it feels like there's something inside and I could really use a drink right about then so I pop open the bottle and guess what pops out?"

"A young blonde genie? Is *that* how a nerd like you landed a girl like Nikki?"

"Did I already tell you this story?"

"No. But does it end with you accidentally telling the genie that you wish you could get the Killers to come to your party?"

"It was one of my three wishes too."

"Speaking of, where's Nikki? I really liked her."

"To tell you the truth: Nikki's pissed."

"Whatever. Now I can have you all to myself! That girl can be pissed and we can party with the Killers!"

* * *

GAGA DIDN'T STAY IN THE booth long. When she went back to Guy I looked out on the crowd, a pulsating mass of leather and denim. Their pint glasses were held aloft as they screamed along.

I texted Nikki. "Looking good in here! You gotta come by."

And she responded, "Going home after."

So I stood there pretending not to be terribly sad.

In the prime of your life you can only be divided by yourself and one. She's the *one*. Older people have jobs and kids and mortgages, things that weigh on them. But we only have each other and I know that she's the one because *I* am the *one* laying all this hurt on myself. She tears me apart and I wish she'd do it more because I feel so whole when we come back together. I'm only on the other side of Rivington Street and I miss her.

I had created something and she would never see it. I could parlay this into a ticket out of bartending. I could throw parties, I could book bands. I could write novels all day long, she could take care of her lingerie business. The difference being that we could build something. Waitressing and bartending are maintenance jobs. But what I do now is different. We could do this! Right?

Right . . .

Why am I so depressed in the middle of this party?

Everyone in the room gravitated towards the jostling corner where the Killers sat. They wanted to overhear them saying something cool or daft or to blaspheme the saintly court of rock 'n' roll, or to stay on hand in case any of them asked who was the band who sang one song or another.

I wanted to go home.

And then I heard a voice: *Oh pretty boy, can't you give me nothing but surrender?* The voice was Patti Smith, crackling around on the turntable.

I stepped on one of those milk crates they use as busing tubs and looked out on the gorgeous room, with all the party kids dancing in the glimmer of the malcontent disco ball.

Life is full of pain, I heard. *And I fill my nose with snow. And go Rimbaud, go Rimbaud, go Johnny go.*

I should toss in a rock 'n' roll killer like "Personality Crisis" by the New York Dolls or "The Clapping Song" by Shirley Ellis. But this was my party and I wanted to hear Springsteen's "Thunder Road." The chill harmonica shimmered through a drumless beat. The crowd stirred. You could hear jokes and phone numbers exchanged, drink orders hollered. The malcontent disco ball didn't dance either. And then the mass began to sway as the piano fired up.

Gaga watched the hair perk up on the Killers' necks and ran over to me. "Tell me you did this on purpose!"

"Of course, honey."

"Ah! Love it!" She joined me in the booth.

"You love Springsteen?"

"Love doesn't begin to describe it." We both looked over at her boyfriend as he laughed and backslapped his way around the room. She shook her head at Guy. "Can you believe he doesn't know any Springsteen? None. He heard the new Killers songs tonight and didn't catch a single Springsteen rip-off." She bounced around in the booth, marveling at the equipment and watching me maneuver the knobs and faders. "Love it, love it, love it! And you know the Killers do too!"

THE PARTY WENT STRONG RIGHT up until four. We pulled the shutters down and hid inside. People still ordered drinks and we all did shots with the bartenders. Jameson, Jameson, Jameson. I cleaned up my records and needles and headphones and whatever. At four-thirty the crowd became too much.

Francesca, one of the managing partners, handed me a thick wad of twenties.

"What'd we ring?"

She looked at me, kind of annoyed. "You got it."

"I got what?" Oh. These are not twenties.

"You got the all-time ring at Motor City."

I can't keep track of each fallen robin

The Chelsea Hotel stood in the middle of Twenty-Third Street, dressed up and a little out of place. At birth, it was the tallest building in New York City. Mark Twain stayed there, Dylan Thomas died there, Sid may or may not have killed Nancy there. Brendan Behan—my countryman—wrote some of his best work in his soundproof room. Patti Smith once loved Leonard Cohen to an earth-shattering degree there. When I first moved to New York, you could live there if the owner liked what you did as an artist. The walls were lined with art from the very talented who couldn't pay their rent. The building was ringed in wrought-iron balconies that looked like foundry type on the printing presses of a mysterious language. The basement had a guests-only bar that was never open and next door was a Miguel de Cervantes themed restaurant called Quixote's. To even stand in front of the place you were forced to inhale a monument to the power of the written word in verse.

Plus, it's gorgeous. I stood on the balcony of room 220, surrounded by friends on my twenty-fifth birthday, and basked at the unbelievable quiet of Twenty-Third Street.

I know the number because Conrad chipped it off the door and gave it to me as a birthday present. The ancient bathtub filled with bagged ice and canned beer and birthday-gift bottles of whiskey.

My little secret that night was one I shared only with Gaga. I felt exuberant, full of the New Year's Eve energy that promised a new age. That morning I had written the final scene in my third-time's-a-charm full-length manuscript *The Confessions of Mercutio*—a retelling of Shakespeare's *Romeo and Juliet*. To tackle the great work, I took Shakespeare's finest character and Romeo's best friend, a long-winded drunk with a knack for getting into situations, and gave him free reign of Verona.

ALL THE GUESTS LEFT AT seven or so in the morning. I found a bottle of champagne in the bathroom and opened it. I wanted to enjoy the Chelsea while I could. Nikki wanted to sleep. We filed into the two double beds, me cozy with the unwrapped plastic hotel cup of champagne, her curling up across the bedside table from me.

I looked up and saw her looking at me, appraising. I loved those little eyes of hers. "Our relationship is changing," I said. "And I just want you to know that I want it to. This is fun and all but . . ."

She smiled. But I would only later find out why. It took a week and she had to go out of town on business. I got hired to play at Luke & Leroy on the following Saturday night and came back to her apartment when she got out of work. We agreed to get pizza for lunch and just have a good weekend together. But I fell back asleep after she first got up.

And the next time I woke up I could see that she was crying.

I know I should stick up for myself but I really think it's better this way

The question remains: Is life just like high school or is high school just like life? Even here, at Rivington High. The bullies, the band geeks, the popular girls. Nowhere is that more obvious than inside the LES panopticon's observation of my breakup with Nikki.

The next day Gaga sat me down at St. Jerome's. "I heard," was all she said, her tiny, intricate hands coming out of her leather jacket, holding my arms, scared I might float away like a child's balloon at a county fair. I figured Guy would hear first and get the most excited, Nikki being single and all. Who knows who told him. Or how excited *they* were.

But when I looked into her big Russian-doll eyes I could tell she genuinely cared. "Have you talked to her?" Even though I saw her almost every night, this was the first time we talked about anything that wasn't at least in part theoretical.

"What is there to say?"

"Lots."

"She called yesterday."

"And?"

"And what? She left her dress from New Year's at my house. She wants me to drop it off at Stanton Social."

"Tell her if she wants the dress she can come and get it."

"I don't want to give her back the dress."

"She's not even your size."

I looked up at the girl. Her lame joke caught me off guard and I accidentally smiled. For about a second. "It's not the dress, it's her. She keeps saying she wants that and her phone charger. But I can't give them back. Why would she need an extra phone charger? Do you think she's with someone else?"

"Everybody needs an extra phone charger. When did you guys start having problems? April? So Nikki is twenty-nine and eight months?" Gaga looked nonjudgmentally into her Bud Light.

"Yeah. Wait. How did you guess that?"

"Has anyone ever told you about a Saturn return?"

"No."

"You can't fight it," Gaga said. "Twenty-nine-and-a-half years after you're born the planet Saturn returns and throws off your whole universe. It tears you away from everything and you can't fight it."

"But I just turned twenty-five. Does that mean I'm in for five years of torture?"

"Pretty much." Gaga had just turned twenty-one. And then I realized that the poor girl was going through the same thing with Guy. "You need to read *The Secret*." Around that time I remember a lot of people my age, very naïve girls mostly, who'd found the power within from this book. According to it you had to *visualize* your dreams. Gaga had *visualized* that one day she would play Madison Square Garden like the Killers. She wanted me to *visualize* getting back together with Nikki. Not to be crass, but *what the fuck do you think I'm doing all day and night?*

"I'm not reading *The Secret*."

"Roll your eyes all you want. But you have to have a vision for what you want. You have to picture it in your mind."

I flagged down Conrad and ordered a Wild Turkey neat.

"Can I ask you something? Do you want to get back together with Nikki?"

"Yeah."

"*Why?*"

"Wh—" I had no answer.

"Can you envision a time in the future where you are with Nikki and things are not like this?"

"Like what?"

"Are you one of those guys who will fuck some girl and then leave in the middle of the night? Or do you stay and cuddle?"

"How could you even ask me that?"

"If Nikki wants you in her life she's going to want you to stay and cuddle. Her—stay and be there for *her*. Don't always be running off to the next party or disappearing into work. Can you envision a time when it will be different?"

I looked over at Guy. "Are you talking about me or him?"

"I'm talking about all of you."

ON THE WAY INTO WORK on Wednesday I had already decided that everything would be okay. Can't be that bad, right? Intergalactic crises be damned. I still had a life to lead. Just had to work out some kinks. We were overwhelmed, Nikki and I. Under-rested. I didn't understand what was going on and there's a part of me that just wanted to let it be. That's mature, right? So I would try to do what Gaga said and envision a time when I didn't feel this way. I had already consoled myself with the fact that I would probably make out with someone else. Would it be someone I knew? Someone new? What a fantastic distraction! The train became a smorgasbord of possibilities. It worked for about fifteen seconds per day, seeing as how every street corner, train station, restaurant, and sidewalk in this city reminded me of Nikki.

On the ride to work my train burst through a cave at the foot of the Manhattan Bridge and glided over its gleaming arch into the morning sunshine. *Next stop on this train is Canal Street.* I checked my phone now that we'd got above ground, hoping to hear from Nikki. Nothing. *Remember that time you got caught in the rain on Canal Street and when you and Nikki went into a store to buy an umbrella you got her a ring instead? That's Canal Street. Next stop is Canal Street.*

I took a deep breath.

This would not happen overnight.

One thing did come to mind. When I finished my last manuscript I walked away from it. Let it marinate for six weeks and came back to it fresh. These things didn't come out perfect all at once. A little distance helped. A fresh look would tell me if I really wanted to put in the work to make it great. This part of our relationship was just a first draft. I would put *Mercutio* and Nikki aside for six weeks. I can do that, right?

Next stop is Fourteenth Street, Union Square. Transfer for L, N, R, 4, 5, and 6. It's also Nikki's stop. You could just get out and walk to her house from there. Stand clear of the doors. The doors shut and the train took me away from the station and into my uniform at the museum.

THE NEXT TIME I SAW Gaga the only thing I could say was that the city felt new to me again. Just as I once looked down at my checkbook and said, "This is my first full month living in this apartment," I now said, "I've made it a week alone and haven't suffered any organ failure." They put up a new exhibit at the museum and I walked into work every day surrounded by new art, new images, new ideas.

When I got paid that Friday I said, "I made it through a full week at work without crying in my uniform." I even went downtown after work so that people could have proof that I was still standing. In my vision I looked at my new world: In it I only ever worked for myself. I had carved out a nice little life for myself in the city and it was full of all the bands and whiskey and Chuck Berry records I'd always wanted.

It was in that time that Gaga went from being just a girl I knew to becoming someone I thought about when we weren't together. That has always been my standard of quality in books and movies and records and decent people. How much you think about them when you don't have to. She lent me strength and smiles when I didn't have any and she let me keep them for as long as I needed.

And at the end of the first month I kissed the first girl who laughed at something I said.

I'm killing it.

I'm doing this.

I'm going to ride this out.

I left working at my beloved museum for good. I needed a fresh start. I needed to work where I belonged. I was ready. I was optimistic.

ON THE WAY HOME FROM my last night of work I got a call from Nikki. "Fine."

"What's fine?"

"Fine I'll come get my stuff if you won't drop it off for me."

Coming and getting my stuff. A pointless and knife-twisting ritual, where you go and get things you don't really need from someone you don't really love. When you tell another person that they weren't worth half a bottle of moisturizer. Where you are ready to walk out of someone's life for good, but not without that novel you never finished reading and never would. Certainly not with the weight of their house keys.

I caught a glimpse of myself in a window and shook my head. For six weeks I'd prayed for Nikki to call or come over. Careful what you wish for. "Now's not a good time."

"Just let me come over."

"No."

"Why? Are you with someone?"

"No."

"I'm coming over."

"Don't." Don't come over until you can promise me that you're over it. Just find me again in six months when we can be together. Leave the dress. It smells like you.

"If I come ring your doorbell, are you seriously not going to let me in?"

"Yes." I took a stand. Like a man.

"Please don't. I'm already in a cab."

WHEN I WENT INTO THE bathroom before she came over I discovered I had a hickey on my shoulder. That girl from the other night, the one who laughed at my joke, had accidentally played a cruel joke on me. I looked at it in the mirror, square on my left shoulder. From the look on my face you might think I was looking through a window at someone else, someone who had committed some terrible faux pas, someone who had walked into St. J's and requested techno. What was her name? I can't remember now. Judging from the pattern of the bite marks, I might be able to identify her from dental records.

Just then the buzzer rang. Nikki was here.

I looked up, scrubbing at the spot as if it might diffuse or come off like Magic Marker. All that campaigning. All those blubbery *I miss you* messages. All down the drain because I decide once to make out with someone like a normal person in his twenties would do in New York City. Also, wasn't I supposed to be sitting out Nikki's Saturn return? Unless it came back around like a slingshot. I should have stuck up for myself, kept her stuff and went back to her in five more months. Even by my six-week manuscript-cooling rule I still had eleven more days. And I still had *no idea* why we broke up.

When she rang again I decided to just tell her the truth.

Then I stood there deciding what I knew to be true. I did this. I was responsible. Not some girl. I made this happen. That's also when I grabbed the three-blade razor off the sink, pressed it against the spot, and ran the blades sideways across it, leaving three stripes across the bruised spot and replacing the hickey with blood.

I ANSWERED THE DOOR PRESSING a wad of tissue to my shoulder. "Very impressive, Mr. Sullivan," was all she said when she walked into my apartment. Since our breakup, I had spent a lot of time internalizing reasons she might find me immature. None of them had anything to do with partying and the hours I'd kept since we met. But I figured a girl like her might find my taste in furnishings a bit too post-collegiate. Since she left I had rid my apartment of any furniture found on the street. I also went through and cleared out any shelving or cabinetry constructed with the aid of Swedish emoji.

My favorite part had been my own design. I built a bed out of two repurposed church pews from a nineteenth-century cathedral in Bensonhurst. At the base of the footboard I had a red leather kneeler.

As if to make clear what she expected that night, she walked over to the bed, shook it for sturdiness, and smiled. I loved that smile.

I poured her a Herradura on the rocks and we sat in silence.

Tequila for a standoff.

She looked at me, her eyes like the enchanting nuclei of peacock feathers. I couldn't stop looking at them. I took my glasses off, hoping that my own myopia might prevent me from falling any harder for her (that's *not* a metaphor).

"I'll go get your dress. I think there's some of your stuff downstairs and—"

"I still want to marry you someday," she said in a deep, mortal voice that called out from her throat. I couldn't see with the glasses off but I could definitely hear—hear the desperation in her voice, in her breath. For once in my life I had nothing to say.

I grabbed hold of Nikki, her body a warm damp ball of misery, crying out of every pore. I held on to Nikki as hard as I could, scrunching us both into a little ball and hiding under the sheets until dawn.

"HOW DID IT GET TO be noon?" Nikki sprang out of bed. She clutched her phone for answers. Hadn't she set an alarm? How much did we drink? She punched in the security code. "Why didn't it go off?" She tossed it on the bed and ran for the bathroom downstairs.

Why *didn't* it go off? I picked up Nikki's phone. That's strange. Everything else about her phone seemed in working order. In fact, right here on the screen is a text. From right before she came over. With my name on it. Which is none of my business. Even though it is in regards to me.

Oh, and then her reply: "I know James and I are perfect for each other, but I miss Brendan."

She walked back upstairs. "I slept through an entire meeting at the factory!"

Who the fuck is James?! "I'm sorry."

"How did this happen? I missed the most important part of my entire day! Ugh! I'm so mad. Like, what's the point in doing anything now? I don't have any appointments until tomorrow and I'm going to have to undo anything decided at the meetings today. Last time I missed one of these they cut our entire supply of fabric *backwards*. This is just the worst. *The worst.*" She gripped her BlackBerry and shook it for answers.

I knew I had to do the right thing. I had to say good-bye to her, let her collect her things, and that would be it. We had a good run, but knowing the information I now know about . . . about *James* . . . I can't, in good faith to myself or to her, let this go on any longer. No reason to toss her out the door. In fact, I should help her collect her things and put her in a cab—make sure she got her toothbrush and spare phone charger. She and I just aren't m—

"If you missed your meeting then you have nothing to rush off to." I took her jacket off her shoulders. "Do you?"

"*Baby*." She said it like a caution. Which made it dangerous. I ran my fingers through her hair, caressing her scalp and wrapping my fingers around the hair at the base of her neck.

"Baby . . ."

She pulled her head away for a second, but kept her arms around me, frowning. "What happened to your shoulder?" She looked directly at the fresh blood scab with the three slices.

"Oh, I must have bumped it."

I wondered, if she had a hickey on her shoulder, would I notice? Would *James*?

Then I decided to find out.

The bellhop's tears keep flowing

"You were supposed to let *her* see *your* hickey," Gaga texted me on my way to DJ at Beauty Bar the next night. Gaga's idea was that I should make Nikki jealous, show her how I've moved on. I couldn't believe someone would do that to someone they loved—let alone that someone would *recommend* doing that. "She did it to you with that stupid James text," she said.

New York City was just as confused as I was that night, and the trains were delayed all over town as conductors absentmindedly missed their appointed stops.

I stopped off at this sandwich shop called Bite two doors from where I had my thousandth pre-spin meal. It's a great place to eat by yourself because you can order and pay and tip at the counter and then they bring the food out to your table and you can bounce when you need to. They had just gotten their license to have beer and wine, which they stored in a lofted area above the kitchen. I never drink before a gig—just during and afterwards—so I declined.

And when I made my order I noticed a dewdrop in the counter girl's eye. "Are you . . . okay?"

"Fine." She punched something on the computer, frustrated, and then tersely added—as if she hadn't taken my order every Tuesday for three years—"We'll bring it out to you." Her voice faltered at the end and she turned away to wipe her eyes with her sleeve.

She said she's fine, Brendan. Let it be. Just walk over to your table and stop projecting yourself on people. You're not going to save the world just by upsetting people at work. And just because you ordered a sandwich from someone every week for three years doesn't m—"Did you break up with him or did he break up with you?"

She burst into tears, great heaving sobs that interrupted the traffic on Fourteenth Street. "What—like it makes a difference?" She disappeared into the loft upstairs. Over the noise of the kitchen she let out only the tiniest gasp of desperation to prove she was still alive.

A bell dinged in the kitchen ("Order up!"). She stayed in the loft. I walked into the kitchen. "I'll take that sandwich."

HALFWAY THROUGH MY SET I got a text from Leigh, the hickey girl. She had a name! She was downtown! Would I come see her later? I got the same text from Gaga.

By sheer force of poverty or the desire to space out my night a little, I took myself on a bit of a walk after my set. Because of some imbalance in lower Manhattan, people walked around as frazzled as the train service had been, always stepping in front of each other, walking out of strange doors and finding, to their own surprise, that they were on the street. But I had stomping grounds now and they needed stomping. I cruised down Second Avenue, past Lit, down to Houston. Normally I'd take a right at Katz's Deli but tonight I decided to say hi over at Arlene's Grocery and then walk by Pianos on Ludlow, just to see what's up, keep up with what's going on. God forbid other people know about a band before I do.

I took a left on Stanton Street, carrying my heavy iron roadie case of records with me.

Oh, *that* James.

He stood right in front of me on Stanton Street. No witnesses or anything. And here I have nothing but this heavy steel crate of records. The James who Nikki's friends all thought of as perfect for her. Is James a critic at the *New York Times*? Is he a restaurateur? Is James an angel investor in the boutique lingerie business? Is James getting ready for his first solo show? A European tour? Here's all I know about James:

James is a fucking waiter at the restaurant where Nikki cocktails.

I gripped the handle to my record case like a pistol.

Calm down, kid. Remember the other thing you know about him: He has a twin brother. Also a waiter. Also might just be walking out of work. What if you're staring down the twin? You'd feel like an ass and it would confuse the hell out of everyone. Besides, you like James. This is all just in your—

"Goodnight, guys." Nikki stepped out the front door of the restaurant wearing a scarf around her neck. She grabbed his hand, giggling at some comment made inside. As though this were just how she did things. I'd rather she just grabbed his cock. "No. Not tonight. We're just going to go home," she called into the closing door. Home. They have a singular home already.

James turned to me and I couldn't believe I could still move. I floated helplessly toward them and wished I had thought to wear someone else's face.

Nikki stopped and looked at me and shuddered. I gripped the rubber on the metal handle of my 45s case. I want to swing it around, smash it on the ground, and scream my head off. Throw it through the goddamn window of Stanton Social.

Instead I swung it with my right hand and used it to keep my momentum going. So I could keep walking.

I nodded my head as I passed. "Awesome." That was all I said. "Awesome. Good to see you, Nikki. Hi, *James*."

LET'S TAKE THE FIVE SECONDS I did not give myself that night and think about something: I just ran into my ex-girlfriend. She was with a new guy. I am going to go meet the girl who gave me that costly hickey the week before. She is wonderful. And tall. And, as far as I know, still uncomplicated by any of the planets. However, because I'm a moron I decided to walk it alone. Therefore I was alone when I ran into Nikki and *James*, instead of letting Nikki see me with someone else like Gaga recommended. If I had run into Nikki alone while I was with someone else this would be a different story.

Let's also accept the obvious: That did not happen.

I met up with Leigh at the Hotel on Rivington. Where the drinks cost twice as much and the music is half as good. I found her at the bar. She stood there with her cute friends, swishing expensive drinks and looking like an ad for something by Cartier.

"How'd your set go?" She smiled. The girl wasn't an idiot. Something had flagged in my optimism in the time since we last spoke. She, charitably, thought it might have something to do with the crowd's reception of the records I played, of some mass-opinion shift against the Beatles.

"Awesome," I said. "Everything is awesome."

"Do you want a drink?"

"Nope."

"Okay."

"Let's get out of here. I need to be further off Ludlow Street right now. Let's go to St. J's."

She motioned to her friends. "Uhm, I think they want to stay."

"I think I want to go."

"Okay, should we meet up later?"

"Awesome."

Everything is *awesome* tonight.

"VH1!" GUY SLURRED AS HE stood outside of Welcome to the Johnsons, another dive on the block. In the autopilot of my march downtown it never occurred to me that I didn't want to go out.

Gaga put me into a barstool at St. J's.

"You look like your head is going to explode," she said.

I sank a nice shot of Wild Turkey into my skull and Conrad looked over. "You want another?"

I slammed the glass all the way on the back row. "King me!"

"What happened?"

"You know all those crazy things you invent when you break up with someone and they drive you crazy?"

"Of course."

"Well. I just found out that I'm not crazy."

"Oh baby." She gave me a hug.

I started crying my dog-shit brown eyes out.

"Shhh . . . you're just upset," Gaga said. "There are a million reasons why she might be with someone else. And probably none of them having anything to do with you."

"When I met Nikki she had a string of psychotic exes who would cause a scene if they saw us or convince her to meet up for tea just to tell her that I absolutely must be cheating on her. I don't want to become one of those guys, but this unbelievably irrational part of me comes out when heartbroken. I don't feel like myself and it is just draining enough that I can't really give a shit about anything else until the next time."

"You need to go home, get some sleep, and get yourself writing again."

"I can't," I confessed. And saying my confession out loud offered no absolution. "I can't write anymore." It had been six weeks since I finished the manuscript, six weeks since my birthday party at the Chelsea Hotel. How do you throw a birthday party for a guy and then set him adrift and screw one of your coworkers? Wondering that had proved more interesting than writing and I hadn't worked since.

"You're going to have to sit out her Saturn return. You know that."

"But I can't." That word fell out of my mouth as a sob. Can't. I can't. "I can't write a word without thinking of how bad I screwed up. And she won't take me seriously. Until I finish this."

"It has nothing to do with that. Girls like what you do, but they want your attention more than anything. If she misses anything right now she doesn't miss your writing, she doesn't miss you at work. She misses *you*."

She said something more but I had to go.

Happy birthday,
Mr. President

That summer I thought I'd learned to do things on my own. I kept busy and stayed in town while New Yorkers disappeared into cabins and the Hamptons. On weekends I rode out to the end of my train line to Coney Island, with its own noise and kids and lights and the pounding surf. Every night after work I found myself down in the Lower East Side with good friends and the music I loved so much. None of us could afford TVs or big vacations, but we did entertain ourselves with the drama of the scene. Gaga's new songs were enough to get her booked at the side stage of Lollapalooza and it wasn't until she'd gone that I realized what a part of life down there she'd become.

I wanted to tell her about a new party I was putting together and so we met up at Beauty Bar when she got back. I could tell from her hollow eyes that something had gone wrong.

When she walked in she slumped down on a barstool, took a breath, looked me square in the eyes, and said in a low voice, "I got a ticket for wearing 'hot pants.'"

"What?" I laughed.

"A bicycle cop came up to me at Lollapalooza, took my ID, and wrote me a citation for wearing hot pants."

"What the fuck are 'hot pants'?"

"I still don't know."

I had hoped for her sake that Lollapalooza could become a steppingstone across the US. They did old-school promotion with programs and ads in magazines, things we couldn't do from here. Her face must have appeared in all the papers out there. "Did people recognize you?"

"Not exactly."

"How do people 'not exactly' recognize you?"

She laughed.

"What?"

Gaga's regular chuckle tickled out of her throat, but today it exploded, rumbling like a bubble from a water cooler. She could barely hold it in. "This girl saw me backstage right before I went on and she screamed, 'Amy! Amy! I love you!'" Gaga whipped her raven-colored mane aside and made this fierce glare come through her dark eye makeup and put on her foggiest East London accent. "And I said, 'Oi! Feck off!'"

The only person to even notice Gaga thought she was Amy Winehouse.

I laughed because Gaga still saw it as a chance to perform. She showed me twice how she made a curtain of her hair and walked off before she could get found out. From the way she squirmed on her barstool I could see she still found a thrill in having a fan.

She tried to change the subject, to ask more about Nikki and the drama she'd missed in just a few days in Chicago.

"But how was the show?"

"It was really rough." I'd never seen her look like anything less than the commander of her ship. Something must have gone really wrong. "I shouldn't say that. I did have a lot of fun." All of this chit-chat, even the silly stuff that she only now found funny, didn't seem to matter to her. Something else had gone wrong. "We had a lot of tech problems," she finally said.

"I love tech problems. Tell me about them."

She cocked her face to one side. "The stage was made of these matched risers, gaffer-taped at the legs. Starlight had feedback in everything and the speakers vibrated her turntables."

"That's awful."

"People were screaming, shouting while we have our limited time on the stage. It was awful." The room before us at Beauty Bar disappeared and Gaga stared back at the empty stage of Lollapalooza and the passive listeners sneering at the feedback coming from her direction as they went from stage to port-a-potty to food truck. That year the traveling festival had moved to Chicago's great Grant Park after many aimless summers of pitching an outdoor concert at fairgrounds and airfields. It still had the overcrowded bill and gaffer-taped wires. "And I'm standing there behind my synth with a microphone in front of me and every minute that goes by is one less song I can play."

"What did you play? 'Blueberry Kisses'?"

"Yes, but I had bought these new turntables with the advance on my record and they gave us a folding table to put them on."

"Are you kidding me?"

She caught herself and looked up at me. "No. Every time I danced the stage would bounce and the record skipped."

"That happens here. Watch." I stood up and stepped on this one spot on the way to the door. Ten feet away in the DJ booth, the record skipped. The DJ squinted at the turntable, couldn't figure out why it happened, and looked up at me. I smiled.

Gaga was angry. "*Why* does that happen?"

"Couple reasons. Come in back and watch where that doesn't happen."

Together we walked through a narrow hallway where a bench from an old barbershop lined the walls. Old beauty products from yesteryear stood in glass cases next to the old price list from Thomas Beauty Salon, where you could still get a beehive hairdo for eight dollars. I led her to the dark, roped-off back room, whose empty checkerboard dance floor menaced the DJ booth in the back room. It was empty except for us and a small bar that opened on weekends and special late nights. She turned around twice to see if we would get in trouble.

"Your tour kit needs to get set up like this," I said. I showed her the two turntables suspended by elastic cord in the private room. Her eyes widened and I showed her a couple of things—how to avoid feedback, etc. Not groundbreaking sonic theory, just the basics of setting up a band like I've done at a hundred shows, mixed with the basics of setting up a DJ booth (which would be reliably torn up). "Walk me through the show."

"Starlight and I came out on stage in dresses and then stripped down to bikinis, performed the whole show, and lit a hairspray can on fire."

"That sounds crazy!"

"It would be here at home with the lights and the fog machine going. But it's, like, three in the afternoon and it's Chicago and windy. I don't give a fuck what anyone says about why they call it the Windy City. Fucking place never stops blowing in your face. We'd blow the smoke machine and in about a second it's gone. The day before was kinda sunny, but we just had these gray Chicago clouds over us."

Tech problems are part of a show. And if the show must go on, the tech problem must get extinguished. We talked about stagecraft and wires and the like until we'd vanquished any future tech problem.

* * *

"LOOK, I'M PUTTING TOGETHER a new party," I told Gaga when she finished.

"Oh . . ." She sounded even more deflated. We'd both gotten used to knowing one person who always had the day off.

"It's at Pianos." I mentioned the name of the rock club between Stanton Social and St. J's.

Her eyes lit up. "You're kidding. Can you get me booked? Ohmygod. I've always wanted to play at Pianos."

"Here's the deal. I've got Sunday nights and I can book the bands, the DJs, whatever. But I need something big. It's so dead in there the barback calls it 'Suicide Sundays.'" I ran some figures with her and she went over the plan with me. This little girl had the business acumen of a mafia don.

"So if we can double what we put in the drawer up front, we can do anything we want in back."

"*Exactly.* And no nickel-and-diming. I'll cover the door charge, the sound guy, everything. The bands get to pick how much they want to charge and every cent will go directly to them."

"This could be good."

"So you're in?"

"I'm in. I just want to play. I'm ready."

"Good. So, look, I might have something for you before that . . ."

THING ABOUT GAGA WAS SHE physically needed to perform, but she had to perform big. Her social intelligence, the way she could talk at your level no matter who you were, meant that she couldn't fake it with a half-interested audience. A DJ on the other hand can work up to the enthusiasm, build it up. A good DJ should read the crowd and *lead* the crowd. I told her I had something for her next week. Something different.

Real different.

Gaga called me later the next Wednesday and I pulled over the Vespa to answer her call. I had twine-wrapped a garbage barrel to the rear passenger seat and filled it with paint, party supplies, glue sticks, pink caulk, and a sparkly paper tablecloth. "You get everything?"

"Yep."

"We still meeting at nine?"

"Yep."

"Are we really doing this?" I could hear in her voice a tremble of intimidation. Why would the crowd at Beauty Bar treat her any better than the one at Lollapalooza? Bombing as a young artist is something you never, ever forget. No matter how many shows you nail because of it. If people in this scene found out about me and Nikki's breakup day-of, imagine what they might say about your band.

"Yep." I hung up the phone and spent the rest of the day in my backyard trying to turn a (clean) trashcan into a cake that read "Happy birthday, Mike!" in pink bathtub caulk. More on that in a minute.

SOMETIMES YOU PLAN A PARTY so well that it can't go wrong. But nothing can stop rain. Nothing can stop the Yankees from playing a number of games well in a row. Or a new game show where amateur singers audition in front of professionals and get voted off. Our biggest competition in nightlife wasn't just other parties but the slow, crushing approach of adulthood and responsibilities that kept people from staying out night after night.

But by ten the back room filled. Dino showed up with Gaga in a trench coat and I was so glad to see him. Dino played bass and guitar in a couple of projects. I'd known him for a few years, but this was the first time we hung out off Rivington. Sometimes at these parties you have to deputize someone as security so the back bathroom can be a dressing room, or hand someone your camera so they can be your photographer. I needed Dino to be her roadie.

"Whatever she needs, man. I need you to do it," I said.

"Got it."

"Gaga, do you know your cue?"

"When the announcer calls out 'President.'"

"Right, anything else?"

"Do you expect me to fit inside of this cake?" I realized then that we had a big problem. I had gotten too small of a barrel. This one barely went up past her knees.

"Are you going to be able to?"

"I'll make it work."

"Okay," I said. "Dino?"

"We got this."

AT MIDNIGHT I CUT THE music right before the second chorus of Rolling Stones' "Satisfaction" (try it sometime: *"I can't get no / NO NO N—"*). Everyone looked straight at the booth and I grabbed the microphone. "Hello everybody, don't you all look beautiful tonight. Can I have a moment of your time? I would like to honor a very special friend of mine tonight. He's brought joy and happiness to all of us over the years, and when I was just a kid looking to make it as a DJ I turned to Mike and he gave me a chance of a lifetime here. And just to show my appreciation, Mike, please stand right in front there because this cake is going to really blow your candles out. Dino?" I handed the mic to Dino and hopped into the DJ booth to put the record on.

"Mr. President"—Gaga's hand pierces through the paper icing on the cake as the record begins. The track played and Mike took

her hand gingerly, like a man helping a lady out of a horse-drawn carriage—"*Marilyn Monroe!*" No one had any idea what was going on. But they wanted to. They all stared agape at this tiny trashcan with a whole woman inside. Dino handed her the mic and she stepped onto the plywood go-go platform.

The crowd couldn't believe it. This was the first time anyone in Manhattan had seen this Lady Gaga, the new performance artist. I played the original recording and her voice shimmered over on top. Her voice destroyed Marilyn's. She belted into that cheap carny mic. "*Happy birthday . . . Mr. President. Happy birthday to you!*"

The thunderous cheer resuscitated the Lady Gaga I knew. Instead of Lollapalooza, where she put herself on stage, hoping that people would come over and check her out, she put herself in a can and didn't ask anyone to see what's inside. But they wanted to know. She stood radiant in the light of the disco spotlight, her chest heaving as she stood with perfect soloist's posture, looking down from her two-foot go-go cube at the birthday boy, smiling. Laughing.

Just as she stood there, about to take a bow to the cheering audience, on the cusp of maybe getting off the tiny stage, I threw on a song with a hard four-on-the-floor beat. "Birthday" by the Beatles. And she go-go danced her ass off, singing the whole time as the exasperated room danced along.

"*You say it's your birthday? It's my birthday too, yeah!*"

Mike and his twin sister were thanking her, posing for pictures, dancing helplessly. People crammed huge tips into her garter belts and she put on a big show, bending over and having them stuff her opalescent sequined bra. I wanted to hold the mood right there, so I threw on "The Clapping Song," a sixties favorite of mine by Shirley Ellis (B side of "The Name Game"). Gaga got everyone clapping along to the school-yard beat. It was Mike's thirty-eighth birthday, but it might be his fifth if I could keep the music right.

Gaga walked across the backroom to the bar, pulled two dollars out of her bra, said something to the bartender, and walked to the DJ booth, carrying two shots of Sauza Hornitos in one hand. She handed me one, rammed her glass into mine and hollered, "I love you, VH1—here's to rock 'n' roll!"

The next DJ was about to go on and I couldn't wait. After spending all day on this damn cake I didn't have any time to eat. I thought I had enough time to go next door to Bite, maybe try and make the counter girl cry real quick. Just then someone came up to me. "Twig the Wonderkid can't stay. We need you in the front booth."

I packed up my operation in back and got in the front booth, thinking I might be there for another hour. I told Gaga I needed to go up front and she gave me this little puppy dog look. I promised her I'd be back.

Antonio (Twig's human name) is there, slightly out of it as usual. "What's up?"

"I gotta go home," he said. Every single time I saw Antonio anywhere he was always wearing the same leather jacket and with yesterday's dried eyeliner. It hadn't occurred to me that he had a home.

The DJ trade-off shouldn't be difficult, but people like to get comfortable back there, to spread out. I saw that he had on a bunch of CDs, so I pulled out my 45s case so he could clean up from the CD trays. I kept my records, even my 45s, categorized by tempo. So I pounded out something to meet up with the Bowie song he had going. Something in the backbeat made me count extra—even though I knew I shouldn't. I didn't even put on my headphones yet—with the two of us crammed into the DJ booth like two guys at a busy deli trying to share off one cash drawer—but I watched for the green light on the mixing board as I cued up the little record. The light went orange. Even better. "You ready?" I dropped the guitar in. Bryan Adams sang, "*I got my first real six-string.*"

When Gaga heard "Summer of '69" she sprang out from the back room and leaped into the DJ booth.

She sang, her hips bumping up against mine, forcing me to dance. And smiled. She sang over the words, " . . . *me and some guys from* Rivington High School *had a band and we try real hard!*"

Everyone in the whole bar had one eye shining on her. I hoped she never played outdoors ever again. She had a new spirit in her. One tied to the freedom of music and a carefree zest. Even we forget: This is supposed to be fun.

"I don't like the music those boys are playing back there," she said. "I just wanna be your go-go dancer. I'm not for lending out."

"Okay, babe, but there's no go-go stage up here in the main room. There's no dance floor either."

"I'll make do."

She hopped up on the bar, hoisting herself on the brass of the beer taps and wearing nothing but fishnets, bloomers, and her bikini top. The fishnets barely reached her crotch. I looked over as she pushed people's drinks aside. She reached over and grabbed a bar rag to wipe the surface while Justin was not looking, and in one swanlike motion she rose up on her white leather heels.

I never did get that dinner break. I didn't leave the booth for more than a minute the entire night. The only thing I did do was join Gaga on the bar to dance whenever her spirits would fade. I earned an extra fifteen dollars this way from people cramming money in my belt. On my final time up to the bar I was so out of it that I crawled up some girl's chair and when I went to put my foot on the bar I ended up kicking a full glass of whiskey-on-the-rocks right at the bartender.

"Hey!"

"Sorry, man!"

"You better watch it."

I looked up at Gaga, who had the biggest smile on her face. Mine too. Even though I'm supposed to be heartbroken and miserable. That night, that summer seemed to last forever. And if I had a choice, I'd always wanna be there.

"Those were the best days of my life."

The music that they constantly play says nothing to me about my life

For the first Suicide Sundays show at Pianos I hired Guy to DJ and Gaga got a band called Semi Precious Weapons to open for her.

I started talking to my barback, St. Michael. He'd had a very successful band in the nineties and did five records and endless touring. Now thirty-six, he found himself checking IDs at bars in the LES and doing awesome things like collecting and auctioning Motörhead merchandise online. He'd been sober for fifteen years, but he made a great bartender. He had full-sleeve tattoos and once a month had to grow his beard out to play Lemmy in his Motörhead cover band.

"How's my young Tolstoy this week?"

"Working hard. But it's driving me nuts."

"Did you talk to your girl at all?"

"I did. But it doesn't get me anywhere. It's just aggravating. It's like she's thrown up a brick wall in front of herself. Like the girl I loved disappeared. How's things with Amanda?"

"She's moving in this week."

"I'll try not to turn my envy into a jealous rage."

"Let me tell you something." He reached an arm out and touched mine. I flinched. No one had touched me in months. He looked at me with his honest eyes. "Your anger is just little Brendan crying out—because he wants to be held."

"Yeah, but—"

"No buts. No anything. That's what it is. You might even hate her for it, but it doesn't change how you feel. Let it sink in."

St. Michael was right.

STARLIGHT CAME IN, BUZZING SOMEWHAT, with fresh makeup ringing her eyes. Gaga strolled in behind her carting a keyboard. Dino acted as their roadie.

"Are you excited?"

"Yes, I can't wait. This is going to be the best show ever!" She gave me a big hug and I felt an electric pulse kick through me. We work in the business of happiness. Sometimes I play records for people who need to hear "Jet Boy Jet Girl." Sometimes I put on shows for people who need a gig. And this is what we all hope for. And that day, my heart, which felt like it could explode every time I thought of Nikki, grew three sizes bigger. The bigger heart could handle the stress and the excitement.

"Did you work everything out with the opening band?"

"Yes, but Starlight has to work tomorrow at nine. So we're going on first."

That came as a surprise. Everyone had clamored over Gaga these past few months, but most hadn't been able to see her play. Tonight would be the first time—for me, at least.

I told her the deal: "Like I told you at Beauty Bar, you can charge whatever you want at the door, because it all goes to the bands. Normally I have a guy doing the door and he writes down who is there to see which band and you get the full cover. But tonight he's DJ'ing upstairs for this new party called Red Light District and Tali De'Mar is go-go dancing."

"No cover. No money. I just want to play," Gaga said.

"And the other bands are okay with that?"

"Yes."

Right then, Justin Tranter, singer of Semi Precious Weapons, walked in with this guy who owned a clothing boutique in Greenpoint called Alter. I looked straight through Justin's soul. Here stood this contrived man in heels, two pairs of panty hose, and a ripped shirt. I could just feel people picking on him when he was a kid. Perhaps some kind of summer-camp exchange had exported my same bus-ride hecklers to make fun of him. He had dry, self-bleached hair and half a pound of eyeliner on, both of which made him look like a truck stop waitress. I loved it.

"Can you believe I got them to play?" Gaga shrieked with joy.

ABOUT HALFWAY THROUGH THE NIGHT everyone at the bar disappeared. Sometimes these shows get a little out of hand. Or the front gets so busy that St. Michael has to come in and help out. Not tonight. I looked out the window to busy Ludlow Street. If tonight didn't go well they wouldn't keep letting me book the acts. Will, the door guy, leaned on his stool, chewing gum, the flat brim of his hat cocked to one side. He shrugged. "What can you do?" I went over to the window and saw the crowds in and outside of all the other places on the street. The smell of wet pencils rose up from the rough-hewn floorboards of the empty room. When you can smell the filth down here, you know something's up.

I walked into the live room. There a rose-lit Lady Gaga had half the Lower East Side wrapped around her little mic cord.

She played her synth and sang "Wunderful." A pitch-perfect song about being twenty-one and confused and in love. It never got released. Starlight backed her up from behind with a pair of records that played her sparse beat.

My voice caught in my throat and right then I caught this look from Gaga as she looked into my wide eyes. She smiled back at me as if to say, "Thanks for noticing, buster."

Wink.

ON THE WAY BACK TO the bar St. Michael looked at me. "What just happened?"

"Nothing."

"The empty demon has left your eyes."

"Really?"

"It's like you're holding little Brendan in your arms, rocking him to sleep." His tattooed arms made a ring holding a baby.

"I think she just did." I had spent these last few years here on a mission. I wanted to find a band that would celebrate and eradicate the peculiar loneliness of youth. It was so sexist for me to think that I would find a group of boys to play music and feel like the friends I never had, to lead me in conversation with girls I never knew.

EVERYONE IN THE ROOM BEAMED at her after the show, but Guy still didn't show up. But for once she didn't beam it back. "Any luck?"

"He's not in there." I pulled out my phone. "I'll text him now."

Gaga finished up a minute later. She just played the best show of her life and amazed the entire room. But not Guy.

I'll never forget that disappointed look on her face when she walked out there and didn't see him anywhere. Maybe she had the charitable assumption that he had to DJ up front but that he'd wait there and support her.

"Where is he?"

"I don't know. He was supposed to be here an hour ago."

"Why didn't he come?" She asked questions I just couldn't answer. If my girlfriend had a show I'd stand in the front row throwing panties at her and cheering. I'd walk around with homemade band T-shirts and custom made, oversized foam fingers.

Starlight walked up with her record bag and her coat on. "I have to work at nine, honey. I love you. But I have to go."

The singer of Semi Precious Weapons walked out a minute later, clomping around in his man-heels. "You were a vision out there."

Gaga looked sad.

"What's wrong?" he asked. "What could possibly be wrong?"

She stopped a tear before it could smear her makeup. "I was expecting someone to be here tonight. And he wasn't."

"Well," Justin said, smiling, "I'm here and if that's not good enough for you then I don't know what is. C'mon. We're about to go on."

He pulled her into the live room in back and shut the soundproof door.

Just then I heard an explosion coming from the back. A sonic valve churned out a crag of guitar. Pint glasses shook under the taps. People outside smoking squinted through the windows to find what they heard. At the bar you couldn't hear the drinks people ordered. I ran in back to investigate.

On stage that little bottle-blond baby bird gawked at his audience and put on the singer equivalent of a bass-face, sneering through his makeup. The guitar went on. The drums materialized in perfect succession as if the amp feedback had stirred them to life. Justin screamed into the microphone the one perfect line that resonated with every soul in the room, "*I can't pay my rent, but I'm fucking gorgeous.*"

Gaga stood off to the side of the stage, headbanging her dark mane all around the room. As their set went on she became lost in the music, bouncing around their chaotic symphony.

I walked back into the bar, which had completely emptied by then. The manager ran over to me, hanging up this little pink Razr phone we had that forwarded calls to us when we couldn't hear the phone in the office. "Brendan, we can't have this," the manager shouted. "Heavy metal on a Sunday night? The neighbors are complaining. I have the sound guy cutting all the mics and the drums are a capella right now and it's still too loud."

"They said they brought their own equipment."

"The guy across the street is throwing plants off his balcony, screaming that he's going to call the cops."

"What can we possibly do?" I said. "They only have four songs. Total. Wait it out."

GUY SHOWED UP, FINALLY, AND gave me this moronic smirk, fresh from—and also smelling like—the bowling alley. "What's up?" He straggled in with a bunch of guys just like him. Leather vests, denim jackets in July, smudged silk-screen band shirts. (I once dated this very wonderful Canadian girl and the only time I ever heard her say anything bad about anyone is when she described Guy and his ilk in a way that sounds pitch-perfect across cultures. "Hosers.")

"You're two hours late, that's what's up. And you already missed Gaga."

"Why?"

"She went on early so Starlight could go to work and you could see her before your DJ set."

"My what?"

"You're the DJ tonight. Did you promote it?"

"Everyone's already here."

"Everyone's already here to see your girlfriend—except you."

"Don't use the G word."

"What?"

"Don't use the G word that you just said."

"You used the G word the first night I met her."

"Listen, we were going to go down to Motor City. I just came in to do a shot."

"Play some fucking records before I kill you."

> # I'm worse at what I do best and for this gift I feel blessed

Normally when a band finishes in the LES, everyone goes outside for a smoke or they rush the bar for another drink. The number one reason to do this is to break away from the band so you can talk shit about them or their bassist or how you wish you wanted anything in the world as much as that band wanted to be the Strokes.

Gaga came out from the door at the opposite end of the room but instead of rushing over to see her late-as-hell boyfriend she exited the back room through the soundproof doors and ran upstairs. The go-go dancer couldn't make it that night for the new party. A legion of neo-devotees of both bands followed her.

I ran up behind her as she strode over to the go-go platform. "What are you doing?"

"These guys need a go-go dancer. And I am a go-go dancer."

WHAT GAGA DIDN'T BOTHER TELLING us at all was that she had been dropped from Island Def Jam. And I didn't get the whole story until later.

When Gaga dropped out of Tisch School for the Performing Arts at New York University, she made a deal with her father. If she didn't have a record deal before her twentieth birthday she would put her dreams on hold and finish school. Then when she had a degree under her belt she could try again. It was about to get more complicated than that, and just in the time that I'd known her she would have all her dreams come true, and then immediately fall through. Which meant that even this summer, the clock had started ticking again. Time was running out.

I got two versions of this story at first. The one I liked came from her: "Dad said, 'I'll give you two months rent and then you're on your own.'" She went to play a show at the Cutting Room and a girl came up to her and said, "Are you ready for me to change your life?" The two went outside and the girl called her producer and said she'd found the perfect voice.

The producer, who was the same guy who called in the middle of the night we met, has another story, which has its place but doesn't concern me.

The story I like best is mine, because I later found out that show was right around her twentieth birthday. I like to think of her there onstage at the Cutting Room, where the cast of *Saturday Night Live* usually went after their broadcast. Gaga would have known that even if she kept trying, she had to honor her agreement with her dad. School would start up again that summer. But *that* night—that night was her last show to honor the deal. And she wanted to go down in glory, to belt out a killer sound instead of waiting to see if she was what people were looking for.

On the way into the show that night she saw a familiar face. Excited, ebullient, and in-the-know from an internship at Famous Music Publishing, a vocalist and songwriter named Wendy Starland. Gaga begged the vocalist to stay for her show. After the show, Wendy wanted to get Gaga in touch with a producer in Jersey named

Rob Fusari, who was in the midst of doing what Kim Fowley did for Joan Jett and the Runaways in the seventies, only he wanted to make an all-girl version of the Strokes for the aughts.

Gaga's dad was the sweetest businessman I ever met. Whenever I saw him he treated me like I was one of his many nephews. He never judged me and he always had a smile for me. But he was a killer businessman. When Rob Fusari first started working with Gaga, he wanted to sign a deal with her immediately, giving him 100 percent of the power to develop, record, and get distribution deals for her right away. Joe Germanotta gave him 20 percent.

The agreement stalled the ticking clock—for the time being. She didn't go back to school.

Later that year—and she never once let on that anything like this had happened to her—Fusari introduced her to Joshua Sarubin over at Island Def Jam. In 2004 Sarubin had been the number-seven-ranked A&R man in the world, behind Clive Davis and that guy who discovered Josh Groban (both of these legends were behind Ben Berkman, who discovered Maroon 5). People in the record industry really like Sarubin because discovered Avril Lavigne. He is famous for saying, "I've never found anything by sifting through demo tapes. But I keep looking." Sadly, this meant that to make it in the music industry, you needed to be in the music industry.

Sarubin liked Gaga when he heard her. I like the idea that he liked her *especially*, because it meant that he didn't have to go downtown and crowd into a sweaty place like Pianos just to hear this new savior of music. He passed the demo up to the legendary Antonio "L.A." Reid, who had just taken over for Clive Davis at Arista a few years before. Pushing out Clive Davis in 1999 was a controversial move, which Barry Manilow called "mean-spirited." Aretha Franklin threatened to leave the label, as did Carlos Santana (they didn't). You know you're fucking something up when Manilow, Santana, and

Aretha are pissed at you. Reid bailed on BMG later that year (Davis briefly re-took over) and moved to Island Def Jam, where he did wicked obnoxious things. I won't really go into how messed up the record industry was at the time, but they were still coming down from the boom-time high of CD sales. They acted like the last king of disco when he finally ran out of cigarettes and blow and found himself standing in a truck stop bathroom with an open-collared polyester shirt, only to discover the clock just struck 2003.

When I first met Gaga she was waiting to hear what Reid thought of her songs.

So this genius was in his office one day in early 2007 and he heard early masters of songs that would later come out in the same form on Gaga's debut album, *The Fame*. I really can't stress enough how desolate the record industry was at this time. Just as an example, Sony Music had 17,700 employees in 2000—by 2003 they had 13,400. That left 3,000 empty desks in the once-grand offices. A friend of mine moved to New York from Boston to work in their studios and the job disappeared while he was on the bus over. They later tore the building down. Soundscan started keeping track of record sales in 1991 and Sony had never had a lower number-one-selling album than when the *Dream Girls* soundtrack sold 66,000 copies. I mention this just so you won't think that L.A. Reid has no taste or is a terrible businessman. The record labels were desperate for a savior, but L.A. Reid took one listen to this early incarnation of Gaga and did the one-finger-slash-your-throat hand motion. Cut her loose.

He even fired the guy who had put the record on.

At twenty years old Gaga had a production deal and still believed in herself. But her first label did not. Gaga's dad had been as supportive and helpful as any dad could to his crazy kid with a wild dream. He had another daughter in private school at Sacred Heart and he wanted Gaga to set a good example. Education had always been important to the family, and young Stefani took her schooling very seriously because she knew that her parents made great sacrifices in order for them to afford to live in a nice home and go to a nice school.

Every child has a moment where they need to break out on their own. When I was a wee one, I packed my lunchbox with raw hot dogs, a bread-and-butter sandwich, and two juice boxes, and when my mother was on the phone, I ran away from home. At the foot of my street was a drainage ditch as wild and uncharted as the forest in the imagination of Max in *Where the Wild Things Are*. I would escape and live on my own as a savage five year old. I got to the foot of the driveway when something stopped me. I sniffled once and turned around at the home I was abandoning. *Isn't anybody going to miss me?*

Joe Germanotta knew that he had done a good job raising the girls, but that they would never stand on their own at home. Gaga ran away and made it all the way from the Upper West Side to the Lower East Side. He let her have her fun and test her mettle. She had run away to join the circus but unlike most fathers, Joe Germanotta saw her high-wire act and realized, with a great sense of pride, that she was born for it. In another era, the Upper West Side dad would come downtown and knock on the tenement building where he would find his crying, despondent daughter under the sickly flicker of florescent light, crashed out on a tattered mattress on the floor. He would come down hard with a mix of tough love and papa-bear wisdom, colluding with the landlord via unsigned checks to get her evicted. Joe had every right—including a signed contract with his own daughter—to do this. But instead of clipping her wings he sat down with his little girl and said, "Hey, mom made lasagna."

Joe then had every right to say to his little girl that she could try again after she finished school. But he didn't. He got on the phone with Island Def Jam, and with a businessman's alacrity and an Italian businessman's mix of charm and terror, he made an agreement to return a part of the record advance if the label wouldn't void the contract. This meant that Gaga could still afford her apartment on the Lower East Side, she would still be a working artist, and she would go out there again. And if he hadn't done that with such precision, Gaga wouldn't have played the songs that night that made my heart swell.

Rock 'n' roll depends heavily on the artist's middle finger. It shirks authority, defies convention, and doesn't like to be told what to do. Most kids get into music as an escape from their parents. It drowns out Mommy and Daddy fighting in the kitchen and it comforts us on the way from one stepparent's house to the next. It wouldn't judge us, and would never be disappointed in us.

Having said that, you really have to hand it to awesome dads. Can anybody in your entire life swoop in and chase the monsters out from under your bed, or have you ever known anyone who wasn't afraid of anything like your dad was?

When my high school sweetheart unceremoniously dumped me in the middle of winter vacation, my own father put me in the car and drove four hours to CBGB, the rock club on the Lower East Side that gave us the Ramones, Blondie, Television, and Warzone. We didn't speak a word about it and if he'd said anything I would have burst into tears and never felt like a real man. Instead he took the day off work and brought me downtown. While my friends were watching TV in their parents' basements or visiting grandma in Boca, my dad marched me into CBGB, vouched for me at the door, and had me sit there on the barstool where Joey Ramone waited to get paid and where Legs McNeil first met Blondie. It was three in the afternoon on a chilly February afternoon and I can still remember the way the bar smelled of scotch tape and damp wood. I still remember the bartender's muddy eye makeup, curved, claw-like press-on finger-nails and her baby doll hairdo. He didn't say any fatherly bullshit or tell me to buck up. He just thought that his son might like to know there is a great big world out there waiting for you when you come out of your room.

We all got in tune when the dressing room got hazy

After the show at Pianos, Michael T. and some of the other big names in nightlife hung around. Conrad came by after he closed up St. J's and we stacked the remaining stools on the bar, lowered the iron gate, and then held a little afterhours of our own.

I liked watching Suicide Sundays become the go-to industry party on Sunday nights. All of my friends were dancers, bartenders, and DJs, and none of us could go out on Friday nights. Sunday was our Friday.

"Who is *that* guy?" Michael T.'s eyes lit up when Conrad went to the bathroom. Michael T.'s sexual preference is straight guys. Guy and St. Michael had known him for years and they actually got along quite well. "Does he partake?"

The guys from the upstairs party came down when they saw Michael T. follow Conrad downstairs. They smirked.

"What?" I said.

"You know about Michael T.'s boot thing, right? He only likes straight guys in cowboy boots. Lures them into the bathroom with coke and snorts it off the boots."

Cleaning up, I smirked at the kids. "You guys gossip too much."

"I'm not *kidding*. He even carries around a suitcase full of different-sized boots."

When Conrad went down to the bathroom, Michael T. went and knocked on the door.

IN 2000 MICHAEL T. GOT together with Justine D. and our friend Georgie to put together a party at a club called Mother on the otherwise dead Sunday night of Memorial Day weekend for all the broke kids who didn't have money to get out of town. They called it "Motherfucker." It was a hit. Gay, straight, scenester, drag queens, rockers. The only way to get in was to dress wild. The nineties rock scene and the Giuliani crackdown had already come and faded out with the inspirational party known as SqueezeBox, many elements of which—including the rock 'n' roll drag band the Toilet Boys—later became the musical and then the movie *Headwig and the Angry Inch*. The kids from Motherfucker were older scenesters, well studied in nightlife history and ready to take over between the waves of nineties excess and the posh bottle-service clubs that followed. Motherfucker became like a movie franchise, every holiday weekend sequel becoming bigger and wilder. They started doing it every three-day holiday, bouncing from club to club, the owners always letting them do whatever they wanted on the otherwise dead weekend. It became the highlight of the summer. A friend of mine once asked Michael T., "What's the craziest thing people do to get into a Motherfucker party?"

And he said, "Pay cover."

Although my introduction to New York City nightlife came as an employee, my real introduction came from Motherfucker. I had a job waiting tables at an ill-fated Jean Georges Steakhouse in Columbus Circle. I worked in a maroon-on-maroon shirt/tie combo. (No one else was hiring.) I had no money, no friends, and no life. But on the night of a Motherfucker party, I crammed this maroon ensemble into my locker at work and changed into my powder-blue tuxedo shirt and velvet jacket. I locked my life in that locker and escaped everything into a ceaseless mass of bodies, music, and joy.

I remember the party and that night and its twists and turns as if it were my favorite movie. Only, I realized with delight much later, this was my new life.

The party was at The Roxy, the former roller disco from 1978 where Fab 5 Freddy sought to unite the downtown punk scene and the uptown rap crews in the eighties, where the Beastie Boys hung out with Rick Rubin and Afrika Bambaataa and Madonna. Only now girls wore the wildest, most carefree summer outfits, dancing all night with chiseled gay boys as they passed around Fantasia cigarettes, the papers colored like a box of crayons. Everyone smiled in small, cheering platoons of freedom. I danced with a girl who wore nothing but a miniskirt and paper cocktail umbrellas glued to her chest and stomach. The go-go dancers they hired that year were all dwarfs, men and women. When you went to Motherfucker you weren't a waiter or a student or a failure: You were simply *alive*.

I remember leaving The Roxy with the sun coming up to share a cab back to a loft I had in Williamsburg, where my bedroom was suspended twenty feet over the living room and accessible only by a rolling wooden library ladder. I ran into a girl from high school named Samantha. She worked at Coyote Ugly, where the bartenders made their money dancing in cowboy boots on top of the bar and making guys pay to do shots out of their belly buttons and relieving first-time dancers of their brassieres. She wanted to go home with a guy she met that night, but I was her backup plan in case he creeped her out. Trying to curry favor, the guy handed me a half-full bottle of Jack Daniels as we walked under the abandoned train tracks of the rusted High Line. "Where did this come from?"

He pressed another half-full bottle of Jack Daniels to his lips as we walked into the daylight, took a big swig, wiped his mouth, and said, "Don't worry about it."

Hours later at work I was smiling, beaming into the empty restaurant with my tired eyes and maroon tie. My body was in uniform and my mind was bouncing with two thousand people dancing to "London Calling" and I knew I needed to stay in this city. Only after we'd been dating for three months did Nikki and I realize that we'd both gone to all the same Motherfuckers and that at one point we would have made eyes at each other across the packed room.

WORD OF GAGA'S PERFORMANCE SPREAD. Also now *I'd* gotten looped into the insanity and landed a regular Thursday night slot DJ'ing at St. Jerome's, my favorite place on earth. The other bands in the scene had supportive friends, maybe even crossover supporters from other bands. Gaga had *fans*. I met up with Gaga later that week at Beauty Bar. She was still beaming from the string of successes.

"Guess what?! Guess what?! Guess what?!"

"What?"

"Michael T. just asked me to host the next Motherfucker!"

The streets aren't for dreaming now

Here is how I got hired at St. Jerome's.

Guy texted me one Saturday: "You want a job?"

The thing was: I thought I had a job. One that I loved because as summer turned to fall I had just started DJ'ing Thursday nights at St. Jerome's. The money was decent and I really liked working with Brent. After ten years of working downtown, Brent decided it was time to get a real job. I would have played every Thursday with Brent for the rest of my life, but Guy had other plans. "Meet me at the bar for training."

Thus he imparted to me the Tao of Guy:

1. "Bar owners always want you to put hot girls behind the bar. I don't like girl bartenders. I don't like 'em. They're slow, they're messy, and they take too many breaks."

2. "If you put a girl behind the bar, you need a man around. Someone to stay in control and keep up the pace. If you want to get a female barback, that's fine. Someone needs to do the dishes."

3. "Actually, I prefer that. You'll be crawling all over each other behind this

bar all night. If you have a guy bartender and a guy barback, it's just too much dick behind the bar."

THE NEXT SUNDAY, AFTER I closed Pianos, I went over to St. J's to learn how to close with Conrad. For the first time in all the years of playing there, I walked behind the bar and saw the damp limes in the mismatched bar mats, the cold blue water of the disinfecting sink, the place where the ice melted overnight. Unwashed bottles of cheap liqueurs stuck to the stainless-steel speed-rack. The supply cabinet included a CPR kit, baby powder, and hairspray. Conrad guided me through his greater teachings: how to set up the bar for the night in such a way that you may easily close it down stone drunk. Always put the keys here, always put the padlocks for the gates here, always leave your inventory sheet right there. Always do the cash drop when you're ready to walk out the door. And don't drink until midnight. "It's pretty easy to get pretty drunk here."

Michael T. came along with me for the ride again.

I liked standing behind the bar. You got a little space to yourself (very little), but in a cramped bar you felt blessed. You got to cross your arms and lean against the beer cooler, smugly raising an eyebrow when someone hoped that you would serve them.

At four A.M. sharp, Conrad turned off the music and screamed, "If you don't work here, *get the fuck out!*"

He cranked the music back up and got back to showing how to do inventory. Count the bottles on your way in and then, at the end of the night, count how many bottles you emptied. Simple. Then he looked up at the crowd, mostly friends. About half of them worked there. He dimmed the music again. "If you're not in my phone, *get the fuck out!*"

Pretty much every single employee of St. Jerome's gravitated back to St. Jerome's around four A.M. Especially if you were already in the neighborhood—diligently drinking with customers and dancing for dollars—and could use an off-duty cocktail. The door guys, the other bartenders, the barbacks—everybody. More than once I have discovered, upon lifting the iron gate to exit, that I had gotten lost inside of this tiny bar and clawed my way out into the morning to a city on its way to work. The bright sun greeted me like a stern parent breaking up a make-out session.

"If you don't work here—*get the fuck out!*"

Above all, this meant that the few mixed-in strangers of the crowd—who no doubt had friends who worked here—might not feel the need to leave. It was four thirty on a Sunday night—a.k.a. Monday morning. "If I don't know you—if I don't go to your fucking parties—*get. The fuck. Out!*" Conrad slammed his fist on the bar and screamed in Michael T.'s face.

"Sorry, Conrad. This is my friend Michael T. He hired Gaga to host Motherfucker next week. What am I even saying? We hung out last weekend?" I wondered—out loud—why Conrad would do this to Michael T. The three of us hung out well into Monday morning last week.

He glared across the bar at him. "Do I know you? Do I go to your parties? No. *So get. The fuck. Out.*"

Guy stood at the end of the bar. He didn't move, and behind that long, unruly mane of his I could see a smirk. It didn't make sense. Michael T. stood up and grabbed his seventies Pierre Cardin clutch and walked out the door. I tried to stop him, even chased him out. He marched home trailing a roller bag of CDs and cowboy boots.

When I walked back in I saw everyone doing these half-drunken high fives. I didn't see it that way whatsoever. They poured a round of Sauza Hornitos shots. "That's not okay."

"That fucking faggot."

"Hey." I turned to Guy. "What the hell?"

He looked down at the shots on the bar. "You want yours or not?"

"WHAT HAPPENED IN THE BAR last night?"

It's Gaga. She would like to know how we could possibly have been bigger assholes last night.

"When Conrad threw everyone else out, he threw out Michael T."

She then, quite charitably, wondered about Guy. Was he in the bathroom while all of this went down in the tiniest bar in Manhattan?

"No. He was there. He was laughing about it."

She let out a long sigh. "He's such a fuck." She had an emptiness in her eyes and if you looked you wouldn't find her. She got this way at times, at difficult moments where she could see her career slipping away from her again. Above all else she knew that she would tread a thin line between artistic greatness and cheesy pop. It all depended on the people around her.

Now I worried that Gaga and Guy would be fired from Motherfucker before the party even began. Now we had a problem: The record label in LA believed that Gaga was the Queen of Nightlife, not some NYU dropout who had never done anything of substance. She would emerge from the downtown scene like the Beatles out of Liverpool. Never bigger than where she came from, just elsewhere.

This was the first time I ever witnessed Gaga displaying mama bear–like protectiveness about her career. It would not be the last.

I was just as worried for my future.

Michael T. had fed me gigs for as long as I'd known him. Great, center-stage gigs where the girls would come up to you afterward as if you were part sorcerer or savant. Now that would dry up because I was in league with these a-holes. I had hoped to parlay this into DJ'ing at Motherfucker. Now my best connection to do so fell through. Because my friends were motherfuckers.

The next night I texted Guy. "Fix this. Apologize to Michael T."

"I'm in the DJ booth right now kissing his ass."

"Don't let him lick your boots."

"What's that mean?"

Change my pitch up

Fall came to the city like a returning friend. Same old friend from out of town, only healthier, tanner, happier. Pants and sweaters, leather and denim replaced the uncomfortable stretched fabrics of the sweaty summer. Now we had comfort and confidence and full crowds. New York is not a college town, though every fall we came back together. The bands came back, flush from summer festivals, where people actually paid cover and relished in their merch booth. The bartenders came back from their summer jobs in the Hamptons and summer islands, where they lived temporarily in dark, steamy, shared-shower dormitories.

Lion's Den in what they used to call Greenwich Village has a perpetual open-mic, making it a rite of passage for all Tisch School of Performing Arts students at NYU. It had the same problem as every music venue in New York City: At one point, a well-meaning music lover partnered up with a cash-from-chaos bar owner. They wanted patrons to sit there and buy as many seven-dollar beers as they could handle, and the door price got split up after. We came to see Dino's band, Ism.

"VH1!" Gaga waved when she walked in. I went to hug her. "Don't touch me—I'm disgusting, straight from dance rehearsal." She had dried mud puddles of eyeliner smeared down her face. She looked as if she had been marooned on a particularly terrifying rollercoaster.

"I love you just the way you are."

She smiled. The way she took a compliment made me feel so much older than her. She took it like a freshman girl who showed up to the first day of high school and had only gotten taller and tanner since junior high. She was just as excited by the attention.

"Where's Starlight?"

"She has to work in the morning. She can't stay out late. Probably the only night she'll be able to rock out anymore is Fridays at St. J's."

"Damn it. I just started Thursdays at St. J's and I wanted her to go-go dance."

She looked like I had just broken up with her. "How come you didn't ask me?"

"Honey, I think you were made for better things. When you have to go to LA, I want you to go to LA."

"There's no way of knowing when that'll happen."

"You know what I read last week? I don't know why this hit me so hard. But I was really upset about Nikki and I was reading about whaling—"

She laughed. "Of course you were."

"I was!"

"No. I mean, of course you were reading about whaling while the rest of our friends get wasted and blow three hundred dollars on scratch-off tickets at the deli."

"Fine, I was wasted and reading about whaling."

"There we go."

"And I was thinking about Nikki."

"Okay, now we're talking."

"And I read about this chapel in Massachusetts where the whalers would go to pray before they left on their voyages. So I was in the basement of Pianos and I read about this harpooner who went under with a whale he'd been chasing. He gripped the rope and wouldn't let go. He shouldn't have drowned, but he did because he couldn't let go."

"So that made you feel better?"

"No, but I realized something. The harpooner had to cling to something, right? They didn't have life vests then and he came out there in a rowboat. *Plus*, those guys had to own and care for their own harpoons. If he let go and lost the harpoon he—stay with me here—would be out of a job. Your whole identity on the ship was based on what you did. But think about that poor guy going over-board when the whale got away. Once you learn to let go, it gets easier to hold on."

"Wow." She digested that for a second, blinking her eyes to grasp the concept. "That was in the book?"

"No. That's just what I started thinking about."

"So you want me to let go? Forget about making records?"

"No. I want you to hold on. But let go of how you thought it would happen."

"And this is working for you and Nikki?"

"Absolutely not. In fact, I'm not even trying it." Gaga laughed. I loved her laugh. "But if you wanna give it a shot, lemme know. Okay?"

"So that's what you learned from reading about a dead guy in a whaling book?"

"The weird part is what really made me feel better. The chapel en-graved this dedication to him, sort of too little, too late. But it really did make me feel better."

"Is it a prayer?"

"No. It's just a Bible verse. It just reads, 'Therefore be ye also ready for in the hour you thinketh not: the Son of Man cometh.'"

"Wow."

"I know, right?" Gaga and I both had religious upbringings. We knew you couldn't top The Book. "Be ready for that time when you're not ready. Be ready for that moment when you've lost faith."

"Believe so big that you can still believe when you no longer have the strength to believe?"

"Exactly."

"So that made you feel better about Nikki?"

"I meant it in your case. With the record label. Be ready for when you're not ready anymore."

"Then I guess I am ready."

"But are you?"

"No, I'm not ready."

"Then you are ready."

THE BAND TORE INTO A very different song, one unlike anything they ever played. It started with some looped guitar, unlike the progression they normally did. The drumming came off as digital, but they were playing instruments. This is still just in the wake of when real New York City rock 'n' roll had just collapsed, leaving a dozen half-realized bands in the dust. When I was coming up in the scene, it was considered respectful and earnest of a younger band to cover a song by an older band they admired. It created an honorable mention, literally. Ism did both when they started singing "Smack My Bitch Up," a somewhat forgotten summer hit by Prodigy from ten years before.

"*Change my pitch up,*" Andre sang, and strummed the rhythm guitar as Dino shredded the lead. Leigh cut in on a thunderous, haunting bass and Mike Higgins kept up with an almost industrial drum thrash.

I had never liked this song, but I loved it now that I saw it being put together.

About halfway through the song they moved into the breakdown and Gaga crawled on stage on all fours. The crowd that once kept talking all goddamn night now pressed against the stage while this feral creature detonated on the floor, crawling around the wires and guitar pedals.

Dino passed her a mic and at the explosive moment where the song devolved into its most stripped down moment she sings one single vowel into the void she left in the once chatty room:

"*AAAAAAAAAAAAAAAAAAAAAAAAAAAAAAAAAAAAAAAA!*" Her reverb channels clanked into each other like the heads of two bad guys in a ninja movie. "*AAAAAAAAAAAAAAAAAAAAAAAA AAAAAAAAAAAAAAAAAA!*" She sang like the lonely captive of a harem.

The stunned room looked on as Andre added one final, punctuating, "*Smack. My. Bitch. Up.*"

The band looked up and for the first time at one of their shows they had a throng of eager fans. The fans applauded. They wanted more. But the band already played a cover song as an encore because they didn't have any other songs.

> # This is the kind of place where no one cares what you're living for

Probably the one thing you never got over in New York City was the thrill of arbitrarily bumping into someone you knew. It didn't matter if you were separated at birth or if you had already seen them earlier at work. *Heyyyy!* Your eyes inflated. *What are you also doing on the same fifteen-block radius where everyone we know always is all of the time?*

Later that week I was at Welcome to the Johnsons, and the girl next to me looked up and said, "Normally I would think a girl dressed like that is a slut. But that girl looks awesome." I glanced over at a girl on a barstool over by the pool table while unshaven ogres waited their turn with pool cues in hand and smiled at the girl like cavemen with clubs in their hands. She had on a backless unitard, tights, and a series of belts instead of pants. It was Gaga. The girl we all used to ignore had become a central focus.

MONDAYS BECAME MY NEW FAVORITE day of the week. Usually I slept in and ordered some lunch, wrote into the afternoon, and then met up with the crew for an early movie and a drink. The leisure of it all seemed extravagant and I never got over how much movie tickets cost. But if you can pay the rent and keep eggs in the fridge and scrounge up enough for a cab or a show, who really cared? Most of us existed in the post-collegiate habits of shared apartments, stolen music, and house parties that featured a punch made with the second-cheapest rum.

This next Monday, I ran into Gaga and some of her school friends at Pianos. Guy held court at a picnic table in the corner, sipping the lethal frozen margaritas. He wore a T-shirt from an extinct metal band with the sleeves cut off. Sweat dripped off the glass in the late summer heat.

Andrew W.K. had come in earlier to play a solo set of all classical piano. Bret and Jemaine from the New Zealand band and TV show Flight of the Conchords were at the bar taking notes. Jay, the bartender, had just got back from tour with A Place to Bury Strangers. He had a glow I knew all too well. It came from your band touring the country in a van you can't rely on, playing clubs you can't trust, on equipment you can't afford to break. Sometimes it's good just to get back behind the bar, where at least you could count on yourself. Jay poured two shots of Jameson the second I walked in the door and had one with me.

Most barstools came up to Gaga's exposed belly button. Watching her crawl up them was sometimes the cutest thing ever because you knew other girls who would do a little hop or get some leverage off the concrete bar, like a swimmer coming out of the pool. Gaga crawled up the rungs like a burlesque dancer. Frequently, she put a knee down on the seat and sat her ass right on the bar.

She had on her new uniform: unitard, fishnets, heels. Adding or removing a slightly oversized leather jacket (a.k.a. "the boyfriend jacket").

Strangers kept coming up to her. "I love your outfit."

"Thank you," she said, smiling. "I don't like wearing clothes."

"How do you two know each other?" a scrappy NYU girl asked.

"We are both associates of Mr. Guy," Gaga smiled.

Unconsciously, I glance over and notice that he'd gone.

Paul, the English manager who hired me, walked over and gave me a devilish little glance when he got a look at Gaga. "Who is this fine lass you have with you tonight?"

"This is Gaga."

"Oh, I keep hearing about you." He then turned to Gaga. "When are you going to grace our stage again?"

Gaga, the queen of the court, smiled. "Anytime you want. I'm supposed to go out to LA and record so I have to save my voice starting next week. But we're playing at the Slipper Room first."

"Good luck with that."

"Thank you," she said.

When Paul walked away she looked semi-despondently around the room. She couldn't find Guy. I leaned over to her. "I think he's outside for a smoke."

She looked sad and I hated to see a pretty girl look sad. "What are you working on?"

Her face lit up. "You're going to love it."

"Tell me every single thing about it." I never had any sisters. But somehow I became one on sleepovers like this.

"I wrote a song about the Killers' after-party."

"You're kidding me."

"No. And you're in it."

"What?"

She sang it to me over the beat of the band in the back room.

I never got over how great her voice sounded. We had friends who were singers because they wanted to be in a band and couldn't play bass. We had perfectionist, never-gonna-get-it friends who cleared their throats, blamed their range on something they'd eaten, and had us just trust that they had greatness in their lungs. Gaga worked with a vocal coach on new techniques that toned her vocal cords like tuning violin strings. Even when she sang along to the background music, she straightened her spine and reached into the back corners of her nimble range.

"It just came out one day in the studio. Can you believe it? I'm so excited."

"Do you write in the studio?"

"Of course. That's the best part. Figuring out what comes out of you when you have nothing."

"I'm the same way. Every day I sit down to do my writing and I usually don't have anything but a vague outline to work off of."

Her eyes brightened. "Are you writing again?"

"Every day," I let out my sheepish smile. "Don't ask me how well it's coming but it's coming. I let go. Now I'm holding on."

"Is this *Mercutio*?" She turned to her friends. "Brendan is rewriting *Romeo and Juliet*. Isn't that brilliant? Such a good story. I can already see it being a big movie. You're going to be huge."

Her friends smiled and nodded, still never quite comfortable in Gaga's new world.

Gaga and I went back to talking about craft. "So by not keeping a notebook, every day you get to surprise yourself like you're reading it for the first time?"

"Exactly. Also, I don't want to be one of those Moleskine-wielding schmucks at the bar trying to look deep," I said. "Being a regular drunk is fine by me."

"*Yes*," she giggled. "I never make notes. I always say if it doesn't stick with you it wasn't that important."

"I'm with you on that."

"When do I get to read it?"

* * *

WE STRUT HER AROUND TO a few other bars as I vaguely hit on her cute friends. Gaga caught stares and admiration on every corner of the LES. Her ego never swelled, but it did fan her fame flame. By the time we passed the streetlight on Rivington, she was glowing.

Her friends basked in it with her, and some of the attention focused on Gaga deflected off on to them. Like most guys, I get easily distracted by pretty girls in small groups. I call them Planeteers. One of them is blonde, one of them is nice, one of them is funny, and one of them is just tall. But when you see a group of five nice girls together, the excitement somehow morphs them into one gorgeous Captain Planet.

Finally settling on St. J's, we slid into a half-moon-shaped leather booth, with Gaga perched on the back like in a fifties beach movie, scrunched up in the back of a packed convertible. We lost ourselves in the night. St. J's was the perfect little place to sit with a good friend and listen to good music and have a good time.

Hours later, Guy came roaring into St. J's with a goofy smile on his face. I didn't make a big deal about it and I went back to talking to Gaga's friends. She went to be with him as he faltered onto a barstool. "Are you drunk?" she asked him. Such a preposterous question when all of your friends were, by profession. He laughed in her face.

Minutes later, I watched him stab another cigarette into his mouth, hop off the bar stool, and walk himself out for a smoke. He never returned.

GAGA CALLED HIS PHONE A half dozen times while her friends trickled home.

"Maybe he's out of battery," I told her. She texted him. "He probably just went home."

"Why didn't he wait for me? I would have gone home with him.

Especially if he needed me to make sure he got home okay. What if he's dead?"

"He's probably just in a basement bar with bad reception."

"Did he say anything to you? Is he mad at me?" In the prime of your life you can only be divided by yourself, and one.

"It's probably nothing."

"What did he say? Tell me everything."

"Nothing. But he had band practice today and you know how they get. It's basically drinking practice."

"Did he say anything? You know how he doesn't like it when we get on his case or tell him he's drunk."

She wanted to cry into her phone and press send. I couldn't stand seeing her like this. "Don't worry about it. He'll call. I'll check up on him in the morning. Do you want me to wait until we hear from him?"

She teared up. "I didn't mean anything by it. I wasn't accusing him of anything. I just asked if he was drunk, like maybe he wanted to just go over to my place. I live two goddamn blocks from here." Guy lived in a remote part of Brooklyn where the container ships docked on the other side of the expressway from the nearest subway.

Poor girl, beating herself up like this over something she said. I guarantee he didn't hear her.

"I don't think he's mad. But the only thing we can do is go calling around and asking for him. And you know he'll hate that."

Gaga fell silent. All that buoyant fame she had moments ago burned out like a table candle. Her lower lip trembled. "Will you walk me home?"

IF THERE IS THE INVERSE of a fag hag, I am it. I'm a straight guy who notices when someone's girlfriend gets a new haircut. I pay for the cab when we go out. I buy you dinner when he's bartending and I only take pictures of you where you look cute and skinny. I notice when you have new shoes versus an old pair you don't wear often.

Gaga had this purposeful step when she walked, which made up for the foot we had in height difference. I'm six foot two and I walk like a busy New Yorker. She clomped down the streets in heels, effortlessly slaloming around rusted hatchways, subway grating, and other sidewalk dangers, forcing me to keep up.

"Look. You know how he gets."

She let out an angry sigh. "He's such a *fuck*."

"You know what I think? His pride took over and he got embarrassed about getting so drunk. He likes to be in control."

"I would have taken care of him. I don't care if he gets drunk, we could have just gone to bed," she said, envisioning her forthcoming loneliness. And just before she started to tear up again she smiled at me in the moonlight and said, "You're such a good friend."

"I had fun," I said. And then I realized that I really did. "I haven't had this much fun since—"

Gaga cut me off before I could mention Nikki. "Since before?"

"Yes. But since before it was good. Months ago at this point. You know how they say it's not over 'til it's over? It was really over before it was over."

"I'm sorry I'm such a mess. I really had fun too. If we could cut out the drama then you and I had the perfect little Lower East Side date tonight."

In the panic of my oversensitivity my heart started racing. "Oh, totally," I finally forced out. I totally had fun and that in no way meant I took my friend's girlfriend on a date. "If we'd met last week and I got your number this is exactly what we'd do. I'd take you to Pianos and totally impress you with how I know everybody in the scene. We'd check out a show and then hit up a few places, end up at St. J's."

"You'd feed me shots until all we could talk about was our favorite records, and then we'd gossip about people we both know."

"And then, like, your ex would pop in drunk and we'd have to pretend we needed to be somewhere else."

"Yes!" Her voice had a flutter to it, but with a creaky wrinkle in it like a butterfly spreading its wings for the first time. "But then it's getting late and you'd have to walk me home. So much fun! My little heart racing, like, 'Ohmygod, is he gonna *kiss me?*'"

Our footsteps slowed down as we got closer to her block. We lost cadence, one of us trying to get the other to lag behind. We had rushed the wrong part of the night with other people's problems. The entire block fell into a silence, filled only with the sound of my keys nervously bouncing along on my leg and the staccato metronome of her clacking heels. At the door to her building we shared an extra moment of silence. If we were buddies she'd invite me up for a little nightcap of whatever she had left to drink. We'd listen to records while I snooped through her bookshelves. If we were on a date she'd invite me up for a little nightcap of whatever she had left to drink. We'd listen to records while we snooped through each other's souls. Tonight didn't feel like either.

She climbed up into the doorway and turned to face me. The step evened out our height difference. She looked at me with those beatific eyes. Time stopped. My heart did not. She caught herself, bit her lower lip, and smiled, looking down at her feet doing a nervous dance. My cheeks swelled up like someone holding back a smile.

I heard myself say, "I'll call you if I hear from him, okay? I'll let him know you got home safe."

"*No*," she said, shaking her head and looking like a wide-eyed harlequin in her eye makeup. "He can never know that you walked me home. He gets jealous."

"Oh, c'mon. It's me. I'm like a gelding." I think I said that just to hear it. "A eunuch."

"Not to him you're not. You come into the bar every week with a different girl and all he talks about is how he can't believe it."

"Oh, that's not true."

"It is." She looked dead serious. "You know how he gets. Especially about you."

"I have a hard time believing that."

She put a hand to my chest and looked me straight in the eye. "If he says anything, you say you put me in a cab when we got separated." She looked down at the hand on my chest, still electric from my beating heart pounding back at it.

"That doesn't make any sense. Logistically. We were never more than three blocks from your apartment. It's just not polite or smart to let a girl walk alone."

"Then tell him you didn't see me."

"Don't put me in the middle of this. You're my friend, but he's my boss. I just care that you got home okay. Goodnight."

I kissed her once on the cheek as a soft gasp of cool air whispered through her lips. My senses paused when I smelled her perfume and felt the softness of her skin. Time stopped again. She gave me a goodnight hug and wouldn't let me go until she thanked me again. I swallowed and marched myself down the street, gearing up for my glamorous subway ride home. I lived one stop from the LES, if you were willing to walk through Big Trouble in Little Chinatown and catch the first B train to my house when it started running in the mornings.

I got about halfway down Stanton Street when I heard a lone siren calling, "Hey."

I turned around at the corner. She stood in the light of the open door to her reformed tenement.

"Y-yeah?"

She paused for a second and swallowed. And then she said out of nowhere, "I love you."

To love and to be loved is an addiction and sadly kind of hard to find a fix.

I put my head down and I didn't want anything at all to happen. But I wanted her to know what I had to tell her.

"I love you too."

Her face was shrouded in the dark, hidden by a lifeless streetlight. She nodded and muscled a smile onto her worry-worn face. I crammed my hands into the pockets of my leather jacket. She saw through me and I through her. We were not just two work friends who had implausibly bumped into each other on the street.

There was nothing more to say. In three words she unraveled a mystery that we didn't know we had spent the whole night trying to solve. Her smile evaporated with her tears and the too-heavy tenement door clamped shut after she sent me a goodnight nod.

LUDLOW STREET SHUTTERED UP LIKE a ready-and-willing warzone. Every storefront had an iron garage-door-style gate that served as a canvas for graffiti tags and spray-painted dicks. Every night was trash night in this mixed territory of commercial and city waste. Rats wandered freely from one Chinese grocer to the next, while roving bands of homeless dudes grabbed bags of commercial trash. They took the thick industrial bags from in front of restaurants and factories and shops, wound them up, and tossed them ahead like they were making a sound-effects record. The glass and plastic in the trash bags clattered ahead on the street, where they were picked up once again and tossed ahead until they met up with a garbage truck at the end of the one-way street. Others picked through the bottles and cans we'd drained only an hour before. Before sunrise, you only saw the bottom feeders of Lower East Side ecosystem. Us included.

Just for the hell of it, I called Guy to make sure he made it home.

I wanted to tell him that Stef got in okay. Maybe he should be a little jealous. Maybe he should feel overprotective. I decided that at minimum, I'd call just to make sure he survived.

Somebody else picked up. "Hello, who this is?" A terse accent screamed into the phone.

"Hello? I'm trying to track down a friend and he's not picking up his phone. Did you find this phone somewhere tonight?"

"Boolsheet. He won't get out of the cab. We at his house." He shuffled the phone a little bit. "Hey, hello? Wakey up. $15.60." He must have gone all the way home to Brooklyn.

"Should I come collect him?"

"Hold on." The driver put him on the phone.

"Are you okay? Your girlfriend was worried sick."

"Don't use the G word."

"Fine," I said. "Your boyfriend was worried sick."

"Rock 'n' rolllllllll—"

And he hung up on me.

Empty barrels make the most noise

I cruised next-next door to 151 halfway into my first shift at St. Jerome's. I needed to borrow a bottle of triple sec. In truth, I didn't imagine that too many cosmos get ordered in a filthy rock 'n' roll bar, but Gaga would probably come visit on my first day and I want to be stocked so I could make her a margarita.

One-Fifty-One Rivington Street was an unmarked door below street level at the bottom of a stone staircase. A beaded curtain sectioned off the small seating areas and made it look like the basement rumpus room of a suburban San Diego home—a home rented out to three community-college students who later dropped out. Some of the beaded curtains had big gaps. Some of the seats were taped up. The bathroom walls looked like some disturbed eighth grader's notebook—all graffiti and stickers from bands you'd never heard of. This included the work of "Bea Arthur," a street artist who used a thick brown marker to tag toilet seats with, eponymously, "Bea Arthur." Because of this prolific artist, your friends would politely excuse themselves whenever they needed to take a shit by saying, "I'm gonna take a 'Bea Arthur.'"

Rachel stood behind the empty bar, also working on her inventory. "Covering shifts already?"

"Katy had a thing at her gallery. I'm just doing her happy hour." Katy was one of us, bartending part-time. Her uncle was Thurston Moore, the guitarist for the band Sonic Youth, and had drawn her into some part-time work at a gallery.

"You getting any action?"

I told her the truth. A bunch of dudes came in from the afternoon hardcore show at the squat house across the street, ABC No Rio. They came in *with their dad*. "They're all pumping their fists to punk rock and not tipping."

"At least you have customers."

"I'd rather just not deal with it. They leave their money on the bar—which I hate—because I don't know what's a tip and what's them being morons and leaving money around. Their dad ordered a round of beers and when I told him it was nine dollars he pulled twelve dollars out and I was like, 'Sweet, a tip.' Then dad goes, 'Uhm, hello. Where's my change?'"

"And you were like, 'Sorry, did you give me a twelve-dollar bill?'"

I smiled. Just us two colleagues taking five to talk shop.

I WALKED BACK IN AND decided to get tough like Guy. When people left their inch-to-empty beers on the bar unattended, I tossed 'em. *Take control of your bar.* Field complaints with the kind of tough-shit attitude that you feared in bartenders. I politely mentioned that they should be more careful in New York City. If you haven't seen their money it was because you gave them their change ten minutes ago and money on the bar was *your* money.

Something about this crew bothered me. I see it in other guys—always guys—when they walk into a place and spread their arms and squat over a barstool like children screaming, *"Mine!"* Even their dad spread his fists wide like a placemat to carve out his own space in the world. I wasn't having it.

One of the kids complained, "Every other bar in New York City lets us leave our money on the bar."

"This," and I could feel Guy smiling through me when I said it, "is not every other bar in New York City."

Dad stepped in: "We tip you at the end."

"This is a bar. This is not a table where you go to get served and then leave your money when you're done. I'm not your fucking waitress."

Out of the eight of them, only one guy looked clean-cut. He decided the best way to placate the group was to start a tab on his Amex, which he would pay with and tip me on at the end. When I checked his ID and realized that I grew up about ten minutes from him, I cut the music, stood on the bar, and shouted over to the DJ—who grew up about *fifteen* minutes from them—to play some of our music from home.

Kyle played an old record that those fuckos just ate up. One of them told us with great pride that he not only knew that band, but he was a groomsman in the singer's wedding. Music: it binds us. Even their white-trash dad got into it.

At nine thirty I wondered what I was still doing there. My shift ended at nine and someone else should have come in. Anybody. My door guy should have been there. The phone behind the register rang. "I didn't know you were covering and I can't get through." It's a bartender I've never met. She asks, "Can you stay for a while? I'm getting my hair done and it's taking longer than it should have."

I hung up the phone and when I turned around I found an empty bar. The assholes fled, taking the last bus back to whatever parking lot they left from. Perfect.

A couple of half-empty bottles sat on soggy beer mats. The bar emptied out except for Kyle the DJ and Sandy, a lone patron who asked, "You wanna do a shot of Patrón?"

I smiled. I liked Sandy.

Sandy was the new girl on the block. She came to town on a modeling contract and already everybody hated her. For the first week I saw her around, she made friends with everybody. Then everyone turned on her. There were rumors about her, but I try not to believe rumors.

I raised a glass to my first shift at St. Jerome's in the Lower East Side. I tossed out drinks and found a small pile of dollar bills and picked it up with my left hand, wiping the counter down with my right.

A straggler emerged from the bathroom and scowled at me, "You stealing my dad's money?"

"What? No. Everybody left and I told you before not to leave your money on the bar."

"We said we'd tip you at the end."

"When you leave, it *is* the end. And I told you I'm not your fucking waitress."

With this he snarled, grabbed the money pile (including my tips from other customers), and ran out the door. And you know what? Good riddance.

ONLY THAT WASN'T THE END. I don't know what he said to his elder on the outside. My guess is that he ran out screaming to a pack of drunk morons all hopped up on two-dollar beer and testosterone screaming, "Dad, the bartender just stole all your money and then he called you his 'fucking waitress'!"

The door burst open and Dad, acting on insider information, led the charge with the moronathon in tow, picking up lit candles off the tables and shattering them on my face. The hot wax and glass shards stuck to my skin. "You steal my money? You steal *my fucking money?*"

"Whoa. Hey. I didn't—"

I ducked the next candle, and the whiskey glass votive splintered on the mirror behind me, coating my face in hot wax. Still, I kept to my thesis: "I told you from the start. Money on the bar is my money." Because obviously this was a man to reason with.

He threw a punch across the bar. He had quite a reach for an old man but he missed. Dad grabbed a Corona from someone's table and chucked it right at me. I deflected it with my forearm, which only made him angrier. I pointed to the door: "Get the fuck out of here!"

"Don't fucking tell me what to do." He picked up a bar stool and chucked it at me. Only, he picked it up by the leg and hit me with the soft leather cushion. In deflecting that I ended up bouncing it back at him. So now we're having a pillow fight.

I looked around for help. Kyle stood in the DJ booth, cranking his tunes in his headphones like an extra playing a DJ in a music video, oblivious to the room. The rest of the crew decided to get involved, throwing full glasses at my face.

Dad grabbed the stool off the bar—by the seat this time—and stabbed at me. Somehow I took two of the pipe legs and leveraged them to twist out of his hands. This pushed him back, which he didn't like. He ran to the end of the L-shaped bar and charged at me, pushing the open cash drawer aside as he lunged for me. I flipped over the opposite end, kicking over drinks and purses. He tried to punch me over the bar once again but couldn't connect. I realized I had now done the stupidest thing you could do in a bar fight—I got out from behind the bar.

Dad then ran all the way *around* the bar and came after me.

The eight of them rushed over. When he stepped out from behind the bar one of them took a swing at me. Before he could connect I threw my head straight back and kicked my legs out, falling back behind the bar. The small of my back landed on the sharp metal sink and I kicked my legs up to get me all the way over. My foot landed on somebody's chin.

Sandy started whipping her purse at them. "Get the fuck away from him! Are you fucking crazy?!"

When Kyle pulled off his headphones, he heard me getting beat by eight guys and cut the music. He leapt out of the DJ booth, pulled a buck knife out of his pocket, grabbed Dad's son from behind, and held the blade to him. "If you even fucking touch my friend again I will fucking cut you. You got that?"

I turned to the clean-cut kid with the Amex. "Get him the fuck out of here." And I dialed 911.

"Put the fucking phone down and I will."

"Fuck you. All I fucking have is the phone. What am I gonna do, hit him with it?"

"Hang up the phone."

"Hello? Yes, officer. That's the address. The suspect is still here. He's about five foot five, gray-haired, wearing a blue plaid shirt. I have his friend's credit card and ID. Hurry."

"Hang up that phone!"

"What's that? They're already on their way?"

The phone said, "Thank you for calling the city of New York. Your call is important to us. Please stay on the line and . . ."

I hung up the phone when they left.

GUY ANSWERED HIS PHONE AFTER my fourth try. People stood in front of every bar on Rivington Street gawking at the eight cop cars. Detectives combed the empty booths and made notes about the damage. I had to tell them that none of it was new. I held the phone with my left hand as I pressed a paper towel into my bleeding shoulder. The rusty pipe leg of the barstool had cut a silver-dollar-sized hole in my back. Dad had left me a hickey.

Earlier I couldn't wait to leave; now I was scared to go.

I went to call Guy so he could hear it straight from me. His phone played a tinny, bothersome version of KISS's "Calling Dr. Love."

"What?" he finally answered.

"It's ten o'clock and Carla still isn't here."

"I'll call her." He went to hang up.

"One more thing. The cops are here."

"What the fuck happened? This is your first fucking day!"

When I told what happened he said, "That's the first rule of bartending: You never call the cops." That cannot be the first rule. "Get rid of them."

"I can't. Somebody else called when the fight broke out. I have to make a report and they need our liquor license and we don't have one anywhere."

"Tell them you forgot what this guy looks like."

"And what am I supposed to do if they're waiting for me around the corner in a van when I get out?"

"That's not going to happen."

"How would you know? This guy charged behind the bar. The register is busted and the drawer was wide open."

"That's different. Did he steal money?"

This guy and his fucking money.

"No. But you're telling me that if a guy robs the fuckin' place you don't want me to call the cops?"

"Get rid of the cops. I'm serious."

HOW I WAS GREETED BY the staff that evening:

Carla: "Why is it so dead in here?"

Her barback: "If you're going to stay for a drink, make sure you write it down on your sheet. Not ours."

The door guy: "Sorry I'm late. What'd I miss?"

Carla never mentioned the fact that I was almost beaten to death because she was getting her weave done. She did, however, ask why I didn't stock the hand towels in the bathroom. Sorry, I used them up when my wounds wouldn't clot.

Guy texted, "Don't say shit to anybody. I don't want to have to hear about this all week."

This fucking guy.

An intense fear crept up my leg when I went to leave. My skin burned from the hot wax. What if they're still here?

"Can your DJ stay a little later? Ours was supposed to be here at ten and he's not picking up his phone."

"Who was it supposed to be?"

"Omri, from Beauty Bar." That's *another* person who should have been on my team in the rumble. Not a goddamn model and her purse.

I don't ever want to step foot outside of this bar forever. So I said, "I'll do it."

IT WASN'T UNTIL ELEVEN THIRTY that I got my relief.

Until then, I had contracted into a ball of anxiety, nervously looking out the window to see if they would come back for me. I shivered every time someone pushed in the door. Suddenly I couldn't remember what any of them looked like. They all morphed into a drunken, trashy Captain Planet. One of them could be in here right now, keeping an eye out for when I stepped out or left for the night.

Just then the door burst open. My heart skipped a beat. And I couldn't believe it when I saw her.

The little angel I walked away from at Hotel Rivington was at the gym when she heard the news.

She leaped into the booth and grabbed me like I was her only son stepping out of a car wreck. And she asked the one question that no one else bothered to ask that night. She looked up at me, tears dancing on the edge of her eyelashes, and asked, "Are you okay?"

"Somehow."

"Did they get them?"

I told her how Guy told me to get rid of the cops and not file a report. "If they file a report he'll get in trouble with the boss. And I guess if they shut down the bar all of my friends would be out of a job."

She called me by my first name, which no one does. "Brendan, all the shitty bars in the world are not worth your life." She hugged me again and it wasn't until I forgot to switch the song and the whole room went silent that I realized I was crying.

Once I had a love and it was a gas

The next time I saw Gaga she walked up to me silent, sheepish, and biting her lower lip. She pointed her toes in and looked up at me. Her shoulders sloped down and so did her gaze. Her thick, dark, raven Italian mane had been fried on her head. All that was left behind were the broken strands of a much-loved doll. What normally swung free and full of life now clumped together, strings of mismatched lengths like a toupee. "What do you think?"

"You're *blonde*."

"They wanted to go with a new look."

I wanted to ask her if this had anything to do with the Amy Winehouse story from Lollapalooza. But we would find time for that later. "You'll look great."

"Are you sure?"

"Yes." I didn't lie. Technically. I was sure that she would look great. Right now she had the day-of haircut and bleach job. Her hair had broken off in some places, mangling her haircut.

After what happened at Lollapalooza ("Amy! Amy I love you!") and other problems, her management at Coalition Media thought she needed a "fresh start." They would later describe her as needing to be "blonde with olive skin." Earlier that day you would have described her as "pale with thick, dark hair." Rivington Street was aghast at the change. Already people talked about her "selling out," which is also known as "doing her job" or "having a job." Alien concepts around here. One thing you can't ignore is that Gaga came to the scene with a major record deal. She started so young and worked so diligently that she could have skipped making flyers, mass texting, and the basic hucksterism that most bands go through. And she didn't.

The first application of blonde didn't take too well. Ashy and a little brassy. Like the LES. She looked like one of the Golden Girls. "They're going to have to redo it," she said as she spread her frozen bangs with her fingers. Before, she had this thick, lustrous Italian hair that hung down, accentuating any of her sharper features. Now she had the kind of dead, gassed-out, NutraSweet-and-iced-tea blonde you see in truck stops. Her hands fussed with it, pumping it up, trying to make up for the blankness it left.

Guy looked happy for once. "How does he like it?" I asked.

Gaga rolled her eyes, and smiled to herself. "He likes fucking a blonde."

MORE THAN ANYTHING I'VE HEARD so far, blonde is a vote of confidence in Gaga. After being dropped from Island, her management team forged a new development deal with Interscope. When people asked how her deal with Island was coming along, she corrected them as if they'd misheard her before. Interscope. It was all about Interscope. But it looked like they would never focus on Gaga as a solo artist. They liked her music. But record company stooges didn't see her as a pop star.

One Monday morning I had to wait around St. J's while Guy fixed the bathroom door hinge.

"Fuck," he said. The former drummer cracked a hollow wood door.
"You need a washer."

"I got it." Guy cursed in a dad voice and didn't look me in the
eye. For all of his bellowing and stern, managerial speech, he never
looked anyone in the eye for more than five seconds. He cranked
away at the nut on the door hinge with his hair covering his eyes and
his frustration. The wood cracked again ("*Fffuck!*") and the bolt sunk
into the hollow door.

I dug into the toolbox. These tools wouldn't fix a thing. Vice grips,
and no wrenches; Allen keys, and only one kind of screwdriver. This
bar—however charming and wonderful and inviting—had the in-
sufficiencies of a college kid's first ramshackle apartment. It was
new and exciting, but if you slammed the door too hard the picture
frames would come crashing down from the wall.

"Here." I handed him a bottle cap that I punched a hole in with a
nail (because they didn't have a punch).

"What's that?"

"It's the dirty rock 'n' roll bar version of a washer."

He smiled. He finished the door with the Budweiser cap. The
overwhelming shittiness of it revived his spirits. In a very technical
sense, I used my abilities to impress my new boss in my first week.
Dad would be proud.

We spent the rest of the day fixing up the place.

"Where'd you learn how to do this stuff?"

"My brother's a mechanic. When he found out I was going away
to school he was worried I would grow up to be a pussy, so he made
sure I knew how to do these things. I could take a look at your El
Camino too, if you want."

"Did you tell your brother you pussed out with those guys the
other day?"

"There were eight of them, asshole. If I could fight two of them I'd still have six guys to go. Do you really want your bartenders fighting customers?"

"You lost control of the bar."

"Are we done here? I have shit to do."

"You work two days a week. What the fuck do you have to do?"

"I'm busy. I have writing and books to read and places to DJ. I'm not going to be a bartender for the rest of my life."

He didn't understand that last part at all. Why wouldn't someone want to be a bartender? Guy would bartend five nights a week here if the boss lady would let him.

WHEN I STEPPED OUT OF the bar's encapsulating shadows, I met the blinding afternoon. I realized for the first time that I didn't have shit to do. It was towing day on the streets and when the sweeper passed it left a damp little trail like a slug cleaning an aquarium.

Conrad had started school. My other friends all had real jobs. I didn't have a girlfriend anymore.

On my way over to my Vespa, I saw something wonderful. It deserved a perfect portrait like *Nude Descending a Staircase*. Only I would call it *Gaga Returning from a Follow-Up Hair Appointment*. A freshly swept Rivington Street guided her as she marched past the chain-linked court where kids from the projects played basketball. She wore high heels, fishnets, a leather jacket, and a small stark-white men's hat.

She didn't see me. But I watched her march past me with a wonderfully smug grin on her face. She had worn the hat to the salon in shame to cover up that bad bleaching job. Now she wore it cocked with pride.

Beneath it you could see her hair had now gone platinum. That's what you call foreshadowing.

Bleaching the surface of her hair made Gaga walk like a star. Her smug grin made it look like she caught you looking at her—and she knew. Most girls who worked all weekend would just plop around on Mondays in workout clothes and watch TV. But Gaga walked briskly down Rivington with a heavy bag. Like most of us, she worked a stop-off at St. J's into her routine, magnetized away from her apartment one block up and over. She came by on Mondays to spend time with Guy. To watch him work, but without all the drunk girls surrounding him. When I saw the way they had their little afternoon routine, I could see that she really did love him. She wanted to be a part of his world, to double count the stacks of money, to help around the bar. To break for dinner when he got frustrated. Then she'd earned her night with him and knew he could relax once everything was battened down.

They teased each other with inside jokes; they had a date rotation of dinner at home, movies, bowling on Sundays, visiting him at work, and band practice. I never mastered that with Nikki and it left us both unsettled, unsafe. No wonder the tiniest problem threw us into a tailspin.

She walked purposefully, like a busy career girl. Gaga had a full-time job now. The boss, the manager, a stylist, and the publicist. And the client she worked for was Lady Gaga.

I watched her walk past and noticed the sort of Lower East Side heads she turned as she marched down the still-wet streets. Hasidim shocked she wasn't wearing pants, guys from the projects checking out the white girl with ass, busybody neighbors scowling that the girl might catch cold, scenesters trying to figure out where they'd seen her before. Nobody here knew who she was, but they all wanted to.

Without turning her head she walked by me on the opposite side of Rivington and kept the same perfect 4/4 walking tempo. I saw the hat tilt just over her shoulder, "See you tonight, buster?"

"Yeah . . ." Busted. You can add me to the list between ghetto boys and scenesters. I was gawking. "We'll get dinner or something."

"Can't wait." She turned her head and gave me a devilish smile over the top of her shades.

And I knew right then she would be a star.

PART OF BEING A REGULAR or an employee of a certain kind of bar is feeling like a part of it. Beauty Bar always felt like home, but I never felt like a part of it. The bartenders and DJs had their own scene. Some of them had worked there for ten years even when I started playing there. St. Jerome's would have disappeared if it weren't for us. The year before we showed up, it was a failing wine-and-cheese shack called Belly. It failed miserably (bartenders were given forty dollars a shift and on most nights they didn't bring in enough to pay themselves minimum wage). So they painted it black and added a DJ booth. We all worked hard to make it a special place. Maybe the neighborhood didn't need one more dive. But we did.

After years of jobs where I felt replaceable—where I felt like my anonymous uniform was just waiting for another anonymous candidate to fill it when I got canned—now I belonged.

But not for long.

Ask me I won't say no, how could I?

I met British Henry a few years earlier when he first came to visit from London. I hadn't seen him since I started working downtown. Back then he worked for Martin McDonagh, the Irish playwright. Henry had a posh, privately educated accent and he always wore effortlessly matched outfits and took long, thoughtful drags of his American cigarettes. We sometimes sat in bars, making up stories about the people around us, rehearsing their lines of dialogue. Henry had a play produced when he was quite young and skipped university in order to get right to the business of playwriting. We both clung to minor successes, to one-acts and short stories published and performed where no one could find them.

He signaled for the check as we finished dinner at Stanton Social. "Can I ask you something, Brendan? I'm hearing you. I like you. I think you're a talented writer. What do these bands and singers and your friend's relationship to her terrible boyfriend have to do with your work?"

I actually had no idea. Usually I'm better at faking an answer.

"You know I think you're a genius," he said.

"That is a bit off topic, but thanks."

"But here's the thing with genius: It still gets confused." The check came and I discovered, thankfully, that the drinks had managed to fall off the total. "I know what you want to do here. With your bands and your parties and your music and your writing. You want to create something for yourselves. You will be the one who writes about it. But you're getting in the way of your story. Right now you're in the thick of it and you can't see out."

"Come to our show next week. I'm DJ'ing and she's go-go dancing, but we're going to slip in some of her music this time. People are bored of bands—it's such a chore. Why stop the music? I'm going to play and then she'll go on and sing. It'll be different."

"Is something going on with you two?"

"No. Why would you ask that?"

"She's just the part of your life that doesn't make any sense."

"Maybe she's the only part that makes sense to me."

"Interesting," the playwright mused.

WE WALKED DOWN STANTON TO Ludlow while large groups of people our age tried to figure out where to make bad decisions. They swarmed together in the cold autumn night. As you passed every venue it was the roar of voices, not music, that marked their vital signs. Everyone always looking for everyone in the uncertainty of night. I caught a girl's eyes, thinking she might be Nikki, and when she looked into mine I knew she wasn't. The strange girl looked back at me and wished that I was who she thought I was. I wished that Nikki thought I was who she thought I was when we met.

"All I'm saying is that it would work as a play," Henry said.

"What would?" I looked over at British Henry, who had carried on our conversation and didn't seem to mind when I disappeared.

"*Mercutio.* We are supposed to be talking about your writing. Correct? All the feedback you're getting and all the difficulties you're having just point to the fact that it would really only work on stage. And I don't have to tell you that English audiences wou—"

"Get out of my way! I'm going to fucking *kill* somebody!" Just then a young screaming woman in a red flannel shirt burst through the smoking herd outside of Pianos, swinging her purse. She shoved everyone out of her way, kicking the doors of parked cars and slinging her leather purse at terrified strangers. "I hate you! I hate all of you!"

The oversized wool button-down hung off one side, revealing a bare shoulder. The red of her eyes matched the shirt. She swiped the purse at a girl in front of her, but she missed and it whipped her around, spinning her on the spiked heel of her shoe. The other girls stepped away as if from a wild animal woken from hibernation. The street went silent as she turned to them, her shirt fell open, and her left breast glared at the speechless crowd. "I hate you. I hate you. I hate your fucking face!"

She turned her back on the gathering crowd and started trying to hail cabs, kicking their plastic taillights as they sped away from her. Part of my job was making sure drunk girls didn't do anything stupid, so I went to hail one for her and I finally got her in, screaming. She kicked the partition and screamed at the Nigerian man at the wheel, "Fucking drive! Get me out of here!"

The car sped off.

Henry never lost the thread: "You want to write about a world in which the Montagues and Capulets are real. At the same time, Dante is exiled from Florence in Verona."

"Which did happen. All of it happened. But no one's writing about it."

"I agree with you. I'm surprised this hasn't been written." Henry nodded with sincerity. "Put some pages together for me and I'll show it 'round in London. But do it for the stage. You really have this dynamite lead, the setting—you just need the story. I mean, you have the ending and then you have this catalyst, this time bomb. And—"

"I hate you! I fucking hate you! *Fuuuck!*" At the corner of Ludlow and Rivington we turned and saw that same girl screaming and getting thrown out of another cab. Bodily. She landed on the street in a pile of flannel and purse shrapnel. Plastic palettes of makeup clattered onto the chilly sidewalk. The open shirt hung off the right shoulder this time, buttoned only at the belly.

I picked her up again and she started screaming at me. For the sake of brevity, I will have to paraphrase her argument: Fuck you, I hate all of you, you all make me sick, fuck you. It is similar to how I felt when I walked down Rivington Street on weekends.

"Sweetie, just get off the street and put your coat on. Relax. Breathe." I let go of her and she tore down Rivington towards Essex. A cab that had a green light came screeching in front of her. The driver's eyes widened as he tightened his brakes. It stopped so close that it banged her purse.

She gripped the strap to punctuate her disgust and slammed it against the hood of the honking cab. "I. Hate. *You!*" The wild woman kicked the grill of the cab that almost killed her. Her boot got stuck and she fell backward into the intersection. The cab honked. British Henry and I were crossing that way as it happened. I picked her up for the third time, which was easy because she weighed maybe ninety pounds. She looked me in the eyes, tears spreading to the corners of hers, and wimped, "I hate you—"

"Shut the fuck up. I hate you too, just so you know." I put her down in a pile on the street. "Fucking breathe or you're going to pass out. Breathe through your stomach. No. Your stomach. Like me, ready?"

I crouched down and wrapped my jacket around her icy skin, holding her elbows with mine. "Why is everyone so awful?" she asked, as if taking a survey.

"Because you fucking hate them. Now breathe. Just fill your lungs as much as you can." I ran my fingernails in her hair. "Shhh . . . just breathe."

British Henry looked nervous, like we'd found a bear cub. "Maybe we should leave her alone, Brendan. We should go."

What was really odd was that the only word for what I was doing with this stranger is "cuddling." I also have to admit that it felt marvelous, but in the least creepy way possible. Then she whimpered, "I'm not on drugs."

I patted her hair. "Who said you were on drugs?"

"You're thinking it. You think I'm crazy."

"Are you crazy?"

"I have schizophrenia and bipolar disorder."

"I'd like to hear more about that sometime. Sounds awesome."

"Why do you think that's awesome?" She eked out the words from deep in her diaphragm, like someone trying to get a word in before the tears took over.

"Because you can be on vacation from yourself. Do you have your medicine on you?" For the twelfth creepiest thing I did to her that night, I started searching through her purse. It was full of makeup, headphones, sparkly underwear, titty tassels, and prescription bottles. Only later would this reporter deduce that she was a dancer uptown in a place where people go to see strippers. "Honey, these are all empty."

"I just want to go home. Can you take me home?"

"I can't take you home like this—can we get a refill somewhere?"

"I just want to go home."

"You can't. You just offended half the Middle East. Allah forbids you from getting in another cab right now."

"He's following me."

"Who's following you?"

"I saw him at work. He's not supposed to be there. And then as soon as I got downtown I saw him again."

"Who?"

"I don't *know*."

SHE STARTED SCREAMING AGAIN WHEN the ambulance pulled up. "Don't put me in there! I don't have any money! Don't put me in there!"

"What a crazy girl," Henry said. "Why on earth wouldn't she want to go into an ambulance?"

"Henry, you're being too English right now. I have a standing agreement with all of my friends where unless I am bleeding directly from an aorta, put me in a cab."

"That's ridiculous." Henry didn't quite understand American health care.

We watched them load the girl into the ambulance, her screams muffled first by the oxygen mask and then by the closed doors. You could still hear her screams over the lights and sirens as they took her up Essex Street to Bellevue. We stood there in the street until she disappeared.

"Wouldn't it be great if you met your wife this way?" Henry asked.

"You can use that in a play. I don't think it would be very believable."

"I can see it now, Brendan. Everywhere else in you life you never mattered. But down here, these people need you. And you need them too. Or at least they want something from you and you want them to."

I took that in for a second. The only question I asked was, Is that believable? The answer was yes. "That's good playwriting, Henry," I said.

"And a really awful way to live your life," he replied.

AND SCENE.

I ain't seen the sunshine since I don't know when

What makes the bars on Rivington different from all others in the city is that the bartenders are expected to plan, manage, and run their nights in competition with each other to see who gets the best shifts. Literally every other bartender in the city shows up for a job like every other hardworking person. But on Rivington you have to advertise: you beg bands to do after-parties and you text your soon-to-be-ex friends.

In the fall of 2007 President Bush was having problems with that country he had invaded. The transition of power hadn't gone smoothly. Those in charge didn't understand the people they were in charge of. Handing over authority seemed a disaster. And on this side of the world I took over for Brent, the LES's most beloved bartender. I prepared to stay the course, even hiring his regular DJs instead of mine. That Thursday night I got there early, dimmed the lights, cleaned the bar, and popped in an old silent-film version of Dante's *Inferno* on the projection screen. And within an hour I was in hell.

Getting jumped on my first night left me a wreck. Every time the music got distorted, I worried that the DJ couldn't hear me scream if I got attacked. When people at the end of the bar shouted out my name for drinks, I flinched. Everyone still came by after their bands played or after they waitressed uptown, only now, instead of requesting songs and asking for drugs, they demanded free drinks.

The following types of people, however, were completely perplexed as to why I would not automatically give them a free two-dollar beer:

1. DJs who spun on other nights in the area

2. Drummers from bands that also contain members of Rivington Street bartenders

3. Girlfriends of on-duty bartenders up the street who don't want to watch them flirt with other girls all night for tips

4. Former barbacks

5. People I had met one time before

The only people who didn't expect free drinks were the drug dealers. They respected that you both had a job maintaining an expensive supply of poisons. Only once did one ask me for a Bacardi and Coke. And he paid. Otherwise, they were content to sit in the corner, sometimes three or more of them coming in and out. You couldn't really fault them for hanging around. It's their neighborhood too. I wished more gangsters would hang around because the ones I knew were really great guys with young kids. One of them was trying to drum up the capital to get a bodega started. Another had his eyes on a barbershop. I would trade one dealer for ten flakey scenesters on the day I got jumped. Two or three of them would have torn those eight guys apart. More than I can say for my so-called friends.

WHEN SHE WALKED IN WEARING the red flannel shirt I couldn't believe it. She had an unstable clarity in her eyes as she scanned the room for her friends. The girl I'd put into an ambulance the Monday before reminded me of an old car I had once. It had a lot of miles on it, but if you tightened the brakes and checked the tire pressure, it would run smooth. The shirt slipped from her bare shoulder again.

She plopped her purse on the bar and rooted through its shiftless, unstable contents as she sat down on another girl's stool. Finally she came up with a rattle of a pill bottle and read the tiny instructions by candlelight before looking up at me. "Could I just get a glass of water?"

"Sure." I placed it down in front of her. And waited.

She popped something into her mouth and went for the glass. When she saw me looking at her she stopped, the pill cradled in her curled tongue as she held water just inches from her lips. "Sorry. Is there a charge?"

"No." I said. And I waited. "You don't remember me, do you?"

She looked up at me, a little fearful. The energy between us felt a little one-night-stand-y, one of us with greater expectations than the other. She swallowed and clutched the front of her open shirt, shrinking her shoulders and making herself smaller like a scolded child. "Yes. You're the only bartender who charges me for drinks." She dug through her purse, defeated, until she found three dollar bills in the side zippered pockets. "That's all I have." She put it down as a tip.

I shook my head and gave her the money back. "Did you get out of the hospital okay?"

Her dim eyes flickered to life like the florescent lighting of a basement storage room. "How you hear about that?"

I looked into her eyes, bright but not quite showing all the vital signs. She had the narcotic glaze of superficiality that looked also like colored contact lenses. "I was the one who put you in the ambulance."

Her mouth hung open in disbelief. Then a shudder of recognition. She brandished a shoulder with two bruises. "There were six of them holding me down while one of them shot me up with tranquilizers. They started screaming that if I didn't calm down they would shoot me again. And they did. I was having a nervous breakdown when you found me."

"Do you feel better now?"

A look washed over her eyes, miles away from the denim and noise of this bar. The look didn't come from the pills, which arrested her movements and kept even her thoughts strapped down to the gurney. The look came from somewhere inside, miles away. "Yes." She smiled.

GUY WALKED IN LIKE HE owned the place. "Why's the music still on?" Authoritative and full of bullshit and he still wouldn't look me in the eye. You can't respect someone like that and I straight up hated it. After taking shit from all his friends all night, I didn't want to hear any more from him.

"I'm cleaning up. We had a good night."

He walked over to the speaker system and turned it all the way off. "Where's your inventory?"

I cleaned one of the bottles with a bar rag. "Almost done."

He turned the register key and the battered machine coughed up the results like a bullied informant. He saw the total.

"You call that a ring? What did I tell you on the phone? I said $1,500 or we're going to have a problem. Right? Is this $1,500?"

I looked at the receipt: $1,385. "If it means that much to you, I'll buy us $115 in shots. And you can still tell the owners you yelled at me. That'll probably cover how many of your friends came in for free drinks tonight."

"This isn't Dark Room or Motor City or *Pianos*, where everyone drinks for free. If my own mother comes in here asking for free drinks, you throw her ass out."

I couldn't do anything about drinks I hadn't sold by then. I went back to cleaning and trusted that by not over-pouring all over town I'd at least saved the bar money. My inventory would look fine.

Then I heard the twin rattles of keys and spokes come through the door. Conrad let himself in with his keys and pushed the door open. He worked Thursdays at a venue down the street called Fontana's but couldn't fight the magnetic force of Rivington Street on his way home every night. For about five seconds I was happy to see him. "How'd the kid do tonight?"

"Terrible," Guy said. "Come help me drink to forget how much I'm gonna get reamed out tomorrow for vouching for this kid."

Conrad rolled a cigarette from a sack of Bali Shag. The stray bits of tobacco scattered on the bar I'd just cleaned.

"What'd he ring?"

Guy told him.

"On a Thursday?" Conrad licked the cigarette paper. "Didn't you say Thursdays were the best nights for the solo bartender?"

I crouched down beneath the bar to hide my fury as I counted the number of empty versus full bottles of liquor in the inventory. Then I heard Guy: "They were. Until this cat came along."

Until "this cat" came along? Until I came along and brought my friends? Until I started DJ'ing here? Until I rang more on Thursdays in my residency than you rang on Fridays with two bartenders? So angry. I stood up.

Guy lit a cigarette and blew it in my face. "Gimme two shots of Hornitos."

I put three glasses down. Guy gave me a look. I asked, "Can I get one too?"

"Not with a ring like that." He clanked shot glasses with Conrad, rammed the bar with the glass, and took it down in one gulp. "You want a beer? Give Conrad a Bud."

He then interrupted every single thing I did for the rest of my shift.

"Can you believe what a year we've had?" he asked Conrad. He pounded his beer down. "And it all started that night I came next door to you just to bitch about my door guy not showing up."

Really, Guy? That's what brought this bar into fruition? Fucking Conrad. I was livid. How many flyers have I made and how many nights have I put in everything I had?

When I finished my work I looked up at Guy, expecting something. He looked around the room, and when he decided I had done everything I could, he put on his leather jacket and Conrad pulled his bike off of the go-go booth.

"So look. It'll take me a while to build Thursdays, but I'll get there. So I want to talk to you about Fridays. Now that I'm not DJ'ing on Thursdays anymore, how are your Fridays looking? You ready to bring me back in?"

He gave a smirk around the room—not really at anyone, since the only person between us was Conrad.

"Here's the thing. I can't really have you tend bar here on Thursdays and then DJ here on Fridays. It won't work. It's too much of the same thing."

"Every other bar in New York City has employees that work more than one night."

He smirked again. "This isn't every other bar in New York City."

Whatever happened to the Transylvania Twist?

Halloween ripped through downtown Manhattan that year like some sort of twisted Chanukah: Eight days of madness in costumes and smeared makeup kicked off the Wednesday before and didn't truly end until the subway ride home that Thursday morning in an ill-fated outfit.

This Halloween marked a complete turning point in downtown life, and some would argue that this was the moment where it stopped being fun. What was once a semi-secret escape for a few became an everybody's-famous fuckfest to sell off-brand energy drinks and vodka to overeager kids who swarmed to online ads and sponsored, bought-and-paid-for mass texts for open bars. I don't have anything original to say about it that doesn't make me sound about eighty-five years old. So I'll just say: We've all had the experience of finding something cheap online that later turned out to disappoint. Welcome to the new world of nightlife.

An icy frost met me at the door to Motherfucker at a club called Rebel. Thomas made me wait at the door in a steady, but not unmoving, line. At the door I could tell something was up. He cleared the sidewalk and the processing area ("IDs out, kids. Everybody's getting in . . .") and when he had me alone he looked me in the eye and muttered, "It is like *Clash of the Titans* in there."

I marched around the bi-level club looking for my friends, to tell them I came to support, see if they needed drinks. In every room, I met up with a few no-eye-contact smiles. Somebody locked the door to the main DJ booth, where I had planned on hanging out. The bartenders pressed on, sluggish and Bhutan. Drunk girls teetered on high heels, stabbing me in the toes. Drag queens clubbed me with their elaborate headpieces as they turned their heads looking for friends and fixes.

Q: What did one scenester say to the other when they weren't partying?
A: God, these people are obnoxious.

My night ended with Conrad, at Welcome to the Johnsons, straining to shut up a drunk girl in the nicest way possible.

At the door I saw Kelvin, completely disgusted with the decade. Kelvin had worked in clubs at the GM level for years and got sick of it. Now he checked IDs four nights a week on Rivington and drank in the bars here the other seven. He sat on a stool while a flock of drunk, loud girls dressed like slutty Little Bo Peeps refused to leave. Nightlife photographers and self-proclaimed reporters circled like fruit flies. Kelvin hung his head in disgust. "It's like you used to go to the zoo to feed the animals. Now they're trying to market *us* feeding the animals."

The day after Halloween brought in a mixed bag of news. After that unstoppable Chanukah of Halloween, I was forced to keep up with the task, to text and cajole everybody into one more night before Friday took over. After seven years of throwing absolutely the craziest parties you've ever seen, Motherfucker disbanded, citing personality conflicts.

Still, Gaga walked into the bar the day after Halloween with a huge smile. "Can you believe it?" she said to me. "That somebody came to Motherfucker Halloween *dressed as Lady Gaga*?"

SHE CAME BACK HALF AN hour later with Guy. Big smiles on their faces. Guy had a smirk a mile wide, the kind you only see on his face the moment he threw down his winning cards. Gaga basked in his attentive light as he put one hand under her leather jacket, gently guiding her in the door by the small of her back. He had on a matching leather jacket with equally sagging shoulders, embellishments of chains, studded spikes, and other bangles clanking along. They were both laughing about something that neither could quite explain. You had to be there.

"Will you make me one of those VH1 margaritas?"

"You mean a Gagarita?"

Under the bar we have, inexplicably, a few proper bar tools (nothing fancy: a muddler and a strainer). We don't have any fresh juices here and our margaritas rely heavily on lemonade from the soda gun and Rose's lime juice.

But when Gaga came by, I liked to try something special for her, something more becoming of a semi-highly-trained bartender. I took all the best parts of a shitty dive bar and made the best of it.

½ lemon, muddled

¼ lime, muddled

1 deli packet of sugar (but usually 7UP and a little OJ)

1 oz. triple sec

2 oz. Sauza Hornitos

Shaken and served on the rocks in a pint glass

Guy went out for a smoke and I smiled at her. "I'm glad you guys worked it out."

"You know how he gets." She took another sip. "We should hang out more."

"Agreed."

"I mean, like, not in a bar with you DJ'ing or bartending. Like in real life."

"I'd love to."

"But he'll kill you if he finds out."

I looked at her for a second, trying to figure out what she meant. "We can all go out together. You guys and"—there comes a day when your friends have all paired off and the only way to see them is on double dates—"I dunno, you got a sister?"

"Yes."

"Perfect."

"She's sixteen."

"Oh."

Guy walked back in through the creaky, insistent door. Before he sat down, she whispered, "Just you and me then. I'll play you the new tracks I have. Bring whatever you're working on. Just don't say anything to him. He'll kill me if he finds out."

"What are you girls yakking about?" Guy sat down and tossed an arm around her.

"Music." I said. Which is true.

Something on the projection screen caught his eye. Gaga tossed me a smile.

"Can we go now?"

"Fine." Guy got up from his stool. "Now remember what I said. Fifteen hundred or else . . ."

* * *

THURSDAY LED TO A DARK autumn Friday. I stayed in bed. I spent the night before in a fit of hospitality, coaxing broke downtown kids into doing something crazy—like buying a drink. My day started with a text from Guy: "Your drawer is $26 short."

I dropped by the bar that night and it felt like I never left. Lady Starlight was dancing in the red light of the go-go booth with a pair of pom-poms and little else. One of Guy's clones headbanged away in the DJ booth, blinded by the disco ball. Denim and leather from the front door to the back bathroom.

Guy flirted with a couple of bar creatures and then greeted me. "I heard you had fun last night."

"Did I?"

"Sounded like it."

Gossip travels fast and slippery on this block. Whatever did or did not happen is inconsequential as long as it did or did not happen with a limited number of pre-approved people. It's not a sin to like someone that someone else likes, but you *cannot* like someone that someone else doesn't like. Extra points available for any kind of achievement that includes anyone new to the scene, but no points awarded for any work done with an unknown.

I ordered a beer and a shot of Jameson and turned to watch Starlight dance to her favorite Faith No More song, "Epic." When I turned back, I saw Guy with his hair in his eyes, making no effort to move his hands from the bottle he'd just opened for me. He stood there, motionless, with a grip on the sweaty neck of the Budweiser bottle. I looked around to see what went wrong. As a reflex, I stuck my hand in my pocket and handed him a twenty. "That's for you."

He nodded and put the bill in his tip jar.

Money made Guy smile. Money made him wink at girls he'd never speak to elsewhere. Money kept him in town when others might take a vacation. Money sent him to Atlantic City on his first day off. Money brought him into the bar to open the safe on quiet Monday afternoons to count the money—not even his money. Just money. Money was my boss's boss. I took another sip from the bottle. Normally the overcooled beer fridge at St. Jerome's produced the world's best ice-cold beer. They lay flat, like treasure in a wine cellar, maturing and nurturing its contents with a fine layer of sediment. That night, it just tasted like buck-nasty beer.

I leaned across the bar and dropped the bottle on the bar mats. And bailed.

Watch your heart when we're together

I got off the D train at Grand Street and took my usual walk through the markets of Chinatown, where the sidewalks stank of brine and iced fish. Some stayed open late, peddling plastic bags of obscure sea creatures, many of them still flapping their gills. Middle-aged men stood on the grease-stained sidewalks, wearing knitted grip gloves with rubber palms. This commute of mine only cost me one stop on the subway, rather than transferring to one of the nearby lines to find an F train, or taking the subway all the way to Union Square, and taking the L train to First Avenue and walking fourteen blocks to Allen Street. The Lower East Side does not go out of its way to be convenient.

I went out of my way to go past Stanton Social, knowing that Nikki worked upstairs. Her network of hostesses and bouncers might see me walk past. I marched with dignity, with shoulders back and with a deep, abiding sadness inside of me. We had been broken up longer than we were ever together. It still didn't get any easier. At Allen, I crossed over and took Stanton on my daily stomp past Pianos,

Living Room, Iggy's, through that blank block of actual respectable establishments on Rivington between Ludlow and Essex, until I crossed Essex and passed along greetings to the various soldiers and sentries I met. Most of them wanted to know if I'd be at Mason Dixon later. There's a party. Someone's birthday. Meet me there. Meet me there at midnight. We'll do a shot.

I have succeeded now in discovering a reason for going out and partying another night.

GAGA'S APARTMENT ON STANTON STREET looked like it was designed by the witness protection program for a young female informant. My grandparents would call it a tenement. One flight up the florescent-lit, chipped-paint hallway on a narrow, echoey, too-steep staircase where your feet clacked on the stone. Like many things in my daily struggle, each step felt just slightly more difficult than I imagined. Carting synthesizers and secondhand furniture up these stairs never got any easier. Sometimes the wooden railing with too many coats of paint was the only thing to keep me from misjudging my step and tumbling to my own slapstick demise.

Her building was suspended in time; the cooking smells rose from the half-agape transom above the doorways. A pair of glass doors separated the bedroom and living room. They also separated this tiny space from the studio category on Craigslist. By dropping out of school at nineteen, Gaga missed out on much of the college-kid experience, but she made up for it by living in this adorable Fisher-Price toy called "My First Apartment."

"Hi!" she chirped at the door. Her hands in her blond hair. "Still getting ready. Come in."

A few discarded pairs of heels were lying on the floor by her door—wounded soldiers on the battlefield. She greeted me with a beautiful smile and then went to mill around and do the kind of last-minute cleanup that we could all dispense with. I think we were the kind of friends that could accept each other as is, but I'd probably do the same thing if she came over to my place.

A cheap flat-screen TV blabbed in the background with its over-exposed colors and gabby spokespersons. She had abandoned flipping channels somewhere in the basic cable range.

Two pint glasses sat in a near-empty drying rack by the sink. A mismatched, unpainted Ikea kitchenette island floated in the middle of the room next to a single stool, last week's mail, and a set of black and yellow Guitar Center studio monitors. She had a pair of brand-new Technics 1200 turntables and a base-level mixer, all stacked up on a shelf, both used just once at Lollapalooza. The uniformity of both her furniture and equipment reminded me that she was still a young girl, fresh out of the nest. Nice girls from the Upper West Side don't have basements full of dated furniture to pilfer on the way to their first apartments. A fresh bookcase on the end held a few re-cords, some books, and miscellany. The entire apartment had the air of something purchased on the run, with a few parental flourishes of domesticity.

A well-read girl with few books. A music super-fan with eight records. A downtown fashion icon with half a closet of clothes. I saw this as a sign of her attachment and not her abdication of the Upper West Side. Anyone from Ohio or Minneapolis who came to New York to be a pop singer would pack every vestige of her former life into the shelves. The Ohio refugee would have a sentimental collection of books, stuffed animals, and cherished, rarely played CDs. Stef's parents housed all the embarrassing photos and piano song-books. They keep guard of her childhood and memories while she stayed downtown to work on being Lady Gaga. The kitchen—and really by extension the entire apartment—served as a command center where she could focus on making music.

All she had were six vinyl records that her producer in Jersey had pressed for Starlight to play over her singing. As a record collector, I already felt a Pavlovian sweat come across my fingertips. I reached out and opened them all. Up until then this was the only music of hers ever pressed.

"Don't mind me, I'm just getting ready," she said while rifling through a makeup bag. "Would you like a drink?"

"Always."

Gaga pulled out a bottle of Louis Jadot Beaujolais—one of the world's finest dirt-cheap wines—and gave me a perfect six-ounce pour in a pint glass. "I never asked you this before, but were you ever a waitress?"

"For *years*," she said.

"I can tell. You do a perfect pour just by sight. I'm impressed."

"Years of practice. But, like, when I was a kid I started at sixteen at this place down on MacDougal. I want to bartend now but—"

"Don't. Bartending takes away your hunger and replaces it with thirst." I had a secret in my pocket. Something that made me quite nervous to share. But sometimes when you're trying to keep something down it's like pushing it against a spring. I had a new chapter tucked in my jacket like a jack-in-the-box, and hiding it from her made my words come out way too profound.

She leaned out of the bathroom door with a brush halfway through a stroke. "That's genius," she said. "But even if I wanted to I couldn't." She went on to explain that Guy wouldn't let her.

"That's a bullshit reason not to do something, but I think you should just stay focused on your music. You'd never want to have to cancel a trip for recording because you couldn't get the time off."

"When they were opening Mason Dixon I asked them if I could get a spot over there and he said no."

"I wasn't even offered a slot."

"Can you imagine what your life would be like if you had a shift at Pianos, St. Jerome's, *and* Mason? *And* you still DJ'd at Beauty Bar? You'd never be able to keep a girlfriend."

I laughed. She had a point. "My schedule's kind of bullshit right now. It's like I work every other day all week. I never get any time away. I like to travel. I like to be moving."

"I'm the same way."

I sat on the couch and she kept tidying up, folding bills into their return envelopes and stacking misplaced fashion magazines.

She looked up at me and could tell my mind was elsewhere. "You were thinking about Nikki." She cocked her head in appraisal and nodded. "You two were really in love."

I felt lost when she said that. Perhaps I preferred to live in a world where my love of Nikki came as a side effect—a by-product of insanity. Hearing Gaga mention it as fact didn't make sense. I started to sweat in that tiny apartment. I stood up to take off my jacket and the pages slipped out of my pocket and fell onto the floor. She gasped. "Is that what I *think* it is?"

Fuck. I had already chickened out on that.

"Did you bring me pages to read?"

"Actually I thought maybe I—I dunno—I could read it to you?"

"Yay!" She did her giddy little clap, bouncing a bit in her bare feet like a little girl. Which—well—she was.

"Yay!" She clapped again. "I've never done a two-person reading before. Do I stand?"

"How about this. Lie down and close your eyes and I'll tell you a story." She smiled and put her head in my lap.

AFTER I FINISHED READING THE first chapter of *Mercutio* I put the pages down and took a deep breath. Gaga looked up at me, speechless. I wondered for a second if she maybe didn't get it or if the pages didn't make sense out of context. In that micro-pause, I had the vague sense that I had just thrown up. All the unease and sickness I felt before left me empty, but satisfied. She opened her eyes at me. "That was amazing."

I looked down at her. "Let me see the pages." She opened them up and whipped through the whole story again, giggling at the parts she liked. "You need to be doing this. On stage. You need to get a group of actors together and perform this in underground theaters until you have someone begging to produce it."

"Huh . . ." I had nothing to say, nothing prepared at least.

She looked me square in the eye. "And you should do the lead. I didn't know you projected like that."

"It's not really a play. I mean, I get that you—"

"Have you ever thought about using the page itself as a canvas?"

"Uhm . . . I mean it's a first draft. It's pretty much exactly how it came out."

"I mean like this." She flipped over the page to the blank side. "I took a creative writing class once. I wrote a story about the worst day of my life."

"When you got dropped from Island?"

"No," she said, as if I should know better. "When my sister fell out of the tree. I wanted to create a simple way of explaining what she had gotten into and what was at stake."

Two stories up

She climbed.

Two

Stories

Down

She

Fell.

She leafed through the pages again. "I like what you say about two sides of things." She glanced over at her command center with her laptop and speakers. "I—" She hesitated just as much as I did. And I knew she had something in store for me. "I have a song with that same idea in mind."

Finally I could exhale. Thank god we're doing this.

"Play it for me *right now*." She got up and put on a track. It began with a harsh beat, a decaying synth horn, and a backwards-bass effect. "Turn it up." I lay down on the floor with my eyes closed to hear it for the first time.

She shouted over the backing track, "I wrote this for him!" She meant Guy. "You know how he doesn't like anything that isn't metal? And he doesn't like my sing-songy piano ballads? So I wanted to write a song he would like. I work on the music to impress him, so I can be close to him. But the more I work on the music it's like the more the music will take me away from him. When I'm famous, I won't have time for him, but if I don't work on the music, he'll get bored and leave me." The track played on to the part where the paparazzi are chasing her chasing him. "And then it's like I call him Papa. Paparazzi." That was the name of the song.

I got it right away, and I liked how it had more to it. "What a brilliant track."

She smiled and bit her lower lip. "Want more?" She looked for the next track. Most of the songs had obscure titling. She put on "Track 2 - Lady GaGa." "This is another one along the same lines, only you know that song you guys all play? 'Girls Girls Girls'? I wanted to write one like it called 'Boys Boys Boys' and you're going to die when you hear it."

She started up a familiar song with a simple structure. "It's about a girl on a date with a boy she really likes. She gets really excited and she really wants it to go well, but she's mostly excited because it's an occasion, not just a hangout date."

"You mean this girl is going out and not just going out to the same three bars with her bartender boyfriend?"

"Yes. In fact, they even go *uptown*."

"Oh."

"They go see the Killers in the Garden and make out in the bleachers."

She played the song, another synth-driver track with a drum machine backup. I instantly liked it. It didn't sound like anybody else downtown. She looked up from the laptop with her lips pursed into the smile of one who slaved away all day cooking up a surprise for her true love. Gaga bounced a little, trying to hold in her smile. The jaunty synth notes brought me back to that early spring night when we'd last seen the Killers. I remembered the crisp air and the expressionless leather on all of our friends' jackets. I remember standing on milk crates and looking out on the gorgeous room, everyone with pint glasses aloft.

"Is this the one you told me about at Pianos, with the—"

Gaga put up a manicured index finger. (Meaning both "Shush" and "One second.")

It was the song she told me about earlier. I didn't believe it really existed. The one about the Killers and how their friend was the DJ.

It's one thing to hear that a friend wrote a song. But this. This isn't some coffee shop singer-songwriter ballad. This is a high-gloss pop masterpiece with tinted windows. This is real. *"Let's go to the party / Heard our buddy's the DJ . . ."*

Stunned. My mouth hung open. I remember the Killers after-party being a thankless task, which annoyed me and Nikki. But then I heard this song and I realized that maybe, just maybe, somebody there had fun.

"Did I hear that right?" I gasped. "I'm in your song—playing a song?" As moronically as possible I say, "I'm your buddy! I'm the DJ!"

Her delighted teeth smiled through the purple stains of the cheap Beaujolais. Despite talking about music, seeing bands, talking about shows, hanging out with other bands, and being completely obsessed with music, none of us had really heard much of Gaga's music just yet. I felt a cool relief wash over me. In nightlife, it barely mattered if a band were any good as long as it got people in the club. But now, I realized what an amazing talent fit into this tiny little girl. The song ended and I looked up at her. We were both a little out of breath when I said, "Play it again?"

Gaga played her own, personal John Peel, playing the unmastered record samples over and over again.

"You're gonna die. Ready? Remember when I came back from Lollapalooza all broken and you had me play with Semi Precious Weapons?" She threw on another track; this one began with backwards piano. But right before the beat begins you hear her angelic voice take in a breath, tuning up her instrument at the last second, like a string section second-guessing a change in temperature. Gaga—the one in front of me, not the one on the track—shouted over the loud studio speakers, "I wrote one about that night too!"

"Midnight at the glamour show on a Sunday night . . ."

I stopped the track cold.

Gaga looked up at me in the silence.

I said, "Sorry. I need to hear that opening breath again." The beauty of it struck me, and it sounded like an angelic choir behind me that night when I sat in the basement of the venue, taking a deep breath and hoping my new idea would work out. Every detail of that night at Pianos, from the Sunday night, from who had to get up early the next day, what people drank, her go-go dancing for dollars, flirting with guys, hanging out with the other bands. She crammed it all into this one track and it *still* didn't sound like an in-crowd record. And just in the background, spouted as a boast and certainly only to herself, you can hear a little girl trying to be her own best friend and tell herself how wonderful she is—even if she's not the person she wanted to hear that from. Even if that person didn't show up.

"This is just the beginning. I don't even want to just be a singer forever. I'm going to be a producer. I'm going to bring in young bands and help them develop. I am going to be the grandmother of pop."

I SCROLLED THROUGH THE TRACKS on her computer when she went into the bathroom. She had a couple of Gwen Stefani songs, but she didn't have that catalogue of music that we always talked about. Judas Priest's "Living After Midnight," "Your Love" by the Out-field (which I assumed was her father's influence), "Fergalicious" by Fergie, "Metal Militia" by Metallica (which she and Starlight had played between songs at Lollapalooza), "Girls on Film" by Duran Duran, "Forever My Queen" by Pentagram, and "Hold On" by Wilson Phillips. And that was it. Again I'd like to read into these in some way. But all the songs really came out of some necessity on the road. I scanned the dates of the tracks. She only got Fergie last winter, which made sense—before Gaga started hanging out with us downtown, but around the time when she still had to impress people at Island Def Jam. Starlight turned her on to "Metal Militia." But then she'd had it longer than she'd had the demos to "Boys Boys Boys" and "Paparazzi."

She opened the door to the bathroom and walked back into the kitchen. "I was just thinking how excited I am for your book."

That surprised me. Were we still talking about that? "I'm even more excited for your record," I said. "But I'm not sure there ever will be a book."

She plopped down next to me on the futon. "What matters is that you wrote it. You perform it really well." She picked up the pages again. "Maybe you could . . . maybe you could just record yourself reading it."

"I wonder if that would suck. It'd probably be better if I read it to somebody."

"You can read it to me." She smiles. "Anytime."

"Maybe you could read the girl parts?"

"I wish. My record contract has my voice locked down."

"What if we mic'd your heart? We could record me reading it to you. It would be like invoking the muse; Shakespeare with dick jokes."

"What if you rewrote it as a play? You could do this as a stripped-down underground production and—" She laughed and right then got a text.

Checking your phone was the new yawning. Contagious. Don't know why. I checked mine even though all my friends were at work or in front of me.

Her phone buzzed again and she said only, "Uh oh."

"What?"

She looked up at me. "Were we going to Mason Dixon tonight?"

"Yeah, why?"

"Apparently it's somebody's birthday party in the back." She looked up from her phone. "And Nikki's there."

That just erased the entire night in my head. I looked up from my seat on the futon and the tenement walls rose high above, leaving me in a chasm of my own devising. "I want to go home."

Gaga's lips started moving again, but I couldn't understand a word she said. Or sang. Or whatever she did.

"You can't ditch me," she said. "We have to stick together. It's Saturday night and my only option is to go down to Mason Dixon alone and watch my boyfriend flirt with other girls for tips. It's disgusting. You have to be my fake boyfriend."

"No."

"It'll be fun." She pulled me up from the couch, bodily, and wrapped my hands around her waist. "Nikki doesn't know what I look like now that I'm a blonde. No one remembers me. I keep having to introduce myself. I can be your fake girlfriend too—you know how jealous that will make her."

I let go of her waist. "It's not gonna work."

Before I let her go, she pushed me away with one of her small hands. "You should have let her see the hickey."

My face went flushed. "What does that have to do with anything?"

"You don't understand girls. She doesn't want you when you're pathetic and walking around alone like a little puppy. She wants you when she can't have you." She fanned out her arms. "Like when you're with me!"

"The answer's no, Gaga," I finally said. "We can go out. But we're not going there. I can't handle it and"—I know I shouldn't have said this next part—"your goddamn boyfriend would be all too happy to see me crumble in front of her."

"Fine. But we're going out tonight. Ever since he started over there on Saturdays it's like I don't have a social life anymore. Pick any other bar to go to and we're there. I wanna talk more about your book."

I let out a deep breath. I felt empty again. "Can I hear that song one more time before I decide?"

We're the dreams you'll believe in

Yellow streetlights shined through a puppet show of leafy shadows, and a few stray neighborhood kids blared music out of prepaid phones as we walked down Stanton Street. A nearby school, closed for the weekend, blanked out half the block. Clinton Street breathed life into the gap as chuckling herds stood outside of tiny restaurants, smoking and commenting on what they just ate and how it lived up to the reviews. Soon the shutters would come down—starting with the bakeries and boutiques—giving the neighborhood its familiar, abandoned look. By Rivington Street, I started to calm down. I recognized the graffiti tags on the mailboxes and found small amounts of comfort in seeing my friend's band's stickers on the street signs.

Gaga dusted her bangs in her reflection on a parked car and then turned to me with a big smile, presenting herself in an off-the-shoulder teal top with a metallic note. "How do I look?"

"Wonderful," I said. "As always."

"See? I can't trust you."

"Not true. I promise to tell you if you ever look fat."

As if announced by a butler, all of downtown society turned to genuflect when they heard the clack of Gaga's platform heels. She escorted me down the block, clomping like a show pony with her thick platinum mane as the streetlight danced off the glitter in her eye shadow. The downtown panopticon surveyed us. The door guys along the way said hello; they knew Gaga went along with Guy, but that he worked Saturdays and I didn't. They approved of this only because they could keep an eye on both of us this way as long as, god forbid, we didn't do something crazy. Like walk up to the East Village.

We didn't go to St. J's on Saturday nights. Our bars, bartenders, and DJs had less overlap than in every other bar in New York City. And *this isn't every other bar in New York City*. The Saturday night crew had their own breed of DJ; they never remembered your name.

Instead we went to 151, St. J's older, sadder cousin who lived in his parent's basement. The door opened and we saw Clarence, and exchanged a hand-slap hug and a single-cheek kiss. Clarence is an artist who has long dreadlocks and a wife and child in Jersey. We have a standing argument. He claims he will never make it as an artist because he doesn't paint pictures about his own blackness. If you're black and an artist you're supposed to paint about being black. I claim that there is no point in making any art that you're *supposed to* make.

I've DJ'd here before and have witnessed the unending hilarity with which DJs set up and take down the booth. Sometimes a pair of cheap, RadioShack CDJs tumbled around in the coffin box. Sometimes they worked. It sits on a disused corner of the backwards J-shaped bar, far away from where the bartender could reasonably serve you. Like a passive-aggressive stepparent, the bar management stuck a series of warnings and notices to the DJ booth. To cement the feeling of this being your friend's parent's basement, the booth plugged into an old stereo receiver underneath the cash register. If the managers thought you had the music up too loud, they quietly turned you down from ten feet away. Like breaking up the fun at a slumber party.

As I made my way through the crowd, I exchanged smiles and backslapped greetings with my friends and their leather jackets. I remembered being very stressed out earlier about something going on in my life, but somehow I managed to drown it out with a little bit of music and a lot of love from a friend.

Gaga gingerly crawled her way onto the barstool, ass out like usual. The bartender looked glad to see us. I don't remember the DJ's name, but I remember how crazy it was to see someone use DJ software for the first time. Like watching somebody play a video game about DJ'ing.

"Ohhh!" Gaga kicked her legs and clapped her hands. "Shiny Toy Guns—I *love* Shiny Toy Guns!"

We ordered a shot each of Sauza Hornitos tequila. I turned and saw Gaga drown in hers before she could come up for air. "I get drunk very easily," she said.

"Oh, I've seen you party plenty, love."

"No. I'm serious. I'm like four foot eleven and I eat my one meal a day and alcohol hits me very fast." She was the same height and size as Amy Winehouse, although Gaga didn't have Amy's warm contralto, the voice that popped and cracked with the precision of old vinyl records.

"Most teeny girls like you end up doing lots of blow just to stay up and stay skinny."

"Meh. I don't."

"None of it is any good anymore."

"Every time I'm in LA they want to take me out and do drugs and they're all like talking a million miles a minute, chatting, blathering, and asking, 'Isn't coke better than it is in New York City?' And I'm like, 'People in New York can *hold* their coke better.'"

Candlelit faces smiled at each other through the din of laughter and stacked glasses. Kids glanced at their hair in the mirror behind the bar, plumping it up a bit with their fingers. Every so often you could spy through the crowd the blue-green-lit smile of a girl who had just gotten the text she'd waited all night for. The soundtrack for our evening came from our most trusted advisor as an expectant crowd glanced at the door and hoped for a surprise visit from an old friend.

Gaga and I went back to talking shop:

" . . . But sometimes an earlier idea becomes something else. Or something I talk about with Conrad turns into a full story later, but that's because it won't leave my head."

"But what you do with it is what matters," Gaga says. "Have you heard my song 'Dirty Ice Cream'? That came out of a joke that I heard down at the bar. But when the boys heard it they were like, 'That's our thing!' and I remember being like, 'Then you should have written a song about it first.'"

"The boys came up with 'Dirty Ice Cream'?"

"Yeah. But they meant it about girls who become *sluts*. So I flipped it around and made it about boys who pretended they wanted to treat you right and then treated you like a slut."

"I get into trouble over that all the time. Once I made up a character after Conrad. He was really into the idea at first, and in the end he hated it."

"Own it. It's your creation."

"When Picasso painted Gertrude Stein, she said she hated it— too frumpy and marmish. She said, 'I don't look like that.' Picasso responded, 'You will.'"

"Ha! You know that song I have 'Beautiful, Dirty, Rich'?"

"Yes. It perfectly describes *Mercutio*."

"Haha. Thanks."

"Did you write that after the show at Pianos too?"

"No. I wrote that a long, long time ago. It's not about my friends from the scene; it's about my friends from home and from NYU. After I got my record deal, it changed me. I owned my own business and I was in charge of it. But my friends I was hanging out with were still partying and still going out and spending money and looking fabulous and they would buy bags and bags of cocaine. But they weren't doing it because they were rich or because they were rock stars. They did it because of Daddy. I'd be out with my friends and you'd catch one of them on the phone with their dad, pretending they needed the money to eat or to buy books or something, and they'd hang up and go to the ATM and take out more money to party."

WE HAD GOTTEN LOST IN the night. I loved that. Hours later my cheeks grew swollen from oversmiling, and our synchronized conversation dazzled with its free-form choreography. I'd locked myself up too long, hidden from my own friends, always acting less bright, less interesting, less excited about theory. Visiting friends filed in and out, but they said little more than hello—giving us our space together. Our conversation had become a dance, a give and take and a romance. I led and she took me to places I never thought I'd see. And together we got lost. When I got to the end of my drink we came up for air, nodding. Getting lost is another word for exploring.

"I—" I let out a nervous laugh. I had nothing to say. "I talk too much. I can't help it."

"It's good that you talk too much," she said. "It means your brain is working faster than your little mouth."

"Sometimes I wish I could shut my brain off. It's . . . it's no fun being stuck up there all the time." I didn't mean that to sound so goddamn sad. But it did. And I still mean it. I looked down at the bar, realizing it was true.

"Hey." Gaga looked up at me through the cowl of bangs and eye makeup. The purity of her eyes startled me. "Anytime you need to come down from there"—she motioned toward my sinkhole of a brain—"you call me. And anytime you want to let someone crawl around in there with you, you call me."

I nodded and looked around the bar. I am the opposite of distracted. For once in my life, I am exactly where I am. "You ever have that day where you're busy running around doing something, stressed, and then you hear the perfect song at the perfect moment?"

"Yes."

"And you feel like your life is a movie?"

"*Yes.*"

"And you feel like maybe everything is going to be okay because things are happening as opposed to falling through? I feel kind of like that now." I searched for the right words: "Right now I feel kind of like that. Only it's different . . . I . . . I mean here I am in the bar I've been to a thousand times and I feel . . . I feel like I'm in a Lady Gaga song."

She smiled and put down her drink. "That's amazing."

"In your music you feel like you can do anything. You feel like you're alive and worth it."

"Anything?"

"Anything."

"You ready to take on the world together?" She held up her drink for me to cheers.

"Yes."

We clinked glasses and she took this as a handshake. I had executed a contract without knowing what I had agreed to. "Good. Because we're going to start by going to that party. Nikki or not."

I almost spat out my drink just to void our arrangement.

All the smart boys know why

A hunting-themed video game at the front door occupied a pair of guys who hid in their virtual duck blind and hunted antlered creatures. Mason Dixon looked like a replica of bars in the rest of the country. The walls had countrified embellishments like horseshoes and Johnny Cash wood-burn wall art. Gaga turned to me, grabbed my hand behind our backs, and tugged me with her tiny claw. "You're with me and I'm with you. Got it?"

I squeezed back. *Got it.*

She let go and we stepped into the honky-tonk. Every blonde girl in the bar made my heart skip. Including Gaga. Every time I turned to her I flinched. The bar snaked around the left side of the room, and from the first curve I spotted a table of familiar faces, normally girls I see when they get out of their waitressing jobs at two A.M. They're all of Nikki's friends. Tonight they have on red lipstick. All of them. They came here for their friend's birthday party dressed like an army of fake smiles. I spun myself around and looked for cover. A few obnoxious, disheveled, out-of-place uptown boys crammed the front booth, drunk and hunched over their pint glasses. I looked out through the sliding barn door and looked with jealousy at the creatures outside. I wanted out.

Just as I turned to run out, I felt a manicured fingernail poke my chest. Gaga stared up at me with a stern look in her eye. "Don't. Ditch. Me."

"I'm not, I just . . . I was looking for—"

"She just walked in. She—turn around—hasn't found her friends yet. Now you sit on this bar stool and smile."

"I am smiling."

"You look like you're being tortured."

"I am. Why did we come here? This is the one bar with all of them in it all at once," I whined. These are the people who think *James* is perfect for her. "We had them quarantined."

"You better get your act together, mister." Gaga slapped my chest and collapsed into my leather jacket, rubbing her head into my chest. When her face reemerged she had an even brighter smile on her face. "Because you just said *the funniest thing I ever heard*. Haha!"

"What?"

"Roll with it."

"Why?"

"Haha!" Gaga laughed and I glanced up and caught Nikki out of the corner of my eye. "Keep looking at me. I'm your date—haha!" Gaga caught her breath and composed herself, stage-like, with one hand on my chest and lots of semi-orgasmic breathing and abandonment.

"What are you *doing*?" I found myself giggling. It was contagious. Gaga kept turning up to me and trying to speak, but she burst out laughing *again*. "Stop that. Hahaaaa!"

Birthday Girl walked over from her table just then and saw me talking to this mystery girl with the platinum blond hair. She brought over a few of her friends and they all failed to recognize Gaga as the somewhat forgettable brunette they'd met a half dozen times before.

Instead, they went into protection mode, trying to figure out who the blonde on their friends' turf was.

Just then Nikki walked over and, through a fluke of the crowded bar, she ended up nudging Gaga into me. Gaga caught herself with one hand on my chest and glared at the uptown offender. Nikki looked over and saw a young girl laughing in convulsions with one hand slipped into my leather jacket.

I hadn't seen Nikki since the night with James. Who was nowhere in sight. She walked straight up to me and we both stopped, just a few feet from each other. She looked me up and down. My voice got caught in my throat.

I still think about you ever day.

Every song reminds me of you.

I can't go anywhere without getting reminded of you.

"Nikki, I—"

Gaga grabbed my right arm with her left and lead me away, spinning my back to Nikki and glaring at her in a stage bicker. "Don't even *talk* to her," she said like a pitch-perfect jealous new lover, and walked me over to the bar, where Guy air-drummed to the music, his eyes squinting and his lips jutting out.

In the tango of Lower East Side lovers Guy lost interest in the two of us as soon as we sat down and talked to him. Gaga, still in character, actually loved this because it gave her a second to catch up with me while Nikki's hot glare tanned my neck. "You're doing fine."

"I want a drink so I can have an excuse to throw up."

"Look at him." Gaga shook her head at Guy. "Blows me up on text all night, hassles me about who I'm with while he's at work, and then the second I get here he completely ignores me."

"Uhm hm . . ."

"Stop thinking about her. Pretend you're listening to me talk about something. Pretend it's interesting. And sexual."

"I am pretending I'm listening to you talk about something."

Gaga looked up at me with those eyes. I couldn't help it. "Don't forget that we're in this together."

Guy swaggered over, stopping periodically to impress his big smile on drunk girls along the way. He made it just a few feet at a time, always glancing at Gaga and I and then ignoring her. Finally he bopped over and put his hands on the curved bar. Unlike at the other dives where we work, here a tiered speed rack of liquor bottles filled an alcoholic moat of bottles, four deep, between us. "Where've you been tonight?" He always opened with this question in the way that scenesters always wondered if they've missed a party somewhere else. FOMO: Fear of Missing Out. But this time he said it to mask the subquestion he really wants to know: *What are you doing here with her?*

"151." The lie becomes the truth. "How's business here?"

"Good. We got the lights fixed and the mechanical bull going."

Gaga trotted off to the bathroom, leaving me and Guy alone.

"How long were you guys at 151?"

I hate questions. First of all because they distract me from waiting for my heart to explode if I see Nikki again. Second because I'm so preoccupied that I'm likely to answer them a little too truthfully.

Guy: "So you have a Saturday night off for once and now you have a thing for my girlfriend ever since you got dumped?"

Me: "Actually I was in her apartment long enough to totally nail her three times. Then we talked about all the books we've read. There were at least eleven of them."

"What?"

"Crazy night!" I finally said to Guy. Then I just tried to focus on something he understood. "This place must be a cash cow."

"Well, it's no *Pianos*."

"Right . . ."

He looked at me. "What's wrong?"

What's wrong. The fact that Guy is the one asking me that question is what's wrong.

"Look at her."

Guy stared over my shoulder at Nikki and even his eyes twinkled. "I am lookin' at her. How'd you ever let that one get away?"

Somehow I just magically convinced Guy I'm not into Gaga by having us both admit that we have a huger crush on Nikki. "Fucking hell."

"You'll be fine," he said. "You always land hot girls."

I decided to change the subject. "Man, that girl loves you, though."

He acknowledges it without pride or feeling—rare for Guy not to pitch something to his ego. "I know."

"No. I mean she really loves you."

"I know."

GAGA CAME BACK FROM THE bathroom just then and teetered onto her stool just like usual. Her dainty mount hit a few kinks before she treated herself to a seat. "This one," Guy said, and smiled at her like she just woke up from being passed out in the bathroom. Just then I looked over at the two of them and I saw something weird. Gaga—who had barely had anything to drink, by my count—acted drunk. Meanwhile, Guy—who barely cared about her when we walked in groping each other—now only cared about her because she was another drunk girl. Something backfired on the way here from 151. "This one's drunk."

"I'm just here to keep VH1 away from You Know Who."

"Why'd you get my girlfriend so drunk?" Guy joked. But in the joke we found the words she wanted to hear. The G word. Guy only got possessive when he got territorial. He turned to me. "You want a shot?"

Before I could even register the question and readjust the abacus of my brain into an answer, I found myself clinking glasses with Guy. He's already poured the damn things and we have one shot each on either side of the bar. We toast. We drop. We meet eyes. We drink.

Supposedly that's part of an old trust ritual. Supposedly we're friends who don't need to reaffirm our trust.

"Where's mine?" Gaga wondered, a beat behind the rest of the band.

"Obviously, VH1 got you drunk enough already." He gave her the dim-eyed bartender smile, in lieu of a toast. He gave me that cold-hearted, "I'll-fuck-you-up" grin.

"We need to . . ." Gaga trailed off. "We need to set VH1 up with someone else."

Guy answered, "*Yes.*"

"Somebody who will treat him right."

As if that were an afterthought he shrugged. "Sure." Guy carried a blank look on his face. He did the social-scanning thing that everyone hates, cruising the bar for more interesting people to talk to, which for him meant drunk girls.

"And we need to keep him away from her, especially now."

"Absolutely." Guy drifted off to the waiting crowd. Away from us.

"It's weird to visit your boyfriend at work and have him totally ignore you."

"Yes," I said.

"So?"

"So. You have your job"—I realized immediately that she had a different frame of reference—"and he has his. Your job is to dance in front of boys and make them pay you. His job is to make boys dance in front of you by making girls dance in front of him."

"Do you mean that?"

"Yes."

"Really?"

"No."

"Okay."

"But we're both being ignored," I said. "Do you think he has time to deal with his employees on his night off at another bar where he doesn't have a management scenario?"

"Why are you talking like that?"

"I'm dying out here."

"Just stay with me. You're better off without her and you will be just fine."

"Do you mean that?"

"Why wouldn't I? All that jealousy that he puts on you when we're out and she's out. All of that is gone. Just stay with me and—"

" . . . BUTNOTLIKEABOOKONTAPE." I'm outside telling Nikki way too much about Gaga's idea of recording the manuscript. I'm excited. I'm vibrant. I've just come from a reading!

I'm also wicked nervous.

Nikki looked up at me and sniffed. "Do you listen to yourself talk?"

"Here." I pulled the pages out of my back pocket. "I made these pages for you. Long ago. You should have them." Then I realized that I'd handed her the pages that Gaga had written on—the ones I meant to save. "Except . . . here . . . here I have more for you . . . the thing is that, Stef . . . Stef . . ."

"Ohhh," Nikki said, "is that your new *girlfriend*?"

Just then Guy came out for a smoke break in this interminable night. I turned to Nikki and said it as honestly as I could: "She's just helping me with the new draft of *Mercutio*. She went to school for theater and she had this great idea—Henry said it too—that I develop it into a play."

I can't play games. I have to be honest. *Nikki, I miss you. I think about you whenever I do anything.*

Guy then hollered out, "Yo! VH1! You ever end up banging that chick? You know that girl you brought by the bar last night?" I ignored him and his on-the-clock drunken antics. "What was her name? I can't remember. I can't keep all the skanks you bring around the bar straight. Oh, hey, Nikki. How's things?"

Nikki drifted off to her friends and then disappeared an hour later. I kept my back to her for a long as I could. But Guy always kept an eye on her throughout the night. His stark glance traced Nikki around the room wherever she went. When she left, Guy fed iced water to Gaga and talked to her until his shift ended. The lights came on at four and I made a very cowardly Irish good-bye.

Life is a mystery

Sundays round out the weekends in a lonely, solitary fix. While the rest of the city sat at home, unshaven and waiting for the good TV to start, I dragged myself through Chinatown and into the Lower East Side, where I worked at Pianos. I always came early to check out the show in the back room, where you could catch comedians like the Whitest Kids U'Know, John Mulaney, Hannibal Buress, or Greg Johnson. Comedy got a different part of my brain firing and I always left smiling, ready to get back at it.

I kept an eye on Stanton Street, hoping and wishing that Nikki would come around the corner. If she would just come in and sit down we could talk. She could see me at work, which she used to love. Out the windows I caught the slightest breeze of action on the quiet streets. Tonight all of the bands on the roster came from out of town. They faced the terrible specter of outnumbering their audience. Sundays in the neighborhood had a peculiar diffusion and when it was dead here it was dead everywhere.

Here was all the advice I had been given so far and what I did with it:

1. *Go out and meet someone else.* Where?

2. *The best way to get over someone is to get under someone new.* Picture me in a strange girl's apartment. Picture it going well. Picture me saying charming things and making her laugh. Picture shirts getting unbuttoned. Picture me checking her undergarments for Nikki's labels.

3. *Find one of her friends and take them out on a date to make her jealous. Nothing has to even happen, but you'll get in her head.* I think I started crying when I read the words "find one of her friends."

When I looked back out the window I saw the face of a little angel. It was the girl who'd given me the hickey. Passing headlights illuminated a little halo around her hair. She had a pair of big-hearted blue eyes and freckled cheeks. And she smiled as soon as she walked in the door.

I had only seen her once since our failed date at Hotel on Rivington the night I saw Nikki out with James. She glowed in the doorway and I nodded to the door guy to bring her right in.

I poured her a Ketel soda and put it on a napkin for her when she sat down. "That's to make up for the drink we didn't have at Hotel on Rivington."

"Apology accepted," she said, smiling. "You know I worried about you that night. That look on your face. It was like you just lost your best friend."

I smiled.

"I have a present for you too." She pulled out a copy of Rilke's *Letters to a Young Poet.* In the book a poet writes back to a young student who'd asked him for advice. He tells him to just write and not worry what other people will think because at best their readings of it would just be fortunate misinterpretations.

When I got home I found she'd inscribed it, "To a talented writer,

Moby rival, and all around cool guy. I hope this brings you joy and peace."

It did.

ON MY DAY OFF THE next day I had nothing to do. Tuesday would begin my every-other-day cycle of DJ'ing, bartending, guest DJ'ing, and bartending. My apartment had become a cave of failure, piles of half-finished books and printouts that only felt like the dirt-fill for the grave I'd dug myself.

I had an early demo of some Gaga songs and I decided to take it for a walk. At the door to my apartment, I took my glasses off and left them on the table and walked out into blurry, mysterious night.

From the second I heard that voice inhale on "Beautiful, Dirty, Rich," I felt better. It felt like the national anthem of the young and broke. I listened to it on repeat. Again and again, sometimes starting it over after only a minute just to hear the intro. What her song meant to me had almost nothing to do with what it meant to her or what it would mean to someone else. But nothing could change the feeling inside of me.

When I came home I texted Gaga: "I just had the time of my life walking around the empty streets of Brooklyn playing your song on repeat for hours. It's amazing. I took my glasses off and listened to it fifteen times. I got LOST."

"Thankyouthankyouthankyou," she texted back.

"No. Thank you. I can't wait to play it next week. But for now I'm just listening to it alone and I am in heaven misinterpreting it."

"Why misinterpret?"

Full of Rilke and probably too much coffee, I wrote back. "The greatest/worst thing about art: it will never be interpreted by the art appreciator as it is by the artist," I texted, "because they are three separate things."

"Ha! I love it."

"Then imagine how much I love your song: I didn't think of that until after I heard it."

I knew then that the inspiration I'd searched for in all of those books would stay hidden. But this city and the people in it I loved so much would form the dialogue and characters, and I had to learn patience because a story doesn't find you all at once the way scenes and chapters do. You need to have everything in place before it can all be destroyed, and your story begins right after that.

Following the girl I didn't even want around

That first week of winter wind in New York is a death sentence. You have appeals and reprieves, but nothing will get you through it but time. I shivered down the street. I headed out for the night and heard the first good news I'd had in a while: Interscope wanted to hear some more of what Gaga had put together. They wanted Gaga to start writing for the Pussycat Dolls, which would put her in touch with Cee Lo Green—the high-pitched vocalist from Goodie Mob—and Gnarls Barkley. The plan being to help Nicole Scherzinger, the lead singer, go solo. Of all the old-school moves they had over at Interscope, putting together a girl group with in-house talent and then having one go solo made the most sense. "That's good news!" I said when I saw her back out at the bar later.

"Do you even listen to the Pussycat Dolls?"

"No. Not at all," I said. "But I will once you're writing for them."

"You're going to love the songs."

"Of course I will."

"No, I mean you are going to *love* the songs. I have one about You

Know Who's always-broken-down El Camino called 'Your Freakin' Car.'"

"Ha!"

She sang, "*I know where you were last night / I saw you with your hands on her / Rubbin' her like you love her more than me.*" Guy proved an excellent source of material for these tracks. Some of them never made it on an album, but she had written "Your Freakin' Car" about how he spends their entire weekend together with his ass crack coming out of his vintage jeans, stooped under the hood on the street down by the waterfront. "Glitter and Grease" was about his piece of shit El Camino. Ostensibly, he's fixing it. But ostensibly we should have a cash register drawer that actually closes.

"That's great." I gave her a smile.

"They're a good mix between what I do and what they are. They have their eye on this one Pussycat Doll to go solo and I'm going to write for her. Which is why I wanted to talk to you."

"What?"

"Now I have to do what you do: I have to take a minor character and develop her as her own entity."

"It's fun," I said, "and terrifying."

"There's one problem. We were going to go on a little vacation to the islands. Nothing big. The good news is I'm going to throw him a surprise birthday party. The bad news is I have to cancel the trip to record . . ."

"When are you going back to LA?"

"That's the thing. I don't even know. But I have to be ready. Like you said that time. I gotta be ready for the time I'm not ready." I started to think of my own half-assed advice. When we went on our fake date to see Nikki I was prepared. I was overprepared. The last time I was really not ready for anything was the next night at Pianos when that little angel came by bringing me a book. I realized something strangely relieving right then: I didn't know a single thing. What had all of these conversations and failures prepared me for anyway? The only thing that did seem to help was giving up. Being ready and rehearsed only put me on the defensive. But being unprepared opened me up for what was ahead. Whatever that was.

"So I was thinking," Gaga continued, "if I can't go to the islands with him, I dunno, maybe he could go with you instead . . ."

"Huh?" I had lost her for a second. "Sure. I'll talk to him."

"IT'S BULLSHIT," GUY SAID, SMOKING outside of Mason Dixon the next Saturday. I don't get Guy, but I do get one thing: This wasn't just a getaway with his girlfriend. This was his big birthday trip.

"C'mon," Dino said, "she'll be back soon and then you can go."

"We can't even plan a trip. Can't even take my girl to the Caymans for a few days. You know how many girls would kill for that? How many would just flip out that their guy could just take off in the middle of the week and hit up the Caymans?"

"What's so big about the Caymans?" Dino offered. "Why don't you go to LA with her? Maybe they could use you on the record. That would be *sick*. Yo, you know that if she ever needed some guitar parts in the studio to call me, right?"

"That's not a vacation. That's more work. Besides. There's no casinos in LA."

The two gamblers agreed, finished their cigarettes, and said nothing else.

"It's done, man. It's like a summer fling that shouldn't have lasted this long." Guy tossed a cigarette down to the gutter. It burned red at first and then sizzled out, disappearing into a thin trail of smoke in the glimmer of a streetlight.

"What do you mean?" Dino said. "You're not gonna—"

"What the difference? I never see her. Even when she's in town she's too busy for me." His voice gathered up a manful, Theodore Roosevelt accent. "She wants to go out on Fridays and Saturdays when I'm at work. I can't even go bowling with my girl on a Sunday afternoon."

"You can't *break up* with her."

"It's gotta happen," Guy said.

Just then a big, drunk idiot comes down the street. Me. I sailed down Rivington in a cloud of whiskey and misplaced optimism for my undisclosed future. "Hey, happy birthday," I said to Guy, and then gave him the hand-slap half-hug.

"Why does everyone keep saying that? My birthday is not until next week."

"Oh." I made eyes with the other guys. First I heard of it was on the text from Gaga to help plan his surprise party.

Dino steadied me: "He wants to break up with Stef." Even in Dino's vacant, drug-smeared eyes I could see a look of terror. Somewhere in the back of his hoovered brain Dino always waited in the wings, careful to help out at shows, hoping that one day he'd get to record with her and show Interscope what he could do. He filled me in on what I'd missed and I looked up at Guy.

"You'd like that, wouldn't you?" Guy turned to me and went to go text her the breakup news.

I looked at Dino. "Just tell him."

Guy looked up. "Tell me what?"

Dino wavered for a second, then launched into it: "She spent all week planning your surprise party at the bowling alley tomorrow. She even went through your phone to find some extra surprise friends."

Guy looked up from that very phone, seconds away from programming in the launch code that would have made their entire relationship self-destruct. He slipped the phone back into his pocket.

Take a look around, see which way the wind blows

A scent of grilled-cheese sandwiches mixed with the glory of bowling shoes and spray disinfectant filled the bar. The windowless, cinder-block bunker took up a huge section of the block among the brownstones and fire-escape village that surrounded Melody Lanes in Brooklyn. The paint colors on the wall all came to match a polyester shirt minted in 1979. A nearby vending machine sold socks, wrist guards, and ball-polishing rags.

A single mural spanned the wall with bowling pins in a wild, airbrushed orbit. A handmade oak-tag-lettered banner hung just under the ceiling, advertising bowling league games and sharing in the pride of local teams (Bay Ridge Ladies, Match Point, Summer Triples). A hand-lettered, framed sign on the wall advertised the unintentionally naughty sounding "Adult Parties!" Which is what the kids of Rivington High came here for today.

"Yo, VH1!" I turned and saw Dino waiting in the bar area with a couple of friends. We merged in among the longshoremen as they commanded the gray-haired, bow-tied bartender to change the channel from one game to another. This is a Sunday in Brooklyn, a time to observe the Sabbath with football.

The entire cast of party kids filed in. Late. Sundays for us came at the end of a long week filled with too many smoke breaks and a little more whiskey than required. Today, my kidneys felt splintered by the wood barrel of last night's Jameson. If downtown were an office building, we would be the gossipy coworkers who harangued each other at the water cooler, talking too loud at the desk of the most hungover employee.

Gaga stalled the ceremony as long as she could, pretending to be on the phone with someone from the label in LA (which annoyed Guy, who was by now in on the secret but no less frustrated with men who needed her in LA). I kept texting her the whereabouts of various friends and scenesters. Your real life can only match the delight of a movie once the whole cast's assembled.

The guest list of a surprise party will never be the guest list of a party you would throw for yourself. It reflects more the ideal social circle that the person throwing the party—ideally the most important person in your life—would have prescribed you. (None of the drunk girls who we see every single night get the invite, for example.)

However, it still follows the same rule as every other party: The person whose name is the least secure on the invite list arrives first (Dino) and somewhat uncomfortably early. Your real friends arrive on time to support the host and to catch up, knowing that once the party starts they will not find time for this. Then it's the wildcard guest—someone who isn't really a good friend but gets the invite to give everyone else at the party something to talk about (Georgie from Motherfucker).

Like a band slogging through rehearsal we all missed our cue when Guy finally arrived. "Surprise!" everyone yelled. Separately.

Gaga came in with her video camera, rolling in behind him. "How amazing is this group?" Gaga peered through the viewfinder. "Years from now people will be talking about the day this group of rock 'n' rollers went bowling. Hey, writer!" She aimed the camera at me. "Did you guys know that VH1 is an amazing writer?"

Guy perked up. He may act like a moron, but he isn't an idiot. Somewhere in the past week I had learned all of Gaga's songs and she had started quoting my manuscript.

I grumbled and shrank and tried to take the attention off of me. "So says the poet laureate of pop!"

Gaga panned the video camera around at the cast. Conrad came over from the jukebox. The Doors' "L.A. Woman" infected the entire bowling alley with its long, stuck-in-freeway-traffic intro release, while this crew of semipro guitar players air-strummed along.

"Right," Guy moaned, putting on his bowling shoes, "like we don't hear this enough on Rivington Street."

"I wanted to set the mood," Conrad said.

I went over to the jukebox and put five dollars in. I'd rather not have any music on than hear the mismatched bullshit that people put on their "Party Jamz" playlist.

"Were you surprised?" everyone kept asking Guy.

His answer got caught in his throat. He muscled a smile across his delicate face, behind the hair and mutton chops. "Are *you* having fun? That's the question. It's not fun if everyone doesn't have a good time at your birthday."

"Were you surprised?"

"Yeah." Guy gave a conspiratorial eye to Dino and me.

"What was that?" Gaga asked.

"Hey," I interrupted, stalling to make someone's life less awkward, "you guys almost talked through the greatest breakdown of all time!" My feet stomped through the drum and horn dissection of Diana Ross's "I'm Coming Out." Guy smiled, air-drumming.

"That is amazing," Georgie said, noticing it for the first time. "I never noticed that before. Are you a musician?"

"I'm a DJ."

"I want to shake your hand. You're the one who threw Michael T. out of St. Jerome's."

"Actually that was Conrad." Guy waltzed off with the boys to talk shop about people and life downtown. Georgie went over to buy Conrad a shot.

"I've been thinking about what you wrote." Gaga turned the camera off and sat with me.

"Oh"— again with my stupid smile —"that."

"It's really helping me to get in the heads of other characters."

I felt like the showoff who executes some kind of trick or backflip and then has to negotiate being impressive in real life. Mostly I just felt like a living disappointment.

"We'll take over the world together. I know we will because you inspire me."

"And you inspire me."

"Who could ask for anything more?"

"I could ask for another drink."

GUY ORDERED ANOTHER ROUND OF Jameson shots. However, I only discovered that he ordered me one after I had already ordered a shot of something else myself. "Never waste good alcohol," Pete the bow-tied bartender said, determined to mix them together. He made us a round of shots that would not have played anywhere else: Alizé, Wild Turkey, Bacardi 151, Malibu, blue curaçao, and pineapple juice. It tasted like your hangover.

"Aren't you working tonight?" Guy asked.

"Yeah."

"If I were your boss I would fire you," Guy said.

"You are my boss," I said.

"Then you're lucky you're working at another bar tonight."

Hope you guess my name

That night I came into Pianos like a guilty husband. Instead of rushing in the door and busily getting about my work, I came early, suck-
ing on too many Life Savers and maybe being a bit too familiar.
Unlike the other bars in the neighborhood, Pianos actually had a
functioning kitchen, and for half price you could get some pretty decent food. I hid in the downstairs office with a seared tuna sandwich
and french fries that I ate like a teenager trying to sober up at an all
night diner after his first house party.

At one point I looked up and saw the booker, who had the over-
priced job title of "talent buyer." He looked up at me like he was waiting for me to finish a sentence.

"What?"

"I said, you look like you had fun last night."

I was too drunk to panic, so instead I looked around at the tableau
I had set on the conference table. Two bottles of water, a coffee cup, a
"Revive" flavored Vitaminwater, half a giant tuna burger, and several
roughed-up bottles of ketchup. "I thought I'd see you out last night.

It was the last Misshapes party at Don Hill's. You shoulda come. It was like a fun little 2004 reunion."

"Hmgh," I grunted through my chewing.

"I saw your ex in here the other day."

Chances of this being any amount of good news: low. "Oh, really . . ." and then just in case you haven't offered anything completely useless, Brendan: "Good for her."

"She looks good. But she's always looked good. I don't really care about that other guy."

You are not going to freak out. You are going to wipe the ketchup off your face and go upstairs and do your job.

There's a story about Frank Sinatra, running late for a gig. Theater packed, musicians ready, instruments tuned. Frank is nowhere to be found. A cab speeds through the streets, stops at the back gate of the theater. Sinatra throws money in the front seat and tears off through the long alleyway, dodging puddles and stray trashcan lids. He skids to the stage door. Then he stops. He takes off his overcoat, straightens his tie, cocks his hat to one side, and casually opens the door, ready to step on stage.

At the base of the stairs I did my gladiator routine. I liked to think of that basement office as our slave quarters and the wide stairwell as our vomitorium. I will go to battle upstairs to earn my freedom. I ball up my fists and mount the stairs like Rocky. Here he comes! The one! The only! The bartender!

At the top of the stairs I see Heidi. Our weekly handoff ritual went as follows. I run up the stairs really enthusiastic and psyched up for the night. She looks at me like maybe she wants to die, and I say, "What's the latest?" And she says, "Nothing. Just tired." And I say, "Your hair looks cute like that." And then she tells me how her boyfriend isn't doing this or that.

"You wanna do a shot?" she eventually asked.

"No, thank you," I said, feeling virtuous.

"Rough night last night?"

"Haha, no such thing for me, y'know! I just know it's going to be a long night for me tonight." Nowhere in that last sentence did I lie even in the slightest.

The DJ came late. I didn't book any of the bands that night, so instead I was stuck dealing with the influx of terrified bands from other cities. Foreign exchange scenesters in tiny thrift-store outfits and too many scarves for the unusually mild weather. The one least involved in the band stayed with the van, nervously checking the rearview and wondering where to feed the meter. The rest of the van came in with a mix of guitars and backpacks full of strings and sticks. We don't have a backstage or a band room or a closet. Bands have to load in their gear, then put it off to the side of the stage and watch it before they go on. Some went overboard. But a band with the basic Beatles/Stones/Killers/Zeppelin setup could probably bundle a guitar, bass, and keyboard into one heavy bag and entrust its safety in the office (but it was harder to keep a coveted theremin from being swiped). If you can plug into a quarter-inch jack and not steal our mics, you are welcome to play at Pianos. After their set they have to load it all up and hope the van doesn't get broken into while they wait for the other bands in their set to finish to get paid.

I didn't notice The Devil when he came in the door, but I guess it always happens that way. There were drug dealers you'd see, and then were the ones you had to call. The code for blow was "the white devil" and then just "the devil"—as in "I just got paid, anybody know how to get the devil here?" This anthropomorphized into just calling the delivery dealer—whoever showed up—The Devil. For the sake of this story, let's just say there was a guy we'll never recognize from these details whom we called The Devil, and that person is free to join the chamber of commerce or run for mayor because we're not going to describe him here. I will add that there was also a premium service at the time run by a guy whose name was not Adam. As I understand it, you would call up and ask for Adam, and then later a dealer would show up and whoever it was would introduce himself as Adam. Adam is also free to run for mayor. The Devil in the booth, somewhat annoying the DJ. "How's it going, man?" he said to me.

I know I shouldn't talk to him and that he'll just end up bothering me and keeping me away from other customers. But here's the thing about The Devil: He tips well. The Devil knows what's up. You give him a couple of Boddingtons and do a shot together and he gives you a twenty. Not bad, right?

"You look like you had a rough night last night."

"Ha."

"Or maybe you're having a rough day."

I clenched my jaw and gave him the eyebrow and went to get another girl a vodka soda. Despite all the complaining I do about my job and being a drink slave, it's a great way to spend a night. I stand at a bar surrounded by beautiful women, and for all those hours I spend feeling worthless at home, I don't feel that way here. I can make you a vodka soda with lime without moving my feet. In the magic of the workplace I can also reach for, pour, and replace any bottle of top-shelf liquor without looking. If you want a bottled beer from the fridge behind and below me, I can tell without looking which one of the eight doors to swing open. I spent four years in college to only make it this far, but how many people I went to college with could do that?

The Devil had about an inch left in his Boddingtons. I pulled the lever on the pub ale and let it fill the glass while I helped another cute girl, using the patented Lower-East-Side Bartender Triage System. The LES BTS carved your crowd into the most important groups for your night, served in order: pretty girls, patient girls, assholes.

I swooped over to bring The Devil a pint. I give him a little wink. He continued the conversation as if I'd left him on pause: "Or maybe you've just had a rough life?"

Instead of getting into it with him I said something meaningless like, "Haven't we all!" More than likely I just affirmed whatever the hell he said and started to help the asshole behind him.

"Do you need a little help?" The Devil continued. I looked back at him. He had a window into hellfire in his eyes. He glanced down and offered me his hand. In it he had a bag of blow and a pen cap for administering cocaine into the nose in adverse bathroom situations.

"Thanks," I said to The Devil and nodded, "but I'm okay." I turned back to the next customer. The Devil shrank away and went on to conscripting another's soul. "What can I get you?"

"G and T," the asshole said. "Heavy on the G."

"Tanqueray good?" Without taking my eyes off him I filled a glass with ice with my right hand and reached over to the back shelf and got the green bottle of gin with my right hand. I fill the goddamn glass with gin and splash a little tonic on top.

"Stiff pour. Thanks."

"If you want it any stiffer I'll have to mix some Cialis in there!"

"Ha!"

"Ha!"

There may be some things that I wouldn't miss

As I was packing up my record bag for my next show with Gaga, Guy called to say that I was fired from St. Jerome's. He wouldn't say why.

"Uhm . . ." he said, searching for the right answer when I asked why. "I don't know exactly why. Look. Be a man. Handle it. That's how life works. Okay? You gotta know how to handle things."

A mere six months earlier I had a very decent, steady job with health insurance, sick days, workers comp, perquisite meals at other restaurants every month. I had a beautiful girlfriend who loved every little awful thing about me. Back then I worked six days a week and loved it. I think. *Now look at me*, I thought. That's how life works, indeed.

"I'm gonna be late," Gaga texted.

"Me too," I texted back from my pile of misery and records.

"Storms in paradise," she texted.

"No problem. I'll be late because I think a bridge just got washed out on the Road to Success."

"See? We're the perfect team."

* * *

ON THE WAY TO THE club I got a call from Gaga. "Are you ready to rock this?"

"You know it!" I said, trying to fool myself with enthusiasm.

"What's wrong?"

"I just got fired from St. Jerome's."

"What? Why?"

"He wouldn't say."

"Wait. When?"

"I don't know. Eight fifteen. Right after I got off the phone with you."

"Uh oh."

"What?"

"You're gonna kill me."

"What?"

"He's such a fuck."

"Stef"—I never used her real name—"tell me what's going on."

"I left some things at his house and when I realized I forgot them I called him to bring it to me and he said, 'Why do you need it?' And I told him the truth. I said, 'Brendan and I have a show to do tonight.'" She never called me Brendan, but the way she leaned on the notes of my name made me think she'd used it against him. It resonated from her mouth to his ears to mine. Something else was going on here. "Then he started grumbling about us always doing something while he's working and I yelled at him because this is my work."

"So what happened?"

"I said, 'When you go to work tonight I want you to bring my disco bra, my lipstick, and my self-tanner because I have a show to do. And we are through.'"

"Didn't you guys just get back from vacation? Shouldn't you be all lovey-dovey?" I said. "And tan?"

Silence on her end. But I could hear the cloven heels of a busy New York City girl clomping through sidewalk traffic.

"Stef. Is there something you're not telling me?"

"No."

"Gaga."

"I don't want to talk about it right now." Her voice broke down at the end and she started crying. My heart stopped.

"Do you want to cancel?"

"No," she stammered. "I want to rock tonight."

A WIDE SIDEWALK-AND-ROPE SYSTEM AT the single entrance/exit kept people in line and errant smokers away from the empty sidewalk. From the outside, Don Hill's looked like a container ship docked in West Soho. This old distribution center was now a hub of imported music from all five boroughs and beyond. At the front door a trusted cast of bouncers and door guys checked IDs and names on the guest list. Like at Pianos, they ask who you came to see—what band or DJ or a promoter, all of whose paychecks depended on that tally. If you ever had a problem or you needed a favor, you could always find the actual Don Hill himself, a gray-haired sixty-four-year-old man in cowboy boots and pressed jeans. He stood at the end of the bar or wandered around playing video poker and erotic photo hunt.

The girl who had been crying on the phone stayed home. And a very different girl came to meet me. Her name was Lady Gaga.

At the corner of Greenwich she strutted out of the cab wielding a handheld video camera. "Look who it is! That my DJ! Hello, world. Say hi to DJ VH1. We have a show tonight at Don Hill's and I'm going to sing DJ VH1's new favorite song, 'Beautiful, Dirty, Rich.' Say hi, VH1!" The video camera was her new thing. Her management wanted to try something new to get Interscope's attention. They wanted to see her downtown, where she belonged. If only they had any idea what happened downtown when she stepped off stage.

Inside, Gaga marveled at the colored interior. She loved the Sailor-Jerry-tattoo wallpaper. She loved the disco balls leading up to the stage, and the series of stripper poles that jutted out like teeth from the gaping whale's jaw of a bar. "This place is very Lady Gaga," she said, smiling at the lighting booth and sound system. "She's going to love it."

I introduced her to Don Hill and he walked us over to the bar to get a drink. Since the departure of weekly party Misshapes, the fate of Don Hill's started to wear on Don Hill. His cheeks hung long, gaunt, and thin.

Don introduced me to Andrew, the bartender. I introduced myself using my proper Irish name. "That's my brother's name!" he said with a smile that reached all the way to his ginger sideburns.

"WHAT HAPPENED TONIGHT, STEF?"

She took a deep breath and sipped a Bud Light. "It's not about tonight."

"Start from the beginning," I said in the half-empty venue. "I've got time."

They had been fighting. Or there had been fights. She felt like he didn't support her. He felt like she was always off somewhere else. They were unhappy. They made each other happy. They could make each other miserable. She said please just stick by me through this rough part. They left this island for another island. Everything was wonderful in a way it never felt like at home. Their phones didn't work, but their relationship did. Wouldn't it be nice if we could just be like this all the time? Guy was the one who proposed that. Sweet, right? He knew of one way to keep them together and happy all the time. She would never give up on music, but maybe music would give up on her. And the next night he had too much to drink. "And he said, 'I hope you fail.'"

"Wait. Let me wrap my head around this. You told me that you wrote 'Paparazzi' about how you're his biggest fan and you'll chase him everywhere and how when you're away from him a single photo of him is priceless to you," I said. She nodded. "But like you said at your apartment last month, you wrote the song and worked really hard on it to impress him so that you'd keep his interest. But you know that the more you impressed him with your music the more the music is going to take you away from him. More time in LA."

She nodded. "And he figured that out."

"So because he likes your song it's actually worse than when he didn't respect your music."

"Because now he feels like the music actually *is* going to take me away from him."

"But why doesn't he get that you love him anyway?"

Gaga was already in the anger stage. "Because *he doesn't get it*. He doesn't get that this is my job. The first time he came over to my apartment he looked around—you know he has that drafty place with a roommate in Red Hook—and when he saw that I had my own place the first thing he thought was it was because of *Daddy*." She mentioned her father not in the patrician manner of girls who never grow up, but rather in the manner of looking down on those types.

"And it wasn't?"

"No. I've had two record deals and gotten booed off stage and passed out demos and done back-to-back auditions and he doesn't *see* that. He just thinks it's *Daddy*. You know that if someone called him and said, here is nine hundred thousand dollars, I want you to fly to Vegas and open up a rock 'n' roll bar, he'd be on the next flight. Or you," she said. "If someone said to you, here's six figures and we want you to give us a bestseller, you'd be home right now working on it."

"I usually write in the mornings, actually."

"So tonight I came into the bar with my hair done perfect and completely composed because I had to show him, *This is what I do.* And I told him, 'One day you're not going to be able to get a coffee in a fucking deli without seeing or hearing about me.' And I walked the fuck out."

Joey Nova came around the corner. "Yo! You ready to go on?"

"Okay." Gaga smiled and started to follow Joey to the go-go platform. "Remember, I don't like dancing for anyone but you. When you're done: We're gonna party."

"Are you doing okay?"

"I'm fine. Let's have some fun."

"Okay."

"No," she said in a low tone and raised her eyebrows. "I mean let's have some *fun* tonight. Can you call anyone?"

I HAD ANSWERED WITHOUT THINKING about it. I just agreed to score drugs for us both and spend our entire night smoking too many cigarettes and talking way too fast about ourselves. Then I started to worry. She had a recording session in LA the next week. What if it ruined her voice?

A few minutes later she climbed into the DJ booth with her video camera running. "Woo! Lady Gaga and DJ VH1 know how to party!"

We danced together in the booth, she in her heels and complicated bathing suit, writhing against me facing the crowd, while I reached around her slim waist to cue the next record. Gaga reached an arm over her head and grabbed the back of my neck. "Guess what, VH1?"

"What, Gaga?"

"I just broke up with my boyfriend!" She cupped my neck in her hand and pulled me down for a kiss. My lips felt like they had just touched betrayal.

You can say a lot of things about me and most of them will be true. But I am not the kind of guy who does what I just did.

RIGHT THEN—AS IF MY PHONE had a feed to the panopticon of down-town—I got a text from Guy: "Make sure she doesn't do any drugs tonight." My heart skipped and my paranoia scanned the room for any of his minions. Surely somebody just saw that dick-move I had just executed, making out with the girlfriend of the guy who fired me two hours ago. My stomach tied in knots, churning the food I had eaten only minutes before Guy had broken up with me.

Gaga saw me with my phone in hand. Her eyes lit up. "Did you make the call?"

"Yeah," I lied.

Another text—*straight* from the panopticon—came through then. "Heard you're spinning at Don Hill's," The Devil said. "You got me at the door if I come by?"

"Do you think it's gonna pick up?" Gaga asked. "I could use the money."

"It's gonna be okay," I said. "Just dance. And we'll work it out."

WHEN THE GOING GETS UNCOMFORTABLE, the uncomfortable get non-committal. I didn't respond to Guy or The Devil. I just wanted that night to disappear. I then came up on the most cowardly solution for the two of us: I would get us wasted. I marched over to the bar when another DJ came on, and I paid for two shots out of pocket and fed one to Gaga. "Woo!" she let out a sorority yelp.

Nova walked over just then. "You kids are crazy." He smiled. Gaga leaned down to me, a little bit tipsy, and said, "I don't know if I want to perform."

"You don't have to."

"I can perform in front of lots of people anytime. But I can't go on stage like this. It's just not right tonight."

"You're right," I said. "We'll dance and have fun and we'll deal with tomorrow when we have to deal with tomorrow."

"Do you think he's upset?"

"Yes."

"Have you heard from him?"

"Yes."

"What did he say?"

"He just wanted to make sure that I was with you and that you were okay."

"Did you tell him I was crying?"

"I didn't tell him anything. Let him wonder. Let him think about what he did for a day. Tomorrow it'll be Sunday. He'll go bowling and everyone will ask about you."

"Do you think," she started, "do you think I should go by the bar on the way home and talk to him?"

"No." And I was glad that I found myself telling the truth. "Get back up there. I'm going to go on again and I want my go-go dancer to be up there killing it."

"I love you, Brendan."

"I love you too, Stef."

AS I TURNED AROUND, I looked over at the door and I saw The Devil's face. He peered around the leather-jacketed ire of the door guy's mullet and pointed toward me. In the nightlife pantomime I watched Mullet motion to the guest list on the clipboard. The Devil pointed to his watch and then motioned to an imaginary car waiting for him outside. Mullet shook his mullet, checked his watch, and spread his fingers out to say that since he had come late and not too many people had showed up he could let him in with one hand of fingers: "five dollars." The Devil tried to make a deal with Mullet. He didn't have any cash on him—but he would if you just let him in the door to talk to his DJ friend.

I ducked behind the partition and Nova stopped me. "Hey, there's a guy at the door who says he's with you."

"What's he look like?"

Nova described The Devil to me. "Is he with you?"

I shook my head. "No."

"The door guy says he forgot his ID but that he'll let him in if you'll vouch for him. You have room on your guest list."

"That's okay."

I was so hard pressed, I called the woman that I love best

The winter in New York bore a chill wind of salt and frozen construction projects into your skin. The icy breath of frigid breezes coursed through long, uninterrupted avenues, billowing up a caustic gust of sanded streets that pit your skin and battered your frozen ears. It slipped into the seams of your clothing. At night, your on-site landlord chuckled himself to sleep among a half dozen space heaters upstairs, snug as a chicken wing under the orange glow, while the rest of the building leaked gusts of cold wind on the chill metal of the lifeless radiator. And you shiver and toss under a half dozen blankets, wearing your winter hat in bed. Every time you ask about the heat, you're met with a mixture of confused answers, grumbling about "going green," and a condescending note about double-checking your windows' latches. In the basement I cursed through the frozen tile floor and discovered a single unlatched window. The top of it folded down so you could clean the outside, and whoever had done this last never put it back on straight. I rattled the glass in the sill and clicked it back into place; gusts of cold air chilled my fingers at the two-inch opening of the chest-high window. With that on track, I slammed the window shut and the slapstick hinge buckled, smacking me in the forehead, blood dripping into my eyes.

That night Gaga met me at Japonais in Union Square. She wore heels, fishnets, a chain belt, and her leather jacket. We had both gotten dumped by the same guy. "Didn't you say you used to bartend for this company?" she asked.

"Yes. I moved to Chicago after graduation and bartended for them for a little while and I was gonna start picking up shifts. Actually . . . something just occurred to me. If I hadn't gotten fired from this company in Chicago I never would have moved to New York."

"Cheers to getting fired!" We clinked glasses.

"You're so upbeat today, what's going on?"

"My last recording session went very, very well."

"The Pussycat Dolls stuff?"

She lifted an eyebrow as she took a sip from her birdbath. "It was supposed to be a Pussycat Dolls session. But it didn't end up that way."

"What happened?"

"I did what you said. I wrote honestly and I took what I was feeling inside and made it into something." She went into detail about the feeling she had dealt with. The arguments she had over and over with Guy. The fights became mixed up in so many other things and all she wanted from him was the love. Behind the Killers' party was the excitement of going on a date and that became "Boys Boys Boys." Behind the fight over the trip to the islands was this feeling that they didn't get to spend enough time together, as if he had to compete with her career. But she didn't want any of that trouble. She didn't want the stress. She just wanted his love. "And I know he loves money. You remember when you told him you couldn't DJ on Sundays because you were going to start working at Pianos and he said, 'Pianos is money'?"

"It's true."

"So I wanted to write something simple like that. I wanted to make it so simple that we didn't have to fight about it. It's like it wasn't even that simple in my mind until I wrote that down."

"If even you don't understand yourself until you read about it you're officially a writer." We cheers'd again.

"Ever since then it's the only way that it makes any sense. I can't even remember being confused about it."

"Good for you. So it's going to be a song or for that Pussycat Doll you told me about who wants to go solo?"

She smirked and her eyebrow peaked sprightly. "No." She took her time swallowing her drink, set it down on the paper coaster, and looked up at me, taking it all in. She had a dainty, almost robotic maturity to her movements now. "The vocal arrangement was too complicated so they had me make reference vocals for her. Akon heard my recording and he flipped."

"How's it go?"

She sang a song for me called "Money Honey." The other patrons at the bar craned their necks with delight, their wineglasses ringing with the reverb of her angelic voice.

"That's so subversive." I smiled. "Like how the Jag and the jet and the mansion are your LA life and your LA life makes your boyfriend jealous because it's like another boyfriend."

"Wow." She thought for a second. "You know what's funny? You're totally right but I didn't think of it that way. When I imagined the Jag and the jet it was the ones I'd seen in LA. But the gifts and the islands were with him."

"So it's different from the Elvis song."

"The what?"

"The Elvis/Clyde McPhatter song 'Money Honey.'"

"I don't know that one."

"I'll send it to you."

"Okay and—"

"Shit." I put my glass down and glared at it.

"What?"

"That's what I didn't do with Nikki. I wanted to compete. I wanted to be bigger than fashion shows and expensive trips. But those were just more distractions. No wonder she left me for that fucking waiter. She didn't want to be impressed, to be adorned. To sit around in bars after work while I scrounged up DJ jobs. She wanted someone to be on her frequency."

I looked over at Gaga. She had tried to explain this to me before but it took a song to understand it. I smiled. But I didn't see my friend. I didn't see the patient breakup buddy.

"It's not always about Nikki."

I retreated into my stool and looked down. She didn't bring me here to talk about Nikki. "Do you have something you want to say to me?"

"I—" she stumbled, her voice coming out strained, "I have something else I want to tell you. I am moving to LA and I'm just going to start over. I love the songs I have but while I have the label's interest I'm going to get all the studio time I can. This changes the whole plan. Instead of me being the singer that toils away and lives in obscurity and makes a slow rise out of the clubs I'm just going to come out of nowhere and take my place at the top."

My eyes widened.

I liked her plan. But it had nothing to do with us. We were the farm leagues for major label bands. Everyone knew a Stroke or had barbacked with the guys from TV on the Radio. We didn't do pop creations. She had just scrapped the whole show. No more dive bar scene. Now it wouldn't look like the old gang of her and Starlight in homemade costumes.

"I'm going to come out on stage at an awards show where no one has ever heard of me. I'm going to blow away the entire crowd and all everyone is going to say is, 'Who *is* that girl?'" Gaga straightened her fishnets with a devilish little grin. "And I'm going to come out on stage and sing the song for the first time in front of everyone. And I'm going to be in my underwear just to let everybody know that I don't give a *ffffuck* what anybody else thinks."

THERE WAS AN EXCITEMENT IN the air as we took our twin stools at Beauty Bar later that night. Classic 45s spun around on all four turntables in the front room and back, and through the dimly lit chorus of gossiping thieves you could see the spotlight at the center of the room on a girl getting a manicure while sipping a cheap cosmo with her free hand. Heads bobbed to the music and with the stark transition from one single to another you could catch a few stray metal hands or the solitary approval of a happy scenester saying "*Yes.*"

Kids smiled into their pints as they huddled together in warm, grateful masses. We watched the daily transactions of friends and lovers, and drugs circled through the crowd. Girls in tank tops shivered outside, wearing nothing thicker than a padded bra, their arms crossed over their goosebumped chests, patiently hoping their friends could smoke faster. When the single-stall bathroom opened, a cab-load of girls spilled out.

Through the dark room, I could see the apparition of smiling faces, green-lit by the text messages they had been waiting for. Beauty Bar was a place where everybody knows they don't need to be on the guest list, but their problems can't get in the door.

I really counted on that staying true. I didn't know that this was going to be her good-bye party.

"There's more," she announced. "I'm getting a nose job." She faced the vintage chandeliers on the ceiling, turning her offending snout in the air. She had the air of a coed who had just discovered where she would put her first crappy tattoo.

I slammed my Brooklyn Lager pint down. The bar took a sip. "*No.*"

Shave-and-a-haircut. "Yep." She drummed her fingers on the bar and tapped her nose twice. Two bits. A devilish grin filled her face. She said it so offhand. I think she put more thought into bleaching her hair.

"No."

"It's holding me back. Do you think I'd be songwriting this long if I looked like the girls you date?"

"Songwriting is work. It's good work. It's—it's not waiting tables."

"It's slipping away from me."

"You cannot get a nose job."

"Might get a titty lift."

"That's unacceptable. Also, you know you will lose all sensation in your nipples if you do that."

"It's not a boob job. It's just a lift."

"Stop it."

"Why? Afraid I'll be your type?" She pushed the stirrer around in her martini glass and shimmied up to me on her stool, leaning her face into mine. "Now that I'm blonde and all. I'll be the girl with a little ski-jump nose and a cute ass. Your exes will die."

"Just because I'm shallow doesn't mean you can be."

She looked over at me and smiled. "I know you're not shallow."

"I'm insecure. It's way different."

"You're not insecure."

"I know I am because I like hearing you tell me I'm not."

"You're not insecure, baby. But you're protecting someone who's insecure. Inside of you, you have a little geeky Brendan who didn't fit in and probably wore glasses."

"It was not cute."

"You have to spread your wings, buddy. You're six foot two, you dress like a champion, and you have a nice, thick—"

"Stop it."

She shrugged. "What? Girls talk."

"You let those Los Angeles people into your head, Gaga. Stop it. Stop them before they destroy everything good about you."

"You don't know what I've been through over there. It's new. It's opening up my way of thinking."

"You're just . . . you're saying things. You're like I was when Nikki and I broke up."

"For *once* can it not be about Nikki?"

That stung. We had done nothing for the past two months but talk about her goddamn boyfriend.

We sat in silence together. Great going-away party. Like I said, the one whose name is least secure on the guest list shows up first. It's me.

The bartender walked over to say hi. "What's the latest?"

"Stef's getting a boob job." I put down my pint. It didn't even taste good. "And a nose job."

"Tonight?" the bartender asked.

"I'm trying to talk her out of it."

"Tell her to try and watch a nose job on video. You'll never make it through the first two minutes. They use a hammer. Like the kind of hammer Amish people use to build furniture."

"That's what you want, Stef?" I said, dadlike. "You want your face to be Amish furniture." I put on my best I'm-not-upset-just . . . disappointed face.

"No one will know. No one has heard of me. You won't even be able to tell. But I will."

"This is just wrong. It sends the wrong message. You're basically telling your fans that it's okay to hate themselves. You're saying that they should all be like you and buy their way into loving themselves."

"Just drop it."

"I won't. Haven't you ever seen Warhol's 'Before/After'?"

She looked at me blankly, swallowing a gulp.

"It's in the Met. I know the Upper East Side is far but it's worth going. Tell me they let Upper West Side girls go to the Met. Here . . ." I looked up the picture. This silk screen looked like an early Shepard Fairey piece with stencil elements, thick outlines, and streaked black paint. The top box says "Before" with a picture of a face with a nose that might be mine, might be Woody Allen's, might be Gaga's. The face's haggish eyes—combined with that nose—make it look like it belongs to a witch, only without the wart. The "After" box shows a tiny ski-jump nose with a jaunty little button at the end. I have a crush on the second girl because I am shallow. At the very top Warhol simply printed the word "RAPED."

She stared at the image until the screen went to sleep, and she didn't say another word.

"I'm cut in another hour," the bartender interrupted, bringing us both back down to earth. "You want to do another shot?"

Gaga looked up, still lost somewhere in the Met, and nodded her head in dumbfounded silence.

THAT LAST SHOT PUT US close to the edge. But not over it. We rode alongside it, feeling the exhilaration of youth in its unallowable future. We collapsed on each other's shoulders. We apologized for being bad friends. We put the blame on jet lag, empty cupboards and empty wallets. We told the other they were perfectly welcome to do and say whatever was right. No judgments among friends. That night we felt like anything was possible. And it was. I had to admit that it was possible that I was going to miss my new friend.

"Where do you feel love in your body?"

She thought for a minute. "In my stomach."

"Describe it to me—in your belly button? Your chest?"

"You tell me."

"I feel love in my stomach, and then it burns, like a candle or a lantern," I said. "It fills in my chest and it gets bright and brighter and my heart starts working and my ribcage feels the flutter."

"Butterflies?"

"For me it's like a jar of fireflies."

"I can feel that." She looked at me. "Do you feel less creative since you and Nikki broke up?" she asks.

"Less inspired. But that's a matter of goals. It's easy to do something when you can tell yourself why you're doing it. I wanted to impress her with my work."

"I wanted to impress him with mine."

"Isn't that stupid? Do you think they want to impress us with their work?"

"Ha! Yeah right. I'm the last person he thinks about behind the bar. Even when I'm right there. But I read that your body has the same response to love as it does to amphetamines. Increased focus, lack of appetite, heart palpitations."

"It absolutely does. Does that make love addictive? Or does it make it habit forming?"

"Maybe we crave them. But most cravings are bad for us. Like your cigarettes," she said. "I read that cravings only exist in your short-term memory. If you can wait seven minutes from when you crave that cigarette you'll forget all about it. Same goes for food. If you can get your mind on something else, you'll forget all about it."

"So you're going to forget all of him by thinking about cigarettes and candy bars?"

"No. But I'm going to break the habit."

"By letting the craving pass? You know I never even think about cigarettes during the day? I think they're kind of gross and a waste and they leave me feeling terrible."

"Right." Gaga smiled. "And I don't love him, I just want to fuck him after I've been drinking. He is an addiction. He's awful and smelly and I waste all my time and money on him. And for what? So he can make me feel like shit?"

"You said it yourself: *Love is weird.*"

"It sure as fuck is."

"I have this thing I say about being in the prime of your life. It's like you can only be divided by yourself—"

"And one, right? Like prime numbers. That's genius. He's the one guy in my life who can get away with treating me like that. He barely reads, he has terrible manners." Emboldened by her next sip she slammed the glass on the counter. She resented him for it. In one of those magical moments of party life the crowd stopped yelling over each other and the DJ missed a cross-fade at the same time that Gaga screamed into the silenced room.

When the music started up again I sheepishly suggested, "Should we go downtown tonight?"

"Ugh. I can't do it. Everyone will want to ask about recording. 'Are you famous yet?' I just want to catch up with you and walk away."

"So that's it, then? Does anyone else know you're leaving?"

She took a deep breath and gazed at the person she had in her mind's eye. Guy. "How about that cigarette?" she said.

"I'm not giving you a smoke. It'll ruin your voice."

"Just one won't. It makes it more authentic."

"You are authentic," I said. "I have proof." Unintentionally, I sniffed.

"Did you want to call 'Judy'?" She smiled.

"Who?"

"Judy is what my friends call cocaine."

"'Judy' is already here." I thought about it. What the heck! Why not have a night out with my friend. And then I remembered a stupid promise that I made to a very stupid man.

Make sure she doesn't do any drugs tonight.

JUST THEN THE DEVIL CAME in from the back room. He marched right over to us and said hi like a shopkeeper still waiting on you to come in and pick up that special order. "Yo, man, what happened last week?"

Luckily in these situations you can always act drunk. "Hey, buddy! Killer party in here. I was just saying to my friend. Everybody's here tonight. Well, almost everybody. And now here you are." We did the straight-guy hand-shakehand, half-hug.

"What happened the other night? I thought you were down at Don Hill's. You even texted me the show details and you couldn't hook your boy up at the door?" Hell hath no fury like The Devil uninvited.

"You should have texted me. I was stuck in the DJ booth."

"I saw you from the door. The bouncer said you said not to let me in."

"Me? No man." I searched around the bar for answers. "Maybe the other DJ? I don't know the guy."

Somehow he fell for that and in five seconds I realized why. God bless capitalism. He leaned into my ear and whispered, "Well. If you're looking for some good blow I finally got those twenty-sacks you guys are always asking for. If you get five I can get you one free. Maybe if you've got friends who wanna buy a hundo, I'll give you the bonus bag."

I looked at Gaga and kept nodding my head until he went away.

"Who was that?"

"Nobody."

"I saw him the other night at the door but he didn't come in."

"He's a vampire," I said. "And the only way to keep him away is if you don't invite him in."

He walks away, the sun goes down

The next day I came to her apartment to get her to autograph a picture for Mike before the Beauty Bar Christmas party. Like the grand dame who won't let you past the sitting room unless she is ready to entertain, Gaga buzzed me in and came down the rank stairs of her fragrant, classic apartment. The florescent-lit hallways gleamed in the shimmer of peeling paint and bumped walls. She lumbered down the stairs in a sky-blue bathrobe tied at the waist, making a small effort to cover up her breasts as they peeked through the polar fleece curtain of their stage.

"I feel like death," she said, rubbing at the nuclear shadow of last night's makeup. "I can't even let you in. My apartment looks worse than I do."

"You know you look fine."

"Ech."

"You should write about this. Right now. This exact feeling."

"I can't," she cried. "It would be like sealing the envelope."

I slipped the photo out of the paper Target bag and peeled the sticker off the cheap frame. She thought about it for a moment with her bare legs crossed, sitting herself on the stairs. Her tiny bare feet pointed down like Cinderella the morning after.

We tore ourselves apart the night before and some kind of fairy godmother guided her home safe because I sure as hell didn't. Maybe part of me worried that people might see us leaving together, or that we might finish what we had started in the DJ booth the week before. There are people who do terrible things when they are drunk. They yell. They pick fights. They go to bed with people they shouldn't. I was not one of those people. Mostly because I always did pretty much whatever I wanted and there was no thirsty, repressed monster hidden inside of me that leaked out with a few drinks. Lord knows I drank. But probably my favorite part of drinking was the little vacation I got from that terrified narrator who sang out from my emptiest cavity, echoing through the layers and worrying me to death.

Her unventilated sadness left the whole tenement feeling stuffy. If she had anything on I would have demanded we go take a walk: The cold New York winter felt like a spa treatment on a hungover face. Instead, she sat there in a pile and took every last inch of her happiness to write a sweet note in silver glitter pen.

The worst part of seeing her like this was knowing that it would only get worse. The day after was the easy part. She would miss him more. See him more. She would venerate him and trade all the men in New York, all the record deals on the planet, all the notes on the scale, and everything she'd ever loved before for a single one of his flaws. At least we didn't do any drugs. As a replacement lover drugs worked like Sweet'N Low, fooling you into believing your craving is satisfied. Drugs weren't the problem. Fun wasn't the problem. Partying wasn't the problem. Being a human being was the fucking problem.

Being the innkeeper of your soul, knowing that people will come and go and use you how they will and that you will have to clean up their mess—that's the problem to have.

I wanted to cry for her, to run the taps and use up all the hot water like a bad houseguest. Crying like that would awaken her deflated heart and prove to her that she was not alone.

She had come down from that great big high we rode together the week before. Once again she looked like that very first Russian doll, shiny and fresh out of the package. The one hidden deepest inside.

"Have you heard from him?"

"No." She stopped and some memory produced a quiver of sadness in her lower lip. Her face soured and then she changed her answer: "*Yes.*"

"Did he say he was sorry? Did he say that he loved you and respected you?"

"No."

"Did he come by and apologize?"

"No."

"Has he been calling at all hours of the night?"

"No."

"What, then?"

When you're young you're in the prime of your life—divisible by yourself and one.

"He sent me a text and—" She started crying until she could only get out the very end of it. I couldn't understand her and so she pulled her phone out of her bathrobe and handed it to me. The screen read, "Bug Bite."

"What?"

"You were there. One night at the bar I got pretty drunk and I asked for a Bud Light, but somehow it came out as 'Bugbite.' It's his little name for me." She looked up at me with her big glassy eyes, holding back the tears. She sniffed, "Bug Bite."

I would have done anything possible to paint a smile on that face right then. She sat on the cold stone steps, her legs shivering. Can you love someone at their lowest? Can you sit on the stump of the Giving Tree and remember swinging in the branches and eating apples? How could I let this happen?

"Come here." I sat down on the step and held her through the flimsy robe the way you would collect a ripped paper grocery bag. She was like a mannequin that had come apart from too much shuffling in a neglected box. I ran my fingers through her dry, bleached hair. I collected the lifeless doll parts of her body and squeezed. Her back had a chilled steam of stress sweat. Being curled up and holding back the tears forced her back to cry. "Look," I said, keeping her forehead pressed against my shoulder while promising to do the one thing I really didn't want to do right then, "I'll talk to him."

Through the collar of my shirt I could feel the warm flow of mascara tears.

Is it in his eyes?

That night I would join a proud tradition of losers who were fired but went back to their old jobs. One thing that's important to remember about a scene—any scene really—is that the employees are half of it. The bartenders, the door guys. The bands don't make a lot, but being there and playing is their job. It felt in a way like I'd been fired from the scene. But I never really would be. I'm like the young exec who lost one of his big accounts. As I put on my leather jacket and boots, I caught sight of myself in the mirror. I looked like Oliver North, dismissed from the military and still wearing his uniform on trial.

I am a soldier.

Few defeats match the intensity of going back to a place where you got canned. First of all, your former coworkers resent you for getting out—no matter what the conditions. They see you with the days off they wish they had—and with the severance you sometimes get to tide you over in the interim. Frequently you just find another damn job, which means you actually have the time for once to hang out and do unheard-of things like go to shows where you're not in the band or working the door.

But mostly, as I discovered that night, you become poison. Most of us get fired for getting caught doing something that every single person you know does. Maybe you drink behind the bar or you let a friend have a few for free and when they slip you a twenty you put it in your tip jar. Never mind. Not maybe. Definitely. Everyone does that, unless their friends don't have the decency to tip. But knowing that you got canned for it meant other people stayed away from you so that it wouldn't look like they sympathized with someone who would do such a thing.

I was a dead man walking down Rivington Street that night. No one said anything about staying away from the bar or taking a week off before coming back here. I had relationships to maintain and DJ slots to fill. Everyone I knew found their way to the bar eventually on a Friday. Because of that I could possibly run into anyone. Starlight, Nikki, Dino, St. Michael, Conrad, The Devil. If I get thrown out in front of any one of them, I will probably have to start hanging out in the East Village.

GUY LEANED AGAINST THE SAFETY rail in front of the hatchway where everyone locked their bikes. With his hair covering the edges of his eyes he looked like an aging starlet trying to hide a pair of crow's-feet from her adoring fans. He smoked what looked like one of many cigarettes, his heavy eyes buoyed by a forced smile. He laughed idly at the social crowd with his hidden eyes, incapable of betraying any emotion.

As I walked up to him a drunk girl stepped in front of me and shrieked, "Hey, don't you work here?!"

The crowd parted and everyone looked at me. I swear they cut the music inside. "I used to. I got fired!" And then, as if I happened to know the funniest punch line in the world: "This is the guy that fired me!" I slapped Guy on the sleeve of his studded leather jacket, pressing the one-size-too-big shoulder against him. He isn't much more than a half size bigger that I, but he always wore hats and jackets in the wrong sizes, as if he thought that he were buying a motorcycle jacket for a bigger badass.

Guy laughed at my bravado and chuckled in my acknowledgement that he called the shots around here. No hard feelings. He smiled. "How about a drink?"

"Fuckin' finally," I said. "Been too long since I could just come in the damn bar and not be stressed out."

"You and me both."

He slapped an arm on my jacket and we herded in the door with the others like the cattle did just before they made our jackets. He walked me into the bar and the message was clear to all around. They must have misheard the rumor. Maybe he just threatened to fire me. Maybe I'd quit, like Brent, and would be an honored guest at any time. False alarm, everybody.

"Patrón?"

"I had enough Patrón working here. Give us some Wild Turkey."

"Fine. I'm gonna do Crown Royal."

"Pussy," I said. As if I ever call people a pussy for drinking a different kind of whiskey. This is what I mean about Guy. I don't understand him, but he has a very infectious persona. I continued as if I didn't care about anything at all. "I'm waiting on a friend. Her family is from Kentucky and they breed horses. They won the derby in '99. You gotta come with us sometime and bet on the races."

"I'd love to." Two dudes in a bar talking about gambling and whiskey.

"They have a box at the racetrack and they know all the jockeys and trainers. They always seem to know who's gonna win too."

The gambler smiled. His face looked like a bartender, but his eyes hid the truth. He gave a grin and flirted with girls and bought shots for people. His arm pumped in the air when they played his favorite Iron Maiden song. And somewhere in Guy, the gambler, he broke even.

"New Year's is a Monday this year," I said.

"I . . . I forgot about that." Guy didn't work Mondays, but he'd assign himself to the shift. Now we were talking money.

"Nice to make some extra money after Christmas, right before rent is due."

"You wanna spin? You've done every other year."

"Done. You, me, Starlight. Just like old times." He smiled. Thinking of old times. "How's it going?"

"Fine," said the party guy. "Great Friday night!"

"No. I mean how's it going?" I said. "Not as your DJ or your employee. I'm your friend and I want to know how you're doing."

"Fine."

"Do you miss her?"

For the first time in our relationship Guy's eyes looked true, not the gambler's indifferent bluff. I could see he was out of aces. He'd ignored her, texted her, gone out of his way to run into her. He'd put on a front to some people. But when I cornered him like this he couldn't bluff. His eyes welled up like hers did when I looked into them. His chin quivered and he looked down at the stool on the corner of the bar. Her stool.

In the Russian dolls of Guy it looked like he had hit the eject button and absconded from the bottom, leaving the outer shell to plod on, lifeless. I felt for him. This outer layer—the one we're all least accustomed to—went on. It worked. It smiled at known faces and never gave away anything about what really went on inside.

"It's . . . hard." In the mirror behind the bar he saw through his twin layers of hair and into his own eyes. The crestfallen soldier turned and wiped his eyes with a cocktail napkin.

I HAD ONE PRESENT TO give that Christmas and as much as I thought I should stay out I didn't. "Stef—I saw your ex-boyfriend out to-night. He misses you more than you think that he's an idiot. Call him."

No man in the world cuts straighter or greater than New York's number 1 cut creator

I spent the rest of that year on the phone with Gaga in LA. We feasted on all-night yak sessions that would soon unravel the mysteries of the world. I wasn't out accumulating brain damage in the Lower East Side. Somehow we would talk and talk into the dark until we both sat in front of plugged-in phones, crouched by the window and hoping for a never-ending reception while our souls and our batteries recharged. We talked about the future, which waited for us on the other side of New Year's, cheering us on and calling out to us like parents trying to teach a child how to swim underwater.

The news from LA changed every day and the record seemed imminent, but formless. Some days there was talk of a Snoop Doggy Dogg verse. Sometimes she had a duet with Akon.

The marketing people worried, constantly, How are we going to present this girl to the world? She wasn't uptown enough for hip-hop; she wasn't LA enough for R&B. She wasn't mainstream enough for pop or pop enough for the mainstream. This was the year of mixtapes, when the record labels not only relied on copyright infringement but treated it as the new A&R.

Interscope began talking to celebrity DJ AM about putting to-gether a Lady Gaga mixtape. DJ AM was the favored boyfriend of Paris Hilton. Only AM had talent. Pure, raw, music-and-the-message talent. Going to see him spin was like taking woodshop from Jesus. You always found yourself looking over his shoulder, wondering how he'd prerecorded a segment or achieved sonic reso-nance with two dissonant tracks, mixing hip-hop, rock, and house. DJ AM was set to take over the world and he worked at an inhuman pace. Vegas one night, LA the next. Interscope wanted this great figure to put his weight behind Gaga.

Gaga wanted me to do it instead.

They gave me the passcode to what I began calling The Vault. They worried that if they emailed me the track it could leak. God forbid somebody hear the damn song (which you could hear for free on her website and record it if you wanted). Only they didn't give me the password for a protected file. They gave me the password for every file.

This is the crate digger's version of the Matrix.

My natural curiosity got the best of me. I could see from the in-dexes that many of the working artists I admired had new songs in the works, many of them in demo versions I could listen to on this server.

These songs were terrible.

Gaga's track blossomed, like a single daisy sprung from a field of horseshit.

"WE DON'T HAVE A RELEASE date yet. That will come but we have to be ready." Gaga called me and told me that she would fly home from LA for Christmas. And one other thing.

"We?"

"Yes. Today I had a meeting with Interscope and they said that I needed to pick a permanent DJ. And I told them that I wanted it to be you."

My heart exploded. I knew she might need me to help out or even book shows or DJ her after-parties. I'd volunteered to do that on the night I met her. But I never thought you'd see me on stage, outfitted behind her. I would be her biggest fan, her greatest supporter, and I would get to ride shotgun. And then a panic took over me. What if I cost her all of her dreams? What if I weren't good enough or I messed something up? What if the record skipped in front of some important industry people? What if—

"Stef. I just want to tell you something and I'm only going to say it once. But just remember I said it." She paused. Who wouldn't be thrilled? Especially someone so adventuresome.

"Okay . . ." she said. She had not expected such a sullen reaction after crowning me as her partner.

"There is going to come a time when you are going to have to leave me behind. And when you think you've gotten to that point, I want you to do it."

"We're not there yet, w—"

"I know. But when that day comes and you have to make the decision, don't blink. I want you to know right now that I support your decision and I understand that you have to make it and that you will only make that decision when you get to a point where you can't turn back. So do it. I'll always be your biggest fan."

She stopped again. In the background I heard some workplace chatter. She must have called me straight from the meeting.

"Okay. I promise. As long as you know that I'll always be yours."

> # Someday, girl—I don't know when—we're gonna get to that place where we really wanna go

I met the choreographer Laurieann Gibson for the first time on Valentine's Day at sound check. Gaga was able to fly home when DJ Alex English booked us for a show at Le Royale. The last time I walked through that club's doors the place was called Luke & Leroy, home of Misshapes and Michael T.'s Rated X parties. I had DJ'd their last night in business, and when I woke up the next morning at Nikki's house we broke up. Gibson had an impossibly glamorous regality to her, touched with an aw-shucks Canadian grin. Her vivacious personality came off on Gaga, who looked up to her for every move.

It was a sunny day in a sunny time. Guy and I had made up enough for me to DJ New Year's at St. J's again. Plus, he owed me. They'd gotten back together.

And in that time I had fallen deeply and hopelessly in love with Leigh. The hickey girl.

"He's being difficult again," Gaga said calmly, as if noting the weather. Something had changed in her.

"That's okay because that will *ground* you," Laurieann said with a nod and a smile, choreographing Gaga's response. "Is he coming tonight?"

"It's . . . difficult. You see, he's . . . it's like here at home he is the star, and I can't . . . I respect that."

"That's good," Laurieann said. "That sets boundaries. You need those."

No one absorbed technique as well as Gaga. In the intervening months she had added words to her vocabulary the way other people learned dance steps. She padded through them with the uneasy legs of a novice. She'd begun to open up to SoCal alterna-speak, the everybody's-okay language of people who did a lot of thinking by themselves.

"I THINK I'VE HAD A life-changing experience since I saw you on New Year's."

"We should talk then," I told her. "I had one too."

"Really?"

"Big time."

"And now you patched things up with Nikki?"

"No. I let her go. Like the harpooner should have."

"Just logically or did—ohmygod, *you're in love*." She gripped her hands together like a bridesmaid clutching a bouquet. "Who is it? I want to meet her!"

Leigh had burrowed her way into my life before I had words for it. Once at Hotel on Rivington, once when she came in to make sure I was okay when I got jumped at St. J's, once when she brought me the book at Pianos. I was the last one to know that I was in love with her too.

"How could you tell?" I looked down and found Gaga's face pressed into my chest, her arms wrapped around me.

"It's all gone. The fear, the anger. You look stronger. The sparkle came back to your eyes. I missed that sparkle when I was in LA. For a long time you just looked so empty. Oh!" She wrapped her arms around me again. "We have to catch up. You had your life-changing event without me and I had mine . . . without him. What're you doing right now?"

"Nothing. You're my full-time job."

She smiled. "I have errands to do, but maybe you want to talk for a few?"

"I have my Vespa." I held up my helmet. "I have an extra helmet. Why don't I just take us around to do some errands and we'll catch up?"

"Ohmygod, that would be so much fun!" She put the helmet on and I draped a scarf around her neck.

WHEN I SEE THIS PICTURE in my head now, I still feel the chill sting of February air, waking me up like an iced coffee to the face. I can feel Gaga's tiny, soft hands in the twin pockets of my jacket as we sail around the West Village in the early afternoon. The cobblestone streets jammed up with cabs, people rushing from one place to another, salt crunching beneath their feet on the frozen sidewalks. A few times in your life you get to have a moment like this. You've done all the hard work and shaken all the right hands and dropped off your gear and done sound check. You can't worry about how the flyers got printed or how you will be received for a show you haven't performed yet. The only thing you can do is hope that tomorrow feels as good as the excitement for it does right now. And even if tomorrow doesn't feel that way after all, it can't change the thrill of now.

"This feels amazing!" she hollered into my right ear as we sped down the avenue. "I miss New York so much!"

I leaned to my right so she could hear me. "I know. What a wonderful way to see the city."

"I *want* one."

"The label will never let you get a motorcycle."

"But it's just so much fun!" She was right. With a swivel of my hips we slalomed around three sharp manhole covers and ducked between two cars as we helped ourselves to the fading yellow left-turn arrow. Gaga held me tight and low, perfectly following my lead as we snaked around the city and made our way uptown.

"I don't want to wear the disco-bra tonight because I keep getting hints from the label that we're going to do a video," she said. "I want to save it for that."

"Crazy. For which song?"

"That new one. 'Just Dance.'"

"Hmmp."

"What?" she asked into my helmeted ear.

"Nothing. It's just I didn't see that really being your first single."

"Me neither."

Later in the trip I said, "I mean, here we are the headlining act for a show on Valentine's Day and we don't have a van. We don't have instruments or anything. We just roll up like, 'Uhh, hello, we're the band.' No guitars, no entourage. Just three girls and a guy who all took different subway trains."

"The first video needs to look like that," she said, almost to herself, and if she'd had on the other helmet I might've not heard her at all. "Or capture that. Maybe the video should just start with you and me. Like we time it so that the beginning of the song is at my apartment in the LES. I climb on the back in the beginning and you have your record case on the very front. I step out into my helmet and I start singing on the way there."

"That sounds awesome. Remind me to wear sunglasses. I think I look too geeky in glasses. And we want to look cool."

"We are cool. We don't have to look cool."

I had on a cheap but thick navy surplus sweater and my leather jacket, which had holes in the armpits. I tried again and again to sew them up with waxed dental floss, but it left me looking like a shoddily stitched stuffed animal. Gaga had on her soft leather jacket, the best one in the store that fit her.

When the wind got unbearable, I shut my visor. At the next stoplight I made the mistake of breathing, which made my visor fog up and then freeze. I could only tell the light went green by the tinge of the ice. In my nylon saddlebags I had a pair of cheap St. Mark's Place sunglasses. I put them on to block the wind and left the visor open.

"Those look awesome," Gaga told me.

"I think it's kind of obnoxious when people wear sunglasses indoors," I said. "Plus, I wear enough glasses as it is. I don't need any more. I just wish they made regular glasses that could block the wind."

"You should wear them more," she said. "It fits your whole persona as the mysterious guy behind the dials, controlling everything."

"You're right. Sunglasses say, 'I've seen everything.' Glasses just say, 'I've read the liner notes of everything.'" We dipped between two cars on the corner of Fourteenth and Sixth, just past the Urban Outfitters. I knew this block cold from late nights at work when the only respite came from the twin forces of the late-night eats at French Roast and the all-night bagel cafeteria. "I'd probably wear them behind you if we had a tour."

Her little paws gripped me tight around my waist, the fists in my jacket pockets Heimliching me with excitement. "Ohmygod, can you imagine if we ever had *a tour*?"

"I'm just as impatient as you are. We just have to hang on. The world isn't ready for you yet."

"Then they should be ready," she said, quoting me and Jesus in the same breath. "For when they're not ready."

"That's when to hit 'em."

Her hands squeezed me harder.

We pulled over at her favorite midtown lingerie boutique and she found costumes for the night, parading them through the half-empty shop for me. Her skin was sun-kissed from the Los Angeles beach and the poolside parties of her new friends.

WE SERVED OURSELVES PAPER MUGS of tea in the upstairs alcove of a nondescript deli where the shopping bags and cardboard drink holders advertised things we would never buy. As we worked on our set list, I showed her how we could signal each other for space in the act by creating loops with the new programs I had started working with. Whatever she had gone through in just a few short weeks without me, I liked it. She had a vision for what it would take and a commonsense approach to each of the steps. Plus, she could now see how I fit into that plan in a way that no one had before. After we ordered tea at the deli, Gaga went to take a phone call. We had just finished shopping in the most pristine underwear store I'd ever seen. She handed me her bags.

I heard her say, "We've met before. When I was about nineteen. . . . My mother still has your book of poetry!" When she finished she kept her eyes fixated on her device.

Eventually the screen went blank and she looked up at me. "That was the best phone call of my life."

"Really?"

"Do you know who Bert Padell is? He was Madonna's business manager in the nineties."

"The batboy who saved Bad Boy?"

Gaga looked at me like I was speaking in tongues.

I said, "He was a batboy for the Yankees and then saved Diddy when he and Biggie got dropped from Uptown Records and helped form Bad Boy Entertainment." My ears had perked up over another thing, though. He was fond of sending people out of his office with his self-published books of poetry.

"Well, that was him. On the phone. Just now."

"What?"

"Someone played him my new stuff and he says he wants to be 'on board.'"

"What does that even mean?"

"It might mean really big things. I haven't even signed with him yet and he already wants me to get to Miami. He says he's got big plans."

"And you know he's legit, right? Your dad wanted to get you working for him years ago."

"Yes. And now he wants to take over."

"Good. I think. Right? That's good. He'll take over for your dad?"

"That means I have to tell my dad he's fired." Gaga and I looked up at each other. Way too many people had gotten that lately.

GAGA'S PHONE RANG AGAIN. AND then again and again. Everyone on Gaga's team in LA, it seemed, had gotten a call from Bert Padell, and ideas were coming in from all sides. A songwriter no one cared about last week was now an act that had people scrambling to meet with her.

We tried to leave the deli three times, each time a false start. The calls kept coming, and because of the cold outside, we didn't head out until the last phone call finished. Gaga tugged at her helmet with one ear on the phone. After several stalled beginnings, the rest of her career would begin at the end of this phone call. "Okay, okay," she finally said to Leah Landon at her management company in LA, the last of many calls. "Okay, I have to go. We have a show tonight." Less than an hour earlier the most excited surprise in her life had been a Vespa ride. Strangely, that still excited her just as much as getting informed that all her dreams were scheduled to come true. I say this because then Gaga did a little impatient dance, shaking the passenger helmet in her free hand and blurting out, "Okay, I have to go and get on a motorcycle now."

You can imagine the amount of squawking that I could hear coming out of the receiver.

"No it's—we're not even getting on the highway. My DJ is going to give me a ride home. We—of course I'll wear a helmet. No. I'm not taking a cab. We have too much to do before the show. I'll—I'll be careful. Okay . . . okay." She handed me the phone. "She wants to talk to you."

"What?" I took the receiver in my hand. "Hello?" I tried to smile like they teach you in customer service.

"Are you the DJ I've been hearing about?"

"Yes. Speaking."

"I just want to be very clear. You are about to give the future of pop music a ride home and tonight you two have a very important show. And I just want your word that you will be more careful than you have ever been."

"You have my word."

"I will call you guys when I hear about the next step, but be ready. And remember—"

"I'll be careful. I promise."

"Because if something happens, I'll come down to the Lower East Side and track you down."

"You have my word."

Click.

"Are we going to your Stanton Street apartment?" I nervously mapped out the route in my head. From the club, I just had to drive her two blocks to Houston and then go across town. But we were inching closer to rush hour in midtown, so I'd have to probably take the FDR—which I promised Leah I wouldn't.

Gaga's eyes hid a little secret. "No, actually. We are going uptown. We need to go to the West Seventies. To my parents' house."

The screen door slams

Central Park is the Times Square of actual New Yorkers. Tourists on Forty-Second Street like to look up at all the advertisements and think, "We're here! We've made it!" And it's true. They have made it to Times Square, New York City. But Central Park is the only place in New York that never changes and always welcomes you back. It cools you off in the summer and the empty paths of white lamps guide you through the crisp trails in the winter. Hills (which were flattened in many other parts of the city long ago) pop up out of midtown like the forest in a children's book. When you get just far enough into the park you can look out and see the tops of faraway buildings—as if you had left the city far behind. Or you'd slogged through the wild to get there. Maybe as a kid you had a backyard or a forest or a tree to hide in. That tree is waiting for you in Central Park.

We wound our way over to the Sixty-Fifth Street Transverse, which cuts through the middle of the park and connects the East Side with the West Side. Right after Madison Avenue we took a left, and the second we entered the park, the two of us landed in dreamland. I eased off the tiny throttle and kept us at a respectable pace. Stone walls rose up on both sides of the driving trench. Ten feet above, the park went on uninterrupted. No traffic, no intersections, no passing lanes. Just the magic of Central Park on a winter's day with the far-away silence of traffic.

In the slow-passing cabs, young couples snuggled together in assumed darkness, their eyes lit up by the jarred lightning of a taxi TV screen. With the promise of an enchanted city just above the trees, anything was possible right then. In its silence it had taken away the chatter, taken away the doubt. Am I going to make it on time? Is the subway running? What time is it? Is my girlfriend leaving me? What did the boss mean, "We'll talk on Monday"? Do I look fat in this? How much longer do I have to work here? How much longer can I work here? Does she even want to be dating me? Where is the train? Wh—? New York City asks too many questions. And sometimes Central Park feels like the right answer.

"It's happening," Gaga piped up from behind me, her voice rising over the wind and the engine noise. "It's all happening."

"I knew it would."

"I didn't. Not until today."

"You know what's funny? You didn't have to do anything differently. You still would have played those shows and written all of those songs. You still hustled all those years and brought your demo tape all over town. You still would have done all of that by now. The only difference is that somebody noticed. It's like what we talk about playing to an empty room."

"I can't think of a better way to celebrate this day than to play a show with you in front of all our friends tonight."

"I'm glad." I could feel it too. We had so many false starts since we'd met. Now it felt like we had to take this chance, before anyone noticed they'd given it to us.

The Vespa pulled us onward with the gathering acceleration of the tiny engine as it descended a small hill. The one way of Sixty-Sixth Street merged into the eastbound Sixty-Fifth Street as we headed west through the park. Gaga held tight as the two lanes converged around a neat point—no traffic lights, no intersections, no commercial traffic. Walls grew higher around us as we got swallowed by the park. Around the next bend we slipped under the stone arch of the East Drive overpass as the fingers of bushes and trees gripped the edge. The mixing board of building lights flickered in the distance. Together we leaned into the curve and came out through the tunnel.

This is the moment. You could have your success and your shows and your tech problems and be tired. You could have a bad photo come out of you in the papers. You could miss a note, be late for a gig. You could fight with you ex and dwell on the past. You could hold a grudge against yourself. But no one could ever take away a moment like this. A moment where everything seemed possible and you realized that it always was.

THE TEMPTATION WILL ALWAYS BEG you to return to this moment. To remember what it felt like to find that feeling and know it for the first time. I could stay there forever. But at that moment I just wanted to go on and on. I gripped the throttle. We had waited for a brighter day to reveal itself and now we were chasing it down together.

"I just love New York so much. I miss it when I'm in LA. I miss you guys."

"We're always here for you," I said. "Central Park will be here when you get back."

"This looks like a video right here." She glanced over the wall. And I knew what she meant. The combined news of the afternoon had fit so perfectly into what was once only a vision. How could we even believe it true? The Time Warner Center hid off in the background trying to stay invisible. The Central Park South hotels checked in for the night, lights coming on in lonely rooms. "They're talking about doing the video in LA."

"Hm. That's weird."

"I guess. But I don't mind. I used to hear record labels say I was 'too downtown' or that they didn't know how I'd play in the rest of the country."

"And now it's like you're their interpreter."

"They think I'm exotic. They're like, 'Ohmygod, so in New York you work as a go-go dancer?' And I'm like, 'Yeah. For only like six months."

"That's part of fiction. You've created a character for them. We all do it. Makes things easier. When you do the video you're going to have to create a character. You're going to have to introduce that character. You can do it. You know theater."

"I should have them fly people out. I need you guys to be there."

"I'll go. I'll definitely go."

"Who else would come? Colleen?" She invoked Starlight's real name. "I could fly you and Colleen out."

"That would be fun. We should get Semi Precious Weapons into it. You know they'd love it."

I could feel her smiling as she bounced on the back like a little girl. "Yay!"

The West Drive overpass swallowed another taxi. We entered into it like a wormhole, with the damp and echoing walls birthing us onto the West Side and into the future. Behind me she sang out into the reverb of the tunnel; it rang with delight the way church bells do when they get to play Christmas music. You have moments like this. Everything after this would change forever. But wherever you go for the rest of your life you will go there with this moment tucked into your back pocket, reminding you that things happen. And being there while they happen matters more than whatever happens.

You have moments like this. And you have them to keep for the rest of your life.

WE PARKED IN FRONT OF an imposing doorman-building on West Seventieth Street. Gaga marched into the unlocked door. She waved and greeted the two uniformed doormen by name as we padded across the loose, trafficked carpet of the entryway. She made a determined left and came to a ground floor door and knocked. When no one came at first, she jiggled the knob and found it locked. "Argh," she grumbled at this momentary interruption of her perfect preshow plan—sound check, shopping, quick tea, ride home. She knocked again.

A teenage girl answered the door. "Hello," she said, greeting the surprised stranger. Me.

"Hi." I must have looked lost. In addition to never belonging anywhere, I also have an ongoing curiosity with the rest of the world. I had never seen the inside of a luxury building, or any owner-occupied building in New York City. The way that the glossed-over details of Gaga's life could exist so plainly fascinated me. The same way that I grew up thinking everyone had a driveway and a rusty basketball hoop, she grew up waving to these same doormen and letting herself into this first-floor apartment.

We walked into a large entry room with tongue-and-groove floors. Everything looked bright and open, with a modest dining room and an open kitchen. A stark, black baby-grand piano sat over by the large floor-to-ceiling windows. Their apartment included the courtyard of the building. I looked into the white stone backyard and saw a tree branch. Was that the tree her sister fell out of in the story?

The stairs were open all the way to the second floor. From there a voice called out in midconversation, "I'll wear it if it works but I don't want to look silly—" Halfway down the stairs a woman wearing a creased white Lady Gaga t-shirt over a more age-appropriate long-sleeved shirt stopped herself. She wore it like a mom, as if Lady Gaga were a college where her kid had been accepted.

"Oh, hello," Gaga's mother, Cynthia, said to me.

It was hard to recall the last time I'd gone to a friend's parents' house. High school? Must have been. Because somehow I got stuck in high school mode. My first words were, "Gaga, I didn't know you had *two* sisters."

The woman smiled.

Gaga smirked at my lame joke. "Mom. This is my DJ."

"Hi." I shook her hand.

She didn't look like the moms I'd met. She had a striking figure and healthy blond hair, and the air of a countess about her. The only proof I had that she was a mom was she kept saying mom things: "Sorry the place is such a mess. We're remodeling."

"I like the shirt on you."

"Do I look silly?"

"No. You look like a mom."

"That's what I'm going for."

"The scenester rule is you don't want to look like you bought the shirt on the way into the show just to wear it. But I think because you're a mom you can get away with it," I said, smiling.

She nodded her head, happy to have someone on her side. "See? That's exactly what I was just saying."

"But then again you're the mom. You get to be supportive with or without wearing the shirt. But you can be a mom wearing it at the grocery store and everything."

"Maybe I'll just do that." She went upstairs to change.

A man emerged on the other side of the kitchen in a baseball cap that had the outline of a woman with teardrop breasts. "Bada Bing!"

it read, after the real-life strip club from HBO's mafia-family TV show *The Sopranos*. I noticed of course that I was under scrutiny and a big part of me rose to the challenge. Fortunately or unfortunately I get underestimated and I always enjoy it because I don't particularly mind getting a chance to prove myself.

"That's not him!" Gaga called out from behind me. I soon discovered that she meant Guy. "You'll meet him tonight, Dad. Like I told you. This is my DJ."

He said my real name, which surprised me. Then he handed me a long business check with the name Mermaid Management LLC and their home address.

"Dad, the dancers said they didn't get your check from the show at Slipper Room."

Mr. Germanotta—Joe, as I was later commanded to call him—looked befuddled for a moment. He had worked his life in telecommunications and eventually started his own company installing wi-fi in hotels. But now his toughest client came to him as the one person he couldn't say no to. I found it adorable. Most of the kids in our scene acted like runaways, orphans working under assumed names who ate ramen on Christmas and drank Wild Turkey on Thanksgiving. I envied her for having a family uptown she could go to for strength and meatballs. "Damn," he said. He had forgotten to bring them the checks at that show. "I'll make up a check for them tonight. . . . How much did we say?"

Gaga grumbled, "What does it say in the email I sent you?"

"I'll have to check."

"*Dad.*" Gaga put her foot down in her own dad voice. "What have you been doing?"

He put on a very adorable voice, like he was one of his own brothers making fun of him, "*Eyyy*, I'm a big-time producer now. I've got three acts to manage and I—"

"This isn't even the right amount." Gaga scowled at the numbers. "Did you even read the email?" Gaga guided her dad with the common impatience of family members arguing over directions to the mall. She was hard on him, honest in the way that only family can ever be with each other and each other's expectations.

"Fine. I'll write another check for the money we owe them. Tell 'em to keep this and say there's a little extra in there and we're sorry for the delay. We don't want to start upsetting people now that we're this close." He went into the other room to draw another check.

Mom came back downstairs in her own clothes, no band T-shirt, and looked right at the look on Gaga's face. Gaga hadn't told her mother she was coming, but—as if by some mother-daughter telepathy—Cynthia seemed to know something big was up. "What did you say you had to tell us, honey?"

"Remember Bert Padell? The management guy we had a meeting with years ago?"

"Of course," Mom said. "I still have his book of poetry."

"He called today. He wants to take over management. He heard the new song and he loves it. He wants to go into business." Gaga's news was met with blank stares. Parents, even showbiz parents, are sometimes the worst people to come to with good news.

"But your father is your manager, honey."

Judiciously, Gaga explained herself: "Yes. But soon it is going to be a little too much to handle." Gaga spoke patiently, but with a firm sense that she had to inform her parents that this wasn't fun and games anymore. "And we don't want Daddy to get overwhelmed. It's about growth, not replacing him."

Joe walked back into the room with the two new checks. He stopped near the front door. "What?" Being the only man in a house with three girls meant always walking into a newly silent room and being told:

"Nothing."

He took a breath and caught my eye. We shared a conspiratorial exhale. *Women.*

GAGA'S SISTER, NATALI, SAT ON the couch, observing the flurry of action. She had the demure plain brown bangs of a girl who had yet to be informed of how beautiful she was. Natali liked to shy out of the way in these family conversations. Gaga was never around and always on their minds and lips and phone calls. No one was more proud of the older sister, and when Gaga flew home from LA that week she came straight over and crawled into bed with her sister, who awoke giddy with excitement.

The truth: Natali and I had been talking on the phone in secret. I pulled her in to do a skit for the Gaga mixtape. Gaga didn't know that, so we had to play it cool.

"Do you go to Sacred Heart too?"

"Mm hmm." She smiled.

"Are you coming to the show?"

"I can't."

Gaga made a cute wail from the other side of the room. "Oh no!"

Natali nodded. It was true. "I have a French test tomorrow."

Gaga's face fell.

I interrupted, "Bring your flashcards to the show. We can work on them in the DJ booth."

Natali smiled.

"What'd you get at the store?" Natali motioned to the shopping bag Gaga came in holding.

"It's my costume for the night." After a few moments of garment appraisal, Gaga explained her outfit for the night. "I'm going to wear the yellow dress with the one shoulder to the show, and then right before I go on stage I'm going to emerge as Lady Gaga with just heels and panty hose and this."

She held up the scrap of underwear. A black bikini with leathered spandex connected to a single slit top by a single strap of fabric down the right side. I'd seen her wear racier things to Beauty Bar.

Mom went silent. When prompted she finally said, "Honey, do you think . . . don't you want your music to—"

"This is part of her character," Stef said, using the uncharacteristic third person to discuss Lady Gaga. "And she dresses like this." Gaga went off to the kitchen to go over some things with her dad.

Mom and I got to talking about music and their excitement and how many of their family members could make it that night. And when Gaga was in the bathroom, Cynthia confessed how much she missed seeing the thick black hair on her beautiful daughter's head.

WITH THE GIRLS WORKING ON details, Joe and I started talking about guy stuff. Joe had planned on ripping up the floorboards the next day. The house had gone on too long, it was decided. New floors, new lights to replace the track lighting. "Don't you think they're too eighties?" Mom added when she heard us talking.

A nice thing about coming from a big family was that you could slip into another big family. It wasn't jealousy, but I did envy her for having parents in the city. Every time I got fired or dumped or got big news I had to get on a bus or a train and wait forever and that's just not any fun. Also, this probably goes along with how I'm more comfortable with strangers than I am with people who know me, but I always have fun with other people's families. They don't judge you or criticize you. Here I came to the door in the same outfit I'd worn for a straight month and Mom told me how much she liked my sweater.

I get caught up talking about home repair with Joe. We're in the middle of talking about nails and different kinds of electric sanders. Mom orders pizza and Natali watches the entire scene, the patient observer.

MY NEW GIRLFRIEND, LEIGH, WALKED up to me after the show. I wanted her to finally meet Gaga, for the two halves of my heart to come together. She had an angry look on her face.

I couldn't tell what was wrong. This used to happen with Nikki too. For some reason seeing your boyfriend at work bothers some people. I'd like to say that if I were in a play or something you wouldn't expect to just come and talk to me on stage. But even saying that out loud just makes me sound like a huge ass. I went over to make it up to her. "Hey, baby!"

She handed me the camera. "I'm gonna leave now," she said sternly. "Happy Valentine's Day. Glad you two had a good time today when you were ignoring my texts." She planted the camera in my hands.

In the camera display was one of the many, many pictures I had taken earlier that afternoon of Gaga trying on lingerie.

I suck at life.

I tried to chase after her but the party wouldn't let me. When I got outside she was gone. When I turned around I was eaten by monsters. "When is the next show?" "When can we get the record?" "Can you burn us a CD?" "When will that new song be up?" "Are you going to be in the video?"

Gaga and her family fed them bags and bags of plain white T-shirts and wifebeaters.

I stared down Seventh Avenue, wishing Leigh would come back. My phone had died somewhere around the five hundredth person I texted about the show.

Little girl, I don't care no more; I know this for sure

On Ludlow Street, the cautious van drivers for out-of-town bands lined the block. Kids wrapped in scarves stood around in their small herds, smoking or watching their friends smoke. Each of them discussing some topic emphatically as if it were a great mystery of the universe that had yet to achieve clarification until just now. The girls smiled through wary eyes, idly checking their phones for a report from another bar. First-time bands loaded up gear into the vans they so cautiously guarded.

At the corner of Rivington Street, I could hear its howl, as clear as the wolf that begins "Thriller." The call of the wild sang out into the night. I had my fun. But I needed to get a job. I needed to grow up. It would take some time. But I got time. Luckily I knew that after a ten-minute walk in Chinatown I could catch the B and take it one stop to my house. I might even get home in time to—

"CHEERS, BUDDY!" GUY AND I dropped our whiskey glasses on the bar at St. J's five minutes later. He hit the button on the smoke machine. Between manning up when I got fired, watching out for Gaga when they broke up, and helping him when he finally decided he wanted her back, Guy and I were better friends than we'd ever been. Starlight danced in the corner, shaking her ass in the red light as the New York Dolls blared on the bar speakers. Even in the dead of winter nothing tasted sweeter than the ice cold Budweiser that lay flat in St. J's refrigerator all day.

Leigh texted, "How's it going, birdie?" Things had gotten rocky with Leigh after the show. But we made it through that first fight, laughed about it, and went searching for another.

"Still in Manhattan. Almost done?" I had—don't judge—gotten over Nikki by dating another waitress. This one a part-time student at NYU.

A brace of scenester girls slipped into the bathroom together, clogging up the line. The two single-stall bathrooms in back held the room hostage. As I waited in line, I felt the ghostly vibration of my phone, which turned out to just be the friction of dry winter fabrics. I missed her.

I looked up and catch a familiar face. The Devil arched an eyebrow at me and just said, "Coke, weed, X . . ."

The greatest trick The Devil pulled.

" . . . Ambien, Oxycontin, Viagra."

The Devil stayed true to his name—he described perfectly a weekend from hell.

"No, thank you," I said like a good boy, and closed myself in the bathroom alone.

"Getting ready to leave midtown. Should I come meet you downtown?" Leigh texted. And then: "I have all my school stuff."

I typed, "Yes. I'm at St. J"—and then I looked up. I should just tell her to go home. I should go with her. I should go home with a beautiful woman and she should read a book next to me in bed. I have made a lot of mistakes in my life. But if you get to read a book in bed with a beautiful woman, you should just in case you never get to again.

I left half a beer on the back of the toilet where someone had tagged "Bea Arthur" on the seat. Just past the go-go platform, I heard a speedy-mouthed girl talking loud into her phone: "Gross, what are you doing *there*," she said. "Come meet me at St. J's. I hear Fridays at St. J's is real hot right now."

ON THE WAY TO THE door I ran into Gaga. She floated in on a cloud of pure happiness. Her heels almost propelled her into the air as she jumped on me and gave me a huge hug. "I didn't know you're in town," I said.

"I leave tomorrow!" She held on to me.

"How did the meeting go with Bert?"

"He's taking over! It's all happening!" She rushed to tell me the news on her way to tell Guy.

"Good, baby. I'm glad."

The arrival of Bert must mean the exit of me. I'd made her promise to do it and I didn't think it would happen so immediately.

"It's really happening! All of it! It's all starting to click."

"Good."

"I'm going to be huge. And I'm taking you with me."

I smiled at this.

"They're filming my video in six weeks. We need to come up with ideas."

"Wow. You work on a record for two years and then one day it all comes together."

"Are you ready to be in the video?"

"Of course. Are you bringing everyone out?"

She smiled. "Just *you*."

* * *

EVERY TIME I TAKE THE J train, I remember the time I came down to New York by myself when I was twenty. I'd had a really bad breakup at some point in college, which, I believe, is now a graduation requirement. My travels around that time vaguely resembled those of a crazy old man whose dog has run off to die. The old man would take the same walk he's taken a thousand times, listening for the tinkle of license on collar, calling out her name and hoping she'll just come back. Everyone told me that I should get out, move to a different city, try something new. Williamsburg, everyone said. Being self-reliant, I took the train to Grand Central and looked up Williamsburg on a subway map. In the great unknown blob that we called Brooklyn, there was the word "Williamsburg" printed in brown ink, stretching from the Navy Yard to somewhere halfway to Long Island. I took the J train to the "g" in "Williamsburg." I didn't find the gentrified college town of skinny kids in identical black plastic glasses. I landed in the 'hood, underneath an elevated train line in the dark. I circled the block a few times, wondering if I had missed a record store or if I would ever get over this feeling of being lost for the rest of my life.

No one told me about the L train or the record shops just north of where I'd gotten off (and quickly gotten back on) the train. But this night, years later, it was this Williamsburg I landed in, and I walked up Union Avenue and waited for Leigh to come out of the L train. These empty streets and boarded-up storefronts stood nonchalantly and I walked through the always-dark shadow of the elevated train tracks. Union Avenue was almost entirely under construction. Gone were the rotting old homes with their ironed slatted windows. These new buildings aspired to live a new life as more than just apartments. They had gyms, doormen, courtyards, and game rooms. One of them would have a bar in the lobby. Entire blocks of old, drab, vinyl-sided homes were plucked off the board like little green Monopoly houses before the big red hotels go down and the rent goes up.

Up the street I could make out a halo of blond hair ahead as Leigh walked out of the Sunac market. She held a pair of chopsticks in one hand and a bag of supermarket sushi and a seaweed salad. Her first words were "Did you eat?"

"No." I actually couldn't remember when I had eaten last.

"I figured. Let me drop my things at home and I'll feed you. Anything going on tonight?"

"Yes."

"Where?"

I smiled. "I hear Fridays at home are real hot right now."

Hanging on the telephone

You'd get one day, one amazing day in late February, where the exasperated weathermen couldn't quite believe the Doppler. You'd wonder for a second if the harsh winter had abandoned you. Defiant girls put on sundresses and took long walks at lunch and braved the outdoor tables and the too-cold slats of the benches in the park, their pale thighs thirsty for sunshine. All around you there'd be New York smiles, the jubilant faces of the community that rose to any challenge. We did it, everyone! We did it! The excitement and the bare legs and the noise of birdsong and voices filled the streets. It held its promise—it meant things were happening, things were coming to life. The sun fed my freckles and dusted off my smile.

The weather only lasted for the day. But you had to hold on to that day for six more weeks and never let it go.

THE VIDEO GOT CANCELLED AGAIN. But the recording continued. With Gaga in California I couldn't book any shows. I didn't have my great go-go dancer that always got me asked back.

The money never seemed quite enough and my creditors still

mounted their confederacy against me. Paying off the electric company meant screwing the gas line for the month. I still DJ'd at St. J's and 151, sometimes filling in on Mondays just to get a few beers and the fifteen-dollar payment for the night. With Gaga away I still made up for our lost time with emails and texts. I knew that people must have wanted her to have her time to create out in California. But that also left her feeling like her friends had forgotten her. I made it an extra point to tell her when people would ask me about her. She loved knowing that her scene went on without her but awaited her return.

On weekends I picked up shifts at a jazz bar uptown across the street from Elaine's, the St. J's of a particular generation of writers. On my way to work every night I peeked in the window, hoping for a glance of the smart gray-and-white suits on Kurt Vonnegut, Tom Wolfe, and Gay Talese.

One night as I was closing up the bar, I talked on the phone with Michael T. He had a Friday night party at Lotus called Tattler, and he wanted me to host the night. When I got there he of course asked if St. J's had burnt to the ground and if Gaga were doing as wonderfully as he hoped. "Michael T. asked about you," I texted her. "I told him you're being brilliant."

She did the uncharacteristic thing of calling me on the actual telephone. "Hey! I'm so glad you called." I was too. Uptown can be lonely.

"Hi, baby! That's so sweet of you to say. What did Michael T. have to say about me?"

"He just wanted to know that you were well."

"I miss my friends."

"I told him that. He says he wants to do a party with you when you get back."

"With *us* you mean."

"So what's up? You going to some crazy LA party with bikinis and hot tubs and 'meetings' and lots of linen pants?"

"Do all of your LA references come from *Annie Hall*?"

"Pretty much."

"I don't really get to go to parties. I'm kinda trapped. I still don't drive and Troy doesn't want me drinking or straining my vocal chords while we finish. I'm only allowed to have white wine and only once in a while."

"You poor LA thing."

"What have you been up to?"

"DJ'ing. I'm filling in at a friend's bar and saving up . . ." I almost didn't want to mention the video. It seemed like such an exotic and amazing thing. People entered contests to be in their favorite band's music video. And lately Gaga had become my favorite band. No matter what happened, I still wanted to do that video.

"Look, uhm, I can't do that show on the twenty-eighth. The one with Theo and the Skyscrapers."

"Oh." I tried not to get discouraged, especially around her and about her. I really needed that money.

"I could swing it if I were out there but it's just not going to happen with me in California."

"No worries." I had saved. Saving is easy when you're planning a trip. Every coffee or sandwich I bought at home was one less I could have on my trip. I economized down to my caloric intake. In the interest of full disclosure, I would like to say that from the very start I knew that California would put me in touch with people who knew people. *Mercutio* was a play now. It had a new script. None of my fantastic digressions mattered and my long-windedness evaporated under the weight of the dialogue. "So what are you doing tonight?"

"Nothing."

"That must be nice."

"I guess. But I miss home. I wish I could finish my days recording by coming down to see you at Pianos or waiting on a stool at St. J's. It just feels kinda . . . I don't know . . ."

"I know exactly what you mean."

"Like do you ever finish writing and just wish you could read it to someone?"

"All the time. Luckily I am shy about one thing, though."

"But you shared it with me."

"You're different." When it came to writing I could never change the subject fast enough. I felt like a mere hobbyist, a model-train enthusiast who wore a real conductor's cap when no one was looking. Writing, even journalism or book reviews, always felt so personal. You know what it feels like? It feels like a friend asks you in public about your psychotherapist. There's no shame and you should be applauded for doing the work that others would rather ignore, but somehow it feels greedy and self-indulgent.

"You're sweet."

Even in New York Gaga and I would never have a phone conversation this long. We might close down a bar and lock ourselves in, but most people don't talk on the phone and it's rude to take up someone's time like this so I felt I should say good-bye. But then I thought of her. Even Guy couldn't call her tonight. He had to work until five most nights. So I decided to just keep her on the phone. "You got any more ideas for this video?"

LA Woman's on the avenue

There's a feeling you get when you look through old pictures and think, warmly, of old friends. You accumulate this feeling at one A.M. once you've forgotten any reason not to feel happy. Because of the obviously complicated nature of life and its basic inescapability, this feeling is a gift. A year earlier things seemed so jumbled, so lost. And then right around the time of Gaga's twenty-first birthday, things just seemed to brighten in that first spring.

Plus, I needed to throw a party if I were going to have anything to eat.

I texted Gaga in LA. "Are you gonna be home for your birthday?" In my mind I made plans for her homecoming. We would have a party at St. J's with the whole gang together. Conrad boozing the piano and Starlight dancing. I'd get back to DJ'ing, where I belonged.

Again, like the other night, she called me back on the telephone, which we never did. "Hey!"

"Hi."

"Did you get my text?"

She had an uncharacteristic cautiousness in her voice. "Yes."

"So will you be in New York for your birthday? I should throw you a birthday party."

She took a deep, honest breath, like the one at the beginning of "Vanity." I thought she might have some bad news. "Actually, I don't think *we'll* be in New York for my birthday."

Wait. "What?"

"Remember what I said about Jimmy Iovine's famous Friday meetings?" She mentioned the Brooklyn-born head of Interscope, who had produced our beloved Springsteen's *Born to Run*. "He keeps everyone late and no one knows why or what they're there for but they have to expect them?"

"At the Interscope office?"

"Yes." She laughed. "Well, they're for real. He just played my new song and made the entire office stay late. I climbed up a chair and danced on the conference table."

"Okay."

"So I don't have a lot of details but when I got your text I thought I should give you a heads-up. Winter Music Conference is coming up in Miami. It's this big thing at the end of every winter where DJs and radio stations and record labels all come together to fight over what they'll be playing for the summer." This is probably not something to be proud of, but I immediately thought of the horn that begins the Skee-Lo song "I Wish." That unbelievably nineties song was the "song of the summer" at the end of seventh grade.

"Of course," I lied. "Winter Music Conference."

"Good, so you know. Again, I don't have any details, but it's been planned for months. We're really late in getting to it and almost everything in Miami is booked solid. But the city will be packed. It's very up in the air but if we can't get booked we might do some 'stunt' performances."

"If you're asking me if I can wire an ice cream truck to be a Lady Gaga Revue truck, the answer is yes."

She laughed, "See? This is why I love you."

"We can hand out twist cones with Oreo crumbs and call it 'Dirty Ice Cream.'"

"Okay, so you're in?"

"A hundred percent."

"Okay. That's all I need to know. Things are happening fast and I don't even really know what it's going to look like yet. But they want to shoot the video."

"Then it's perfect. We can do this Winter Music thing and then we'll go straight to LA and shoot the video."

She paused. I had just invited myself to do quite a lot of things. But in this single phone call I knew that all of her dreams would come true. "Okay. Now the only problem we have—" The phone went silent. I checked it twice to see if I'd dropped the call. God bless American Telegraph and Telephone.

When she finally told me the problem, I could believe it. Guy. "I mean. He's gonna think—"

"Don't worry about him," I said. "I'll take care of that."

"You could try and make it sound fun. Like tell him that I'm going to be busy but that he should come down to Miami and hang out with you and then be in the video with us."

"Of course. He'd be into that. He likes trips and . . . and"—I was trying to figure out a reason that he would want to be in a music video—"and *himself*. The guy's whole life is a music video. He'll love it."

Gaga wasn't convinced. "Yeah . . . but if he doesn't come . . ."

"Oh, and I don't have to stay with you. I can take care of myself once we get to LA. I have friends out there."

You know when you're out to dinner and someone else'll ask the waiter for separate checks? Or you'll be exhausted at a party and someone else tells you they're going home first? Or you show up to class without your assignment and the teacher announces an extension? That's the breath of relief she gave me. "Oh, well," she said to be polite, "that's good to know because I don't know what I'll have to do before the shoot or how long I'll be there. I don't really have all the answers now but it's good to know at least."

"Don't worry. We'll go to Miami and then straight to LA and I'll take care of it. The Beauty Bar in LA can get me a slot. Maybe we could do a show together like old times."

AFTER I HUNG UP THE phone, I almost jumped when I heard a voice behind me: "You're going to Miami?" Leigh had a concerned look on her face. Through my tunnel vision I had forgotten that I had only just stepped out of bed with her when Gaga called.

"Uhm . . . it's up in the air right now. They're working out the details—"

"And then Los Angeles." Her blue eyes clouded over as if she were a kid who learned that Dad couldn't make it to the recital.

"Again, it's up in the air. But she just needed to know that someone could come with her. Luckily, I'm underemployed."

"What about the bar?"

"I'll get someone to fill in. You—" Then I remembered the task I had a head of me. I had to deal with Guy. "You should come with me. Do you want to be in the video? It could be fun. As it stands now we're going to Miami just to play a show. It's basically a free trip. All I have to do is DJ like four songs again." We both had flashbacks of the Valentine's Day show. I tried to put another image in her head. "We can have hotel sex!"

She smiled. But it faded quickly back into reality. "When I agreed to give you one more chance you said things would be different."

"I know, but—"

"And even then everyone said you were hung up on your ex. That you were bad news."

"I'm great news. I have great news. This *is* good news."

"And then you just say yes without talking to me about it."

"Listen, Leigh. You—"

"No *you* listen. I'm going to go to work now and you're going to decide if you really want to be in this or not."

Don't show your face in broad daylight

Here's how I found out it was really, really happening:

On March 14 I got a text from Guy: "Stop texting and emailing my girlfriend. Stop calling her on the phone. And stop following her around the country."

I texted, "Can we just call it a truce? I'm going through some heavy shit with my girl." I found myself borrowing his farm-boy cadence and lingo. When I said Guy had an infectious personality, I meant it in the biomedical sense. I didn't talk like this, ever. But the only defense I had wouldn't make him feel any better. But I already had a tall, beautiful woman in my life. It was impossible to keep one woman, let alone two, and I didn't need to go screwing around with my friend's girlfriend/bandmate.

"That's great. Leave my girl alone."

I didn't know exactly what he was talking about until I got an email asking me to approve the flyer and the flights to Miami and Los Angeles.

We're born only to fade away

That Saint Patrick's Day, Conrad and I got the old band back together for a reunion show. We set up our party at Arrow Bar, which used to be next to Opaline, where the original Rated X party had been. Arrow had a reputation of being a hangout for the DMS crew. Before I ever heard of the downtown scene I knew about the Lower East Side from bands in the DMS crew. In the early days of pre-expert Internet we heard that DMS stood for Droppin' Many Suckas, Doc Marten Skin[head]s, Demonstratin' My Style, and later—when they started to incorporate more Latin kids—Demonstrando Me Stilo. I always had great respect for the DMS crew, the way you automatically revere the seniors when you are a freshman. If you hate anything about them, you hate that you are not them.

I opened up with "Dead at Birth," a hardcore song by my friend's band, Death Threat, and for some reason this hopeless song always made me feel better. I grew up in the music scene, literally and in the greatest sense. Whatever core values I have about scene unity, being open about scene history, and giving respect to those who came ahead of you not only came from the scene, but probably from the liner notes to a song about respect, unity, or music history. The songs in my home music scene sounded detrimental or abusive. But if you can understand the lyrics, you can get a big boost. *"I got nothing but I still got friends / I'm fuckin' broke but I still make ends."* Those two lines could have summed up this entire project.

The bartender looked over as I started the song. "You know these guys?" he asked. I told him who I knew in the crew. "I toured with them years ago," he said. I smiled. In the hardcore scene, you develop a personal mythology about the bands you've seen. None of them get to last very long. The important part was that you saw the bands when you could. Every scenester from home had a wall in their room with flyers lined up. And the purist would only put up flyers to shows they had actually been to. I had all of the great ones in my little bedroom when I was a kid.

But when I looked down I saw The Devil had invited himself to the party. The bar had a rolling DJ booth with two turntables and no CDJs or anything. My record spun around the turntable and The Devil had placed a tiny vial of coke on it. The bottle spun around and around.

I looked up at the room and couldn't believe no one noticed The Devil on Saint Patrick's Day. "No thanks." I handed him the vial back.

THE NEXT DAY I TEXTED St. Michael. "I'm going to Miami for Winter Music Conference."

"Nice! I've never been."

"I need you to tell me something so that I don't get into trouble down there."

"You don't need it."

"I just need something to tell myself if I get into a situation."

"No. You don't need it."

"I think I need something to tell myself or to do if I feel like I'm going to slip up."

"No you don't. You don't need it."

"What?"

"Simple as that. You don't need drugs and you don't need a girl and you don't even need me to tell you this. If you did you'd be in trouble. But you don't need it."

"Really?"

"Let's put it this way. I haven't had a drink in fifteen years. Did I ever need one?"

"No."

"Did I ever want one?"

"Probably."

"Now you see the difference?"

Whosoever shall be found without the soul for getting down

If you had to pick a single rehearsal space in New York City to get excited about, you would pick Smash Studios. You could rent a room for just a few hours to have your first band practice. You could have a music showcase, shoot a video, or record your entire album. Smash Studios had the promise. The possibilities. If you were a young band at Smash Studios, you were already having the best day of your life. Rehearsal spaces and recording studios lined the hallways like some kind of rock 'n' roll high school. At the front gate they sold official drum sticks and T-shirts as if Smash Studios were your all-time-favorite band or theme park. In the back room they had a wall of video games and couches. Whatever happened while you were in Smash Studios, you would remember it as the best day ever. When I got there I found my way to a room that looked like a dance studio all the way in the back. The speakers in the room were blaring "Just Dance," and inside I saw Gaga rehearsing with the same two dancers we had on Valentine's Day.

Choreographer Laurieann Gibson was there. I really liked her outlook. She was upbeat, supportive, enthusiastic, but specific. Her feet tapped out the beat and drove her hips into a swivel every time she heard a sound she liked. Laurieann heard music with every part of her body. When she saw me walk into the room—heated to avoid injuries this close to showtime—I took off my jacket and she appraised my body like a chef always on the lookout for new ingredients. "I'm gonna get you *dancing* in this video." She was convinced I would become a dancer one day and told me I'd make it as long as I could count to eight. She walked me through a few of the steps. We looked in on Gaga doing a run-through in the next room.

Something clicked in my brain—actually, in my body first. I didn't quite know it at the time, but these new people in Gaga's life had opened her up to new things, things that our narrow little music scene didn't allow. That made them off-limits. Which made them hot.

At the next break Gaga came out wearing short shorts, a sports bra, and a loose-fitting gray shirt. She had the smear of old eye makeup on, most of it sweated off during rehearsal. She greeted me with fresh energy. "Oh, I'm so disgusting," she said, like a college athlete coming fresh from practice.

But the Gaga I knew seemed erratic and lost, milling about the room like someone in the kitchen preparing a big dinner. In one room they rehearsed dance steps for the upcoming "Just Dance" video with Laurieann Gibson. They played a low-quality version of "Just Dance" on repeat from a burned CD.

I watched as they ran through the video once. It seemed completely different from anything we'd seen before. But in a good way. The dancers added gravitas to Gaga's leading movements and they followed her with an obedience that anticipated every turn. When she would pop they would bow down and exalt her as a living god. Towards the middle Gaga perfected a perfectly choreographed trustfall with the dancers, where she did a pop and then faded away from center stage by falling backwards into the dancers, who then caught her. I really loved knowing that the four of us would do this together and it made us feel like a band the way we would need each other in the show.

"What did you think?"

"Great!" I said.

"Aaron will get you set up," Gaga said, presenting me with a young bearded guy in a flannel, who set me up in another rehearsal space. Aaron fit the bill of a studio kid, the kind of shiftless, quiet sort that would maybe hang around on the couch while bands recorded even if he didn't work there. He wore faded black jeans and never offered any unprovoked response. Harmless as a bodega cat.

Aaron and I negotiated the proper machine. I would jack directly into a single amp that piped into the house system.

Gaga had a spring wound too tight that day. She came out in smudged sunglasses. I saw her in leotards six nights a week, but today she wore the off-the-shoulder movement clothes of a backup dancer.

That day she switched gears fast, rapidly catching her breath before pounding into her BlackBerry between rounds. She spoke to everyone with clipped frustration, as if they had made her late for something and she had to catch them up on it. Time, which had crept by all year, now sped up for Gaga and she went off to chase it. "Do you remember, Aaron?" she said. "Do you remember when I'd bring label execs in here and they would just have no reaction?" Gaga had a special fondness for the space and for him. She acted as if this were a battlefield where she had suffered an early defeat. She rented it today to restore her honor. "Do you remember what they'd say? 'Uhm, I don't really *get it.*'" She put on the affected voice of an uncool label exec: "'Maybe we could come see you downtown sometime.'"

Gaga was buzzing, her tongue quicker than usual. The tentative sing-songy tone of her voice had disappeared. I didn't like it.

* * *

THE DANCERS HELD THEIR FINAL pose at the end of the next breathless run-through. By then her mother Cynthia had joined me in the booth. Before they could take a sip of water, Gaga ran over to us.

"So?"

We had both forgotten that we were supposed to be the supportive and impressed people in her life. And Gaga noticed. I had a girlfriend to apologize to later. Gaga's professionalism, however, made us both realize that we had no say in the matter and no opinion that really mattered. But she still needed us. "What did you think?"

"Good, honey," her mother said.

"That's *it*?" She spoke in quiet, exasperated tones, saving her voice for the road and *livid* she had to waste any of it on us. She turned to her mother. "Where's my cheering section?" Then she turned to me. "And *where's* my enthusiastic DJ?"

"It's great," I said, weaker than I could muster. Although it really didn't matter. Gaga did not look like herself. She had a robotic demeanor, and her mouth hung open in a new way that I hadn't seen in the quiet, shy girl who came over and introduced herself to me only a year earlier. Her humorless eyes were pools that hovered just below thirty-three degrees Fahrenheit. When she did speak, it came out in a rapid-fire checklist of divergent thoughts that would all coalesce around our upcoming show. Very businesslike. A pair of Doc Martens would need to be purchased. The dancers and the DJ needed to go in the same cabs at the airport and one would be reimbursed. Bags were not going to pack themselves. We had time for one more run-through.

She got up, and her dance moves were so refined, so exact, it was as if you could hear the hydraulic tendons of her muscles pumping away, executing a program. That's when I first noticed her body. In the months that she had dated Guy, I never bothered to look. But Gaga now had the firm texture of a sculptured animal. Her California tan and bronzer provided just the right amount of shading to her newfound marble features.

"Have you been working out?" I said, mostly to change the subject.

She turned, pleased. "Damn right." She held up one of her tiny arms and flexed a bicep. "Three hours a day."

"It shows."

The real Gaga floated to the surface and for a quick second we looked like two friends catching up at the gym. She looked at me as if for the first time and let out a breath. "You look great, by the way. You're going to be great in Miami. The second club we're playing is a big gay party and the gay boys are going to eat you up."

"Laurieann said you have a great body," Sheryl, a dancer, chimed in.

I nodded and looked over at Gaga and then realized that Sheryl was looking at me. Although I don't work out or anything I had trimmed down that winter. Truth is: I couldn't really afford to eat. The jazz club fed me on the weekends, and the rest of the week I ate canned tuna and peanut butter. Sheryl remarked, "Are you a dancer?"

"No," I said, my ribs visible through my last clean wifebeater. "I mean. Not like you guys. I like to dance."

"See? I told you." Laurieann floated back into the room with the enthusiasm of a great teacher and that candy-counter smile.

OVER ON THE OTHER SIDE of the room, the dancers talked technique and kept up with their stretches while Gaga made a phone call. Their movement clothes reminded me of something. They wore calf-length leggings, gym shoes, and the kind of loose, off-the-shoulder clothes torn from other clothes. They looked like dancers to anyone familiar with the background scenes in the straight-to-VHS smash hit *The Making of "Thriller."*

"Just Dance" started up with an unmistakably clear sound, firm vocals, and stark reverb. The girls took their positions as Gaga made her usual acknowledgements.

And then everything fell apart at once. I cut the music

"This is all wrong," Gaga yelled at no one in particular.

Laurieann made some last-minute adjustments to the routine and snapped her fingers in an eight count to show them where to switch. "I need to remind you now," Gaga said, flashing a scowl at me. "You cannot let those tracks out of your sight. I can't have this record leak."

"I already mislabeled the tracks."

"What?"

"Even if someone steals my laptop in Miami they'll never find it." Once upon a time, DJs were so territorial about their set that they would tear the labels off their records, sometimes number them or give them nicknames.

"You did?" Gaga squinted at my screen.

"Yes," I said, a bit short, grumpy from my perpetually empty stomach. "*I'm a real DJ.*"

"Ha! I like that," Laurieann snorted. "'I'm a real DJ.'"

We went through "Just Dance" one more time. The end devolved into a less-than-perfect finale. The dancers were tired, the room had heated up, and they were in danger of overpreparing.

"Where's my count-off? Where's my team? And *where's* my supportive DJ?"

YOU ARE NOW ABOUT TO discover why I have gotten fired from every job I have ever had. Gaga whipped her hair around to make me get on point and I, instead, played Michael Jackson's "Thriller." Gaga stopped dead. Then she got impatient. This is studio time we're wasting. Gaga worked for years to get this far and this wasn't time to fuck around. But I wasn't playing.

The girls had their backs to me, and Laurieann—facing us— clapped along. As if on perfect cue, the dancers both pointed their toes and moved their arms to the right in the zombie pose. Laurieann got into it.

My favorite part about being a DJ is how emotionally invested into their music people get. You can play the latest and hottest any-time, but if you really sit down and try to find ways to bring back old songs, you will end up bringing back old memories. I loved working in Beauty Bar and having some rapturous girl run over to the booth because I'd just played a song she used to love as a kid and never heard again. Beneath that small smile on her face was a giant iceberg of memories, moments, and happiness. The song was just the part of it that surfaced.

Laurieann Gibson was that girl. I walked out from behind the booth, clapping along. She lit up like a kid in front of a birthday cake. With effortless grace she counted off the steps, her head bob-bing. " . . . five, six, seven, eight!" *Switch.* The dancers smiled and glanced briefly behind them to smile at me. Everybody shifted ef-fortlessly into song as if we were in a musical. They drowned in their dance, dragging their zombie feet to the beat. Only instead of fol-lowing Gaga, Laurieann led the group. "This was the first dance I ever choreographed!" She threw her hands around to the beat, telling us a bit of the story. "I wasn't even in school yet and my older sister needed to do a dance routine for gym. I put the whole thing together and I knew then that I wanted to be a choreographer." She looked back at me and smiled at the switch.

"We had to learn the entire thing for a job once!" Sheryl shrieked and clapped along, telling everyone about this job they had once done where they had to do the Bollywood "Thriller" dance for some TV commercial. It was hard to hear. But that broke the rehearsal. It turned from the drudge of practice into joy. We didn't *have to* rehearse, we *got to* dance. Gaga smiled as she looked back at me, shaking her head and clapping helplessly along, putting her new dance steps to the beat.

After that we ran through the Miami live show. It went perfect.

ON THE WAY OUT THE door Gaga pulled me aside and apologized for earlier. "I'm sorry. I just want this to go right."

"I'm going to be there with you at your best and I can put up with your worst."

"It's just they're grumbling about my weight. I've exhausted myself working out and"—she took her sunglasses off—"it's the stress. I get chatty and cranky at the same time."

"Hey," I said. I didn't want to contradict her feelings or the work she'd put in without me in LA or her need to check every possible thing off the list before our big weekend. But I added one thing. "You don't need it."

If this is it, please let me know

On March 27, I looked in my tour bag with a mix of excitement and terror. That's it? A lot was riding on what would happen as I packed my three pairs of underwear, two shirts, and my equipment. It couldn't have been midnight, but I made the executive decision to stay up all night. I checked and rechecked my equipment, careful to bring a backup system in case anything went wrong. Extra cables and a spare pair of needles.

Leigh had packed me a little lunch to take on the plane. In the past few weeks I managed to save a few dollars for my trip. She walked up the spiral stairs from the kitchen. She started to cry at the door. "I just realized how much I am going to miss you."

She gave me a huge hug and she cried with her whole body, faltering from chin to elbow. Her skin felt hot to the touch and her knees wobbled.

"I'm going to be back."

"But you don't even know *when*," she whimpered. St. Michael would say that on the inside Leigh there was a baby crying out because it wanted to be held. We gripped each other like two airline passengers who had survived a water landing. We used our relationship as a flotation device. We didn't have anything else to hold on to.

"I need you to trust me that this is a good thing and that we're doing the right thing. This is what it was all for. The years of waiting tables and taking shit and letting other people treat us like they did. It could be over. If I do it right. This could be a good thing."

"Don't you come back talking all LA like that."

"I won't. C'mon. It's me."

"Are we broken? Is it all over now? You and I."

"Never," I said. And I wished I could have been sure of that. I've seen this happen to bands before. You have a girlfriend and she thinks that you're the most adorable thing to play a bass guitar. Then the band becomes another girlfriend, dealing with the band becomes a chore, and it only gets worse. Leigh knew that Miami meant fans in bikinis, and Hollywood meant those cartoonish and embellished devotees you see on TV.

"Will you call me when you land? And call me when you get to your hotel so I know you're safe?"

"Yes, honey."

"And will you call me to tell me how it's going?"

"Yes."

"And will you tell me you love me?"

"Yes. Any time you want. I love you. I knew I loved you before we started dating. I love you just the way you are."

"And you promise you'll come home? You won't run off with a backup dancer and leave me here in New York all winter?"

"It'll be spring when I get back. Can you believe it?"

"Can we go on bike rides and get dinner together?"

"Yes. If this works out we can do it even more. We could even do something crazy like go out for dinner on a weekend."

"Or get brunch and not just because we have to be at work in an hour?"

"Or maybe we'll do something else after this. Maybe it won't work out and I'll go work for a newspaper again."

This straightened her countenance. "No." She walked over and straightened the lapel on my jacket. "You'll be great. You are great. You're going to do great. I'm just going to miss you. But I know you really want this to work out."

"I'm barely doing anything while I'm there."

"But you can finish *Mercutio*."

"And I will."

I went downstairs into the living room one last time to double check my bags. If I forgot even the smallest piece of equipment, I wasn't sure I had enough money to replace it. I felt like I was moving out or getting sent away from school. And I still didn't even know when I would ever get home.

"Hey, Brendan," Leigh called out from upstairs.

I walked up, following her voice. "Yeah?"

She stood in the middle of the room. I looked around to see if anything was the matter. Her lower lip quivered. "Nothing," she said. "It's just that tomorrow when I call out your name I won't be able to see you."

Get me to the airport; put me on a plane

For my good-bye tour of New York City, I took the subway to Union Square for the millionth time. On the Manhattan Bridge my phone buzzed with sweet messages from Leigh before the train went back into the tunnel in Chinatown in a smooth, labored arch like a magician's deck of cards flying from one hand to the other. At Union Square I came out on the western edge over a neon sign—COFFEE SHOP—and made the surprisingly long walk to Beauty Bar.

The city seemed empty that night as I walked past the furniture stores and closed sandwich shops. I was the only man for 238 blocks in every direction, as alone as I had ever been. In these situations you hope for the best, dream for the greatest, and then sorta expect things to work out but with a bit more disappointment and headaches.

The dancers lived in one of those Manhattan minimum-security prisons for models. I had heard of the fabled model dorms over the years. The buildings had multiple uses, but a large number of them were rented out by indentured models who were fronted the rent money by an agency that would nickel-and-dime them through fashion week. Usually a live-in madam would weigh them each day and serve warnings to girls who couldn't drop weight in time for runway season. Leigh was one of them once.

The entrance had gates like a college campus, where you could swipe your card in for security. Only, just like in luxury buildings, you could get in by telling the overtired doorman the name of any human being on the planet. Then when they say "Huh?" you just make up the number of any plausible apartment—keeping in mind, for example, that a seven-story building will never have an apartment that begins with the number eight.

Upstairs I found Katie and Sheryl lying on the same mattress. They had set alarms but were in no way up, and just barely awake. They both had with them a sort of school bag complete with airplane supplies—laptops, magazines, headphones, and sunglasses. And they both had one of those rolly suitcases that looked like it had been fabricated out of the trunk and wheelbase of a Toyota. They also had a couple of backup costumes for the shoot. I now had the great position of baggage handler on the tour.

Katie had done some featured dancing in the montage-heavy dance movie *Step Up 2: The Streets*. Sheryl taught at the dance studio. I did not actually know if they were roommates or not, but they did have that familiar comfort of two girls in a high-pressure academic environment.

They had wildly divergent personalities. Sheryl was the female Asian version of a tough-talking, Marlboro-smoking wartime sergeant. Katie almost perfectly resembled the neophyte main character in dance movies—somewhat shy at first and then she comes alive in the final sequence. The time between then and when she would in fact come alive depended on a montage that had yet to begin.

"Are we really going to do this?" Katie said from the bed, the hood of her sweatshirt shielding her eyes like overgrown bangs.

"It'll be fun!" I said with my usual Disney-like enthusiasm. "Ugh," Sheryl said. "I just want this day to be over."

BEGIN MONTAGE: Young group of impossibly hip kids in various layers of clothing step out of a typical building in lower Manhattan. They wear sunglasses at four-thirty a.m. and scowl at the inherent self-righteousness of a passing jogger. Manhattan yawns in the morning light, and the rising sun reflects off the yellow cabs as they speed down a deathly silent Park Avenue. The midtown tunnel on Thirty-Fourth Street, damp with morning dew, swallows them up only to spit them out on the other side of airport security, wrestling laptops back into their bags in bare feet while the security staff scans and rescans their studded belts. The team collapses on the floor in front of their gate, ignoring the desire for coffee from the off-hours Starbucks. The male member suddenly remembers a bag of costumes left at security and runs through the crowded airport only to return triumphant moments later with all of the matching hats and sequined accessories. On the flight there is no remaining luggage space. The man sews the holes in his leather jacket with dental floss. Seconds later they are woken by the ding! that follows the captain turning off the fasten-seat-belt sign. The man casually brushes off a slight amount of backup-dancer drool from one shoulder as he helps the other get her bag. After what seems like an eternity (they all have to pee) they walk down the Jetway, which opens directly into another cab. There is no time to go to their hotel. The group, still wearing their in-flight PJs, enters an elevator at Winter Music Conference *in medias res* for sound check of their first rooftop show. There are tech problems. Cut to a single, smug still-shot of the DJ presenting the sound engineer with the missing cable, fresh from his luggage. Everyone around the room has a lot riding on sound check. There is muttering from the hastily introduced record-label execs. People who once only existed as email addresses now have to interact with each other in real life. The DJ steps behind the lifeless booth, flicks just the right switch, turns on a wireless microphone, and for

the first time Miami Beach hears the infectious synthesizer opening to "Just
Dance." Instead of waiting, the girls take their places. Gaga taps the mic,
and slowly the audience draws around her. Label execs clasp their hands
in prayer, thanking the young man who can't be heard over the music, but
whose mouth flaps, "No problem," and then, "I'm a real DJ." The party has
not really begun, the public isn't allowed in, Winter Music Conference hasn't
begun. But you wouldn't know it from the flashbulbs and the dancers who
hit every cue perfect, nor from the DJ who flips all the right switches in choreographed perfection, nor from the singer who should save her vocals for
later but just can't help belting out that single that made every single thing
in this montage possible. They walk off stage with their luggage through
the doorway to the rooftop, which opens up ten blocks away at their lush
beachfront hotel rooms.

MIAMI

Rockman lovers driving Lamborghinis

Rental cars lined the palm-treed streets with the bright stucco buildings beaming back at the hopeful faces on Collins Avenue and A1A. Winter Music Conference was the largest of its kind, and it not only included music and new musical acts but every breathing product associated with music. New artists schmoozed DJs and radio programmers, and satellite radio stations schmoozed the new networks, often by scoring an interview with a new artist. And just as music magazines were supported by ads from Red Bull and Levi's, Winter Music Conference depended on the strangest of trade shows. On the roof of the Raleigh Hotel, at the Armani Exchange party alone you could talk with the reps from Skullcandy headphones, Stanton electronics, and a whole slew of off-brand energy drinks and phone apps. Inside the glass penthouse the Armani Exchange people seemed like an afterthought—their new line of sunglasses was the star.

The majority of the Armani Exchange party went on indoors with a breed of DJs that I just don't get. They were a small herd who had their sets all worked out, and they only played the clean version of songs for Internet radio. In many ways they were more underground than our music scene because, well, people actually came to see us spin. Some of them had big names that I recognized. I felt some of that competition you hear about, like how the navy thinks that the air force is a bunch of jackasses. Then I remembered that I'd only slept two hours and I let it go.

Thankfully there was one company representative on the roof with a new product to help me. Café Bustelo, the dirt-cheap bodega brand of coffee, was trying to launch a canned coffee energy drink to compete with the Starbucks Doubleshot. I must have had about eight. They gave out T-shirts and tote bags that read "I ♥ Café Bustelo" and that were inspired by the bright yellow sacks of ground coffee you can find at the bodega.

I am also quite grateful that Stanton electronics had a booth at this thing. Stanton makes, among other things, phonograph needles and DJ headphones. Normally I would be opposed to product placement and posing for free endorsements . . . but this professional DJ somehow managed to leave his needles and headphones at home. Their representative became my new best friend.

Throughout Winter Music Conference there was the spirit of a swap meet. No one knew who would come to this thing, but in staffing alone they had plenty of people. Vendors traded sunglasses for headphones, and needles for a case of some unheard-of energy drink. Besides the fact that everyone here was constantly reapplying sunscreen on their pasty necks, it seemed like any other conference in any other part of the country, where people from the same industry overlapped and worked with people in another industry. Everyone was halfway familiar with each other. Until that curtain went up, we were, after all, just a bunch of young employees on a business trip. Many had clients to entertain later that night and we would still need to get up for breakfast in the hotel and check in for various conference meetings. Once upon a time this conference might have featured dozens of CD singles and hungry DJs trying to snap up the two constantly sought-after copies on vinyl of next summer's hottest hit. But that was another time. Not that any would be sold at Winter Music, but in past years you might see record collectors and rare vendors selling to the hungry crowd. Now, not so much.

But what about everything else that cool music sells? They still have to design new kinds of cars into those eye-catching, hip, young boom boxes on wheels. People from the Muzak service gave panel discussions on marketing your music. Even without the once-booming CD there were still huge open-bar parties sponsored by Stoli vodka to toast the winners of the International Dance Music Awards. The entire event was tinged with the excitement of meeting important people face-to-face and learning about your industry. But more than anything it seemed like a chance to meet the top brass, to regroup at a music retreat, and to hear from the great voices of a crumbling empire—every panel should have been called, "So, What Do We Do Now?" And it all came glowing in that first month of beautiful Miami sunshine, where the clouds came around smiling and the amount of free shit in your bag made it all worth it. Conferences—as lame as they can be—do have that flavor of youth that comes from the fidgety lessons of how to succeed at things you haven't failed at yet.

Like in all schools, of course, there were little cliques, but the nature of WMC sort of forced us into little groups at mealtimes, just like students in the school from *Harry Potter*. On the one hand you had the Label Whores: a group of hired faces who went around promoting records and getting phone numbers and asking about cool parties. The Label Whores made a sluttish moan when they heard you were a DJ and they always found time to invite you to have a beer with them later. Always the same phrasing. Then you had the Gearheads, who rushed around in band T-shirts with things clipped to their belts in case something needed an emergency gaffer taping. The Gearheads were a nice bunch, mostly because their job for the weekend was to wind cords and make sure that no microphone in their quiver ever gave feedback. They were as evangelical about their particular religion of music-processing equipment as anyone in a youth group might be about their church or sect. Right behind them, and sometimes dependent on them, were the Mean Girls, a group who flew in from uptown neighborhoods all over the world to present this plebeian universe of fashion disasters with this summer's coolest accessories—not that you dweebs could appreciate it. The guys associated with this group were also Mean Girls because they were even bitchier. Like the Mean Girls in school, they are also the ones who have to say no the most. No you can't come to our fashion launch in the penthouse without a press pass. No you can't have a free pair of the expensive sunglasses that we all wear. No we don't want to come outside of the penthouse and watch your band on the hot roof. We're wearing eight pounds of fucking foundation—not that you've heard of it.

The Mean Girls had an offshoot of guys and girls from the record labels who made you think they ran the show. They became known as Pro Tools. Even though they were crashing the Armani Exchange party, they ran around, commanding things they could never really understand. "Can you turn up the bass in the *whoosywhatsit* . . . ?" they would say, trailing off like the hotshot in Spanish class who couldn't conjugate a simple verb. The Pro Tools liked to move around the room adjusting and fine-tuning things because the existence or disappearance of a recording career may possibly be due to which way a free promotional CD got placed on a stray lounge table. Pro Tools liked to shake hands; they liked to meet *and* greet. They sidled up to the bar with impossible dietary restrictions on their alcohol-free drinks: "Diet Coke, not too much ice, and a *splash* of Coke with a lemon twist. Thank you, Charlie. It was Charlie, right, Charlie? That's for you, Charlie." Much of their work took place behind the scenes and they enjoyed watching it, although they stood hawkish on the empty roof, waiting for things they had arranged weeks ago to begin. Pro Tools had set this up extremely last minute on the rooftop stage of a packed event. We weren't on the official WMC schedule. They didn't actually do anything or get involved in any way. Observing what they had prearranged was good enough. They stood off to the side with the smug satisfaction of a father who had just orchestrated his only daughter's shotgun wedding.

Then there's that group on the fringe. Every high school has one. They sit at the edge of the parking lot, smoking cigarettes and looking jaded and disaffected as if while the rest of the class came home from practice and hit the showers, they had to work late. Their eyes cast low and unmoved by the circus around them. They didn't have to be there but somebody made them come. Other outsiders found themselves attracted to the abuse of this crew, sauntering up to them in tight jeans in the Miami heat, pulling a crushed pack of cigarettes from their leather jackets and trying to bum a light as if there were no other way to start a conversation with the other outcasts. The Mean Girls' baggage handler and the Pro Tools' driver and the Gearheads' assistant sound tech. They seemed to have flown all the way to South Beach to sit around in sunglasses, smoking and looking as if they might fall asleep in the back of their next class. They were us.

One person stood out from the middle of this crowd, honored by vendors and sought after by others from the in crowd, the AV club, the student press. You can imagine how great it was to discover that the most popular girl in school that Winter Music Conference 2008 was Gaga. She walked around this little study hall before classes began and said her hellos to everyone. Us bad kids thought of her as one of our own—even making her a special leather jacket to match the backup dancers, which only increased her stature, if only because it was ill-fitting and therefore impermanent. The Mean Girls wanted to give her sunglasses, and the Gearheads evangelized her at sound check. She was the new girl with a fresh start who hadn't declared herself a member of any group. Yet. Gaga, the girl who wasn't even invited to the party, quickly became the guest of honor as she smiled politely at her own army of Pro Tools. Gaga had wanted a recording career at sixteen, and dozens of people had told her no by then. And a good Italian girl never forgets her enemies. "You work with so and so over at that other label? Did you know such and such from this other label when they worked there?" Many of them grew red in the face when she could point them out by name. *She knows I exist!* As usual Gaga had her own interwoven Rolodex memorized—the new girl in school already knew who had gone out with whom.

It would take all of us—the Gearheads, the Pro Tools, Mean Girls, Label Whores, and us bad kids—to pull this off today.

The dancers stood in the shade, smoking and watching Gaga lap up the attention. We discussed what they might expect of us for the rest of the afternoon. Did they have a dressing room where we could leave our stuff? Should we try and get to our hotels? So far I had stayed out of the cliquish details. I had to meet with the Pro Tools and borrow from the Gearheads and handle things with the Mean Girls (although I didn't get a goddamn pair of sunglasses). I actually did want to borrow someone's WMC badge and go to the one thirty P.M. "Intellectual Property: Songwriting & Publishing" forum. Because I'm lame. Instead I mustered my best, most disaffected voice and turned to the bad kids: "You guys wanna get out of here?"

WE WALKED TO THE DAMN hotel because we're New Yorkers. Also: It's less than ten blocks. The avenue was lined with a fresh mix of palm trees, sunshine, outdoor cafés, and creatures walking around in bikinis. Male and female. The recession hit Miami like global warming hit the North Pole. Nothing seemed to change, but you felt that a new hotel or a just recently built venue might come crashing down like a great sheet of ice. You looked around instead at Miami's own Polar Bears—those chubby, white-haired, bald old guys who zoom around in bright white Lamborghini convertibles. Polar bears on an ice flow. They would be out in any season, hunting fresh young models flown down on bikini-catalogue contracts. The entire ecosystem of South Beach stayed intact. As long as the models could migrate down here following a school of dollar bills, the Polar Bears were happy. When the Polar Bears faced extinction, so did Miami.

The dancers went to nap and I had the perfect montage of my own.

DJ enters the wicked-nice hotel room, drops his one bag on the chair, and jumps from the sofa to the other chair and into the adjoining suite. He jumps on the bed for every job he's ever been fired from. He leaps in the air, dancing and singing a song that doesn't yet have a music video. He bounces around as if gaining inspiration for the exuberance he will help capture on stage and on film in just two days. He checks the clock. He has twenty-five minutes to get to the beach and back in time for the show. Should he just wait? Ha! His pasty frame heads to the door in a baby-blue bathing suit with a singing-elephant pattern. (Shut up! They were a gift!) Door opens directly onto the beach across the way and he is instantly surrounded by girls and boom boxes; topless women in designer sunglasses groove around him in another universe. There will be no tan lines in our new universe. The hard work begins in twenty-three minutes. But these twenty-three minutes are what all the rock-star posturing stands behind. These are the goodies. He leaps into the ocean with a baptismal vigor that washes away all that New York jadedness. He discovers muscles he hasn't used in years, and the great waves of South Beach toss him around with the effortless magic of a chiropractor, realigning his spine as if he never slept on a plane or carried a crate of records. He comes out refreshed, he comes out exuberant, he would jump on the bed in any hotel room for miles if only to share the joy he feels right now. He is ecstatic. He is happy, unassailably happy. He has also managed to lose his hotel key.

Gaga makes sweet praying-mantis love to a salad at an outdoor table on A1A with Troy Carter, Leah Landon, and various other people from the management company. Everywhere there are small huddles of work friends going over strategies and talking about the incompetence of other people in their department. Pro Tools scoff at the Mean Girls and the Gearheads squint in the sunshine to check their email.

DJs begin playing the official WMC sessions at ten in the morning and the record labels are eager to get songs placed with them now. Each WMC location had a series of DJs flown in to work in rotation. Most of them don't get paid. Additionally, all of the hotels and restaurants and clubs have their own roster. Record labels and other exhibitors have their official WMC space and then they hold an after-party elsewhere in the city. In that sense it's a bit like the running of the bulls in Pamplona. Millions of people come to town to watch the dangerous procession of talent. The local restaurants and hotels up their prices and have a set menu for the week. People come to see the bloodshed, as great talent falters in the ring.

Gaga makes a minor point about the difference in presentation between the two shows. On the roof of the Raleigh we have sort of a live demonstration of the record. It will be bright and the audience will not be as captive as we would like. If anything they will just stand around and clap when they have to. But again, more important DJs and radio programmers will be there so it's better than just running into them at the party and surrendering a copy of the single. They need to be approachable, ground level. She doesn't want to make a direct comparison to eight months ago at Lollapalooza. But you can't help it. The main event—and we should work hard for both, of course—will be at Score Miami tonight for the Nervous Nitelife party. There the audience will be more mature gays who've had a few drinks. Before we go on there will already be that pulsating, energizing house music blaring. The Score Miami show will be much better for pictures.

Troy looked perplexed.

He nodded his head, a little bit lost, and didn't seem to have heard the end of what Gaga said. She had ended on an upbeat note, saying that they were doing two very different shows today. That's a good thing. It's twice the exposure without creating overexposure. At the first they will get the record out to the right hands, and then later in the night they will get it to the right ears.

But Troy seemed fixated, either lost or somewhere else entirely. "Gaga?" he said.

"Yeah?"

"Is that skinny white boy over there your DJ?"

She turned around and saw where she had lost Troy. There I am, looking like I'd been working in nightlife for three years and had never seen the sun. I've not only lost the hotel's keys, but I've forgotten its name. In order to find the hotel I decided to retrace my steps, which meant walking directly through the patio tables of all the restaurants on A1A in a pair of swim trunks, squinting at the names on the hotels behind the restaurants.

Gaga called out my name. I had never been relieved and embarrassed at the same time before. She giggled at my short swim trunks. "What are you doing?"

"I had twenty minutes for a swim and I . . . uhm—"

"Took a swim?" Gaga supplied. My dripping hair nodded in agreement. Gaga told me what they were talking about up until my ghostly apparition had haunted Troy.

"Exactly. That's what we've always been talking about. Trying to get past the scenester's lament of, 'Uch, I'll see them at the next show.'" I didn't really want to spend any more time standing there in my swimsuit. But I still didn't know where to go. "Well, I guess I must be heading back." I took a step forward.

"To your hotel?" Gaga pointed to it with her fork. Behind me.

"Right," I said. "I didn't know you could get through that way."

Check out the hook while my DJ revolves it

Back in my room I suited up like a superhero. Tailored black jeans so tight I couldn't put my phone in the pocket. I turned the belt around sideways and clipped my phone to the front like a belt buckle and clicked on the screen, which read, "DJVH1." I wore a wifebeater and a black bandana with my leather jacket. Back home I probably would never dress like this all at once, but I felt like I had to represent the sort of people that I'd normally roll my eyes at. I had to embody downtown New York even while I was out of focus.

I walked to Gaga's hotel on Eighth and Collins and when I opened the door she saw me in full regalia for the first time. Her mild mannered friend Brendan in the glasses had stayed back home, probably sitting at St. J's with a library book tucked into his belt. Gaga answered the door in a bathrobe, and she stepped back when she saw me and looked wide-eyed through her half-done makeup. "You look fantastic. Where did you get those jeans?"

"You like them?"

"I love them. The gay boys are going to eat you up."

The backup dancers came in the door behind me in matching

captain's hats, leotards, and leather jackets. When we processed in all together like this we really looked like a band. We belonged together. We really were that group of disaffected outsiders who sneered at the Mean Girls and cut class.

Gaga went back to the chair where a makeup artist fine-tuned her face. I sat on the bed and borrowed Gaga's laptop to email Leigh. The dancers collapsed on the floor. Directly on the hotel carpet. It was the first time anyone noticed them. But these poor girls had to get up at four A.M., fly to Miami, and do two shows, which would last until almost four A.M.

The makeup artist stopped working on Gaga's lower eyelashes. She glanced at Gaga's otherwise heavenward gaze as if to make sure this was okay.

I looked down at both of them on the carpet. "Girls, I have one question." And then in my best Gaga voice I sang the line from the song. *"What's. Go-in' on on the floor?"*

"Exhausted," Sheryl muttered.

"We haven't slept," Katie said with a finality of decree.

I opened up Gaga's laptop and the first screen I saw was the music-editing software GarageBand. On it she had open all the tracks for the show, all lined up side by side. It looked as if she had started to make one long show file of all of them premixed or spaced out in between. I wondered for a second what she wanted with all of that. The mix was bad, I could see that much. Wasn't this my job?

The old joke goes like this: "My father worked for the same company for thirty years and they replaced him with a little machine with just one button. The worst part is the next day my mother went out and bought one." I already felt like I maybe didn't matter so much out here. But now I felt it for sure. The game changed. I already knew that. We used to have to put on a show. Now we had to—we needed to—put on a display.

* * *

TROY CARTER DROVE US IN a rental through the dense traffic to the show. Troy stood about five foot five and had the kind of smile of someone who had just shared a laugh with a good friend. "My daughter said to me today, 'Daddy, can I get Lady Gaga on Limewire?' And I said, 'You better not!'" Troy survived the nineties working for Bad Boy Entertainment. He held on as a surviving war general who looked back on a given year and thought, We lost a lot of brave soldiers out there.

After a few blocks he stopped in front of a yacht showroom. It reminded me of the real estate offices we had all over Brooklyn. Condos for sale that hadn't yet been built. Tiny, theoretical buildings where everything you hated about living in New York City had been considered and designed out. Here it looked like classroom models of the Titanic. Roughly the same size, but obviously counting on the tiny shipmates and crew. That boat was whiter than I am. If that boat could, it would wear K-Swiss shoes to the tennis matches. "You see that model boat in the window? That's not even built yet. You have to order it custom. We're gonna come back here next year and that boat's gonna be called *The Fame!*"

We all looked around and laughed at/with Troy. The rest of us hadn't paid bills this month. We would have rather had just a steady gig. A steady gig is like the fifties musicals with a steady girlfriend. Something we could count on. Let our bad days be bad days together.

"Are we almost there?" Gaga asked. Troy nodded. Gaga turned and asked me to hand her the cassette Walkman and headphones from her bag in the trunk/the eighties.

Troy, who was even a bit older than I was, looked down at the cassette player in mock disdain. "What is that thing?"

"I have to do my vocal warm-ups." Gaga went through an operatic vocal warm-up in perfect Latin. She started at a perfect middle C and worked her way down and up the octaves until her voice opened up.

To catch anyone singing along to their headphones is usually funny. Even Troy couldn't control his laughter. I didn't laugh. A pop singer who takes the time to warm up her vocals like an opera singer will always have a leg up over the rest of the bands who sit around drinking and smoking their vocal range away.

THE PENTHOUSE OF THE RALEIGH had transformed into the World's Fair for musicians. They broadcast live from one corner, doing the play-by-play on visiting DJs as if they were figure skaters coming up to do their routine. Stanton demoed new kinds of turntableless equipment that could fit in your record bag and work as a mixer, MIDI controller, and scratch surface. I couldn't believe it. It felt like that story of Helen Keller going to the Chicago World's Fair in 1893 to meet the creator of the Braille typewriter—only a lamer version of that. The story of the DJ Who Can't Lift That Many Records or Even a Single Turntable Meets This Fucking Guy.

Many famous DJs had come up there to play and I started to feel the competition. Remember the seven pilots chosen for Project Mercury—which became the space program—who were supposed to be the best of the best? They were among pilots who had been trained by those who had broken the sound barrier, the first to double it. And then they joined the National Aeronautic Advisory Board—later, NASA—where they would never get to fly anything. They would just sit in an automatic capsule and ride into the stratosphere and parachute down. Meanwhile, in their training they fell years behind the other pilots. I felt a bit like that here. If I were touring with a major label act, surely I had to be among the best.

But I would never get a chance to prove it. Not that I had anything to prove. Right?

DJ's in our scene at home are territorial about their nights, venues, mixes, dancers, signature style, song choice, and outfits. If I moved up one more step with Gaga I would be out of their league. I wondered then if I would ever play in the Lower East Side again. And if I did, would I be that guy who doesn't stop going to high school football games?

AT SHOWTIME I STARTED WITH the Wendy Carlos theme from *A Clockwork Orange* and added a beat to it. Gaga opened right into the vocal intro to "Beautiful, Dirty, Rich." Her vocals sounded no different than if they had heavy reverb. For so long we had thought of "Beautiful" as the main song, the downtown anthem about party kids taking money from their parents. She made the "shame shame" finger motion with one hand on her nose during *"we just like to party like to p-p-party party!"* like you would if you wanted to motion to a friend for cocaine. Rather than looking like a bunch of performers pretending to be downtown kids we looked like we were performing an original creation inspired by the scene. The Miami sunshine only intensified our dirty jackets and choppy haircuts, like stage lights on the cast of some bohemian drama.

Towards the end of our first song something unbelievably terrible happened. I had prepared for every conceivable outdoor problem, testing the turntables and making sure that the roof was solid enough that the dancers wouldn't shake the table if they jumped. I was ready for rain or worse. But I hadn't planned on one thing. Right in the middle of a song a great big gust of wind came through the roof. It made Gaga look like a star as she sang into the microphone, the wind in her hair and flapping around in her blouse.

But it also blew the record clear off the table in the middle of a song. I watched as the needle skated across the surface. We all know that awful sound. It skipped off like a knife dancing to the edge of an outdoor café table on A1A when a gust of wind caught under the tablecloth. The needle went clanging jauntily off the table, chipping, catching, and dulling on the outer ribs of the platter as the record took flight. I wanted to cry. However, no one noticed. This was mostly because the record had nothing to do with the audio heard on the roof. Because the sound tech had ignored our technical rider, I had to switch to an automatic system and leave the records on the turntables just to have something to look at. I was embarrassed at first but definitely not anymore. We pulled off a live music video, complete with transitions. I bent over to get the record off the floor and no one seemed to notice. If anything, they saw another record spinning on my other turntable and figured I had gotten lucky. And I had.

The crowd grew noticeably excited when "Just Dance" began. People came to WMC not just to see their favorite band two weeks before they came to New York or LA. They came to see what's next. Some people pulled out camera phones. Many previously bored photographers suddenly crouched down and machine-gunned the place with shots, as if hoping to later recreate the moment in stop-motion.

But then we had another problem. I started sweating when I realized something: Not only had I pulled off the transition in a black leather jacket in the Miami sunshine, but in a minute, we were going to have cameras rolling on a song that had an entire verse with a male singer. We didn't have a male singer. We just had me. I suddenly realized that I would have to sing that verse, since I couldn't justify skipping over it and I hadn't preplanned how to fade it out. Gaga needed that verse to catch her breath before the big dance. If they had paid attention to our technical rider I could have made the easy transition from verse three to five. But if they had paid attention to our technical rider, the whole show would have sucked: That gust of wind would have blown the record off the table at a pace that would have made even Gaga's real vocals sound fake.

This is what I meant about astronauts versus pilots. If I had realized this in a normal setting, I would have been able to pilot my way out of it. Instead I would just have to grab a hold of the stick and hope for the best. Just a few days before, that verse included guest vocals from Akon, a handsome black dude from Senegal. Now it included something closer to my range, Colby O'Donis. I only had the Akon version. I dropped my leather jacket on the roof and stood there in my wifebeater and bandana. The Miami sunshine evaporated all of the sweat from my back.

The dancers and Gaga had planned an interlude around the Colby/Akon verse. As they started to strut around the stage I stepped up to the microphone and sang over the autotune of the track.

Some of the cameras snapped photos but most stayed with Gaga as my verse wound down. Gaga looked over the shade of her sunglasses at me and smiled when she realized I was pulling it off. I came out on the other side of it alive, bolstered by a few cheers from the crowd on stage. The dancers wound themselves up for the interlude by pulling out the big disco ball for Gaga to ride around on during the breakdown.

At the end of the show, a small circus put Gaga in the center ring. The dancers went off to the side to catch their breath and I had to take down the set. I noticed they looked a little winded so I grabbed two water bottles from one of the vendors and walked them over to the shade. "You guys okay?"

"Just tired."

"Go take a nap. I'll handle sound check."

Sheryl asked, "Are we going to get to sleep tonight? Our flight to LA is at like five in the morning for some reason."

"Probably not."

They looked sad, and I couldn't stay long. Because I had a birthday cake to wrangle on the way to sound check.

This time around for me baby, actions speak louder than words

I can describe our next venue in three words:

OONTZ OONTZ OONTZ.

Score had a near-constant scene of slightly older gay dudes hanging out in what looked like a beach bar at an outdoor mall. The inside had cathedral ceilings with pulsating strobes that bounced off disco balls. The Pro Tools went in the back way with me and hid Gaga's birthday cake in the kitchen so we could surprise her with it at midnight.

I actually started to see myself as more of one of the Pro Tools. If there were a job for traveling around the country and making sure shows went well, I'd be all over it. The DJ booth had two CDJs on a balcony above the main dance floor, facing the stage below. They ignored our technical rider again. It was, thankfully, indoors and far from wind. I started to wonder if we should start putting CD turntables on our rider. They suck and I had way too much music on vinyl. But I wondered. I told myself to work on a permanent solution for next time.

I didn't know that this would be my last show as Lady Gaga's DJ.

* * *

"CAN YOU IMAGINE HOW WONDERFUL these are going to look for middle-aged gay men?" Gaga held up our first real piece of merch: a little disco ball on a keychain with a tag that read, LADY GAGA JUST DANCE.

I loved merch. T-shirts, buttons, patches, printed bandanas, numbered posters. Merch is a scenester's lifeblood. It helped opening bands pay for gas and separated the tried and tested scenester from a person who downloaded the greatest hits. Somehow I envisioned our first piece of merch to be those little buttons that we called Scenester Merit Badges, which you can only get at the show when you see the band yourself live and in person. But I could dream. I stuck a keychain in my record bag. This was all part of the new plan. Come out on top.

Leah gave us each an envelope with our show pay at sound check and added a fifty-dollar per diem. With that fifty we were supposed to get meals and anything else we needed. I was in heaven. For this whole year I'd lived off of the food at work and canned tuna. I walked down the Lincoln Road Mall in the temperate early spring. South Beach didn't have the grit and sirens that the rest of Miami did. Even the stores had the clean, user-friendly sterility of a hotel minibar.

I peeked in the window of Café at Books & Books. Nothing presented the possibility of life like a bookstore. You could find records anywhere or read about an author, but where else could you stop, drop, and roll around in an author you'd never heard of? The bookstore looked like a dream, all the titles you wished you'd read all laid in pristine stacks on the tables. Why cock your neck at funny angles and read sideways? I had never been to Miami before. Passing this bookstore, for no reason, made me want to stay. It made me want to *browse* and *sit down* and *take in the sights*. I had to go, but I wanted to stay. Someday I'll go back to Miami, I promised, and I'll eat at this café and go into the bookstore. I will browse and sit down and take in the sights. I'd always made these promises to myself. *Someday I won't have to wait until tomorrow.*

As the sun went down, Miami started to hear the call of the wild. Some of the boutiques locked up for the night, leaving the lights on in the big picture windows, making them look like little dollhouses with lifeless, perfect furniture and alphabetized books. The cafés bustled with the tense excitement of people on vacation. Several of them had saran-wrapped plates of demo food and artificial approximations of mojitos with plastic ice cubes in a one-to-one scale replica of glass roughly the size of upturned parasols. I walked down Ocean Drive to get back to the hotel and stopped off at a Johnny Rockets. I'd never eaten in one before and I had in fact not eaten once on this trip.

I emerged one burger, chocolate shake, and fries later. The weight felt good on me and I promised myself I would eat again.

Let's have some fun, this beat is sick

Somehow in the magic of WMC every single thing we had done at sound check came undone before we went on. Aptly named Nervous Nitetlife had packed the club. Someone on the roster of DJs had unhooked my equipment and worked off of two CD players. I never learn. This was what you get for leaving a nightclub and eating dinner once. Some enterprising little joker also went to the soundboard and turned everything off except for the DJ booth, meaning the vocals we had perfected that afternoon were gone. It didn't occur to me that the DJ who probably worked there every Friday night came into work and robotically checked the booth and put it back the way it needed to be.

Something else I didn't realize that afternoon: The club had an elevated booth opposite the stage. Everyone would have their backs to me. That part I didn't mind. But it would make no sense once I went to sing the male vocal of "Just Dance."

My phone rang. "We're changing the set list," Leah said. She went into a long explanation that would have probably made a lot of sense if I weren't standing in the balcony of a thundering gay club.

OONTZ OONTZ OONTZ.

She continued to explain her carefully discovered opinion.

And over din I yelled, "*What?!*"

Gaga grabbed the phone from Leah as I made my way down the ladder to go outside. "Here's the deal. We're going to cut the intro down. So instead of having the audience stare at us wondering, 'What movie is that song from?' we will just have it on at the beginning."

"Okay. Thirty seconds or so."

"Yes. And this time let's leave more space between the songs, none of that overlap."

"Okay. We got this."

"And we're not going to do 'Just Dance.'"

"Really?"

"Yeah. 'Beautiful, Dirty, Rich,' 'Paparazzi,' and 'Disco Stick.'" The song that was to become "Lovegame" was still then known only as "Disco Stick." "We can play 'Just Dance' at the end like on Valentine's Day."

"Good. I think people should hear it, but it is weird having a verse with that guy on it without him on stage."

"Exactly."

"Gaga?"

"Yeah?"

"You're gonna be great."

THAT NIGHT GAGA CAME OUT onstage with a new persona. She acted utterly sexual with a drawling speech like her Marilyn Monroe at Beauty Bar. She took all those years of being an outcast and rolled them into the ultimate out-of-place: a young, hyper-sexualized woman from New York in a Miami gay club. They ate her up.

She grabbed shirtless boys out of the crowd and danced with them, sometimes on top of them, as they lay on the stage floor. An amazing performance for a girl who wouldn't even look at another man in front of her boyfriend. At the finale she froze in position mid-dance, and the crowd screamed the self-tanner out of their pores. I cued up "Just Dance" and loved how the lead-in of the synth created the perfect anticipation before the beat.

Go Shorty.
It's your birthday.

Troy did not. "Yo! You're going to lose this crowd." He waved angrily at the DJ booth from out on the dance floor. He looked ridiculous. A corny older guy trying to make requests to a DJ twenty feet in the air.

Maybe it was the lack of sleep but after a year of working with Gaga one on one, I didn't really care to have all these Pro Tools telling us what to do. Especially so late in the game. When I checked my phone, I saw that I had a text from Leah asking me to adjust the vocals. It didn't come through until after the show. It just seemed amateurish that the vocals wouldn't be taken care of at sound check or that someone couldn't come up in the booth and tell me to adjust them.

"Can you get me out of this? It's in 119." I turned to the house DJ and we talked like airline pilots as I flipped the switches on the board. It would be meaningless to try and write it down verbatim, but here's how it would sound to pretty much anyone else:

DJ1: Peanut butter taxicab washout?

DJ2: Yeah. And tax the pope.

DJ1: Colony water tower on Mars?

DJ2: With bacon.

DJ1: Got it.

The other DJ kept the floor packed with the same excitement that Gaga brought. It was funny. I followed a Lady Gaga performance with a Lady Gaga song and it wasn't big enough to fill the void. You had to take the music up a notch to its most basic and sonic form just to keep the air of excitement in the room.

I found Gaga and Leah in an upstairs balcony. They had a magnum of cheap white wine. After three years in nightlife I had been looking forward to having a stiffer drink after the show. But I made do with the white wine.

Gaga gave me a big hug as she scanned the room for any new fans or media. "By the way," I said as I held my sweaty friend, "Happy birthday."

She gave me a great big smile and we hugged again.

My friend Igor had come down from the city for WMC on his own dime to take pictures for the *Village Voice*. I told him that I wouldn't have time to sleep and he could have my hotel room. After a minute of bullshitting together, some of the Pro Tools brought out the cake that we'd spent all day shielding from the Miami sunshine. It was the kind of cake with a little ball you'd have decorated for your kid's soccer or basketball team, only we had it done up as a disco ball. "Happy Birthday, Gaga," it read. "Cheers to you and *The Fame!*"

There was Gaga and her disco ball bloomers and her disco tie and her disco ball cake. She blew out the candles. More pictures! Gaga reached out to me and sat me down on the couch next to the cake. "I want to put it into your mouth."

The hired guns went flashing. Most of them were either friends or people from the label. But it didn't matter. We were a young act at Winter Music Conference and to all appearances we had just played a sold-out show and gotten mobbed by the paparazzi. And it was someone's birthday! Gaga planted me in the banquette and we took turns stuffing cake in each other's mouths. We were the prom king and queen of Winter Music.

The hard work and the travel and the six 6:00 A.M. flights would begin again tomorrow. We would have a series of very long days ahead. But for now we would just sit in our balcony and have our cake and our white wine like Marie Antoinette.

SIX 5:00 A.M. FLIGHTS. DID I say 6:00 A.M.? It's really 5:00 A.M. I went back to my room with Igor and got him a copy of the key. The dancers split after the show and I agreed to go get them at 5:00. On the walk home I went by all of the café tables from before, now gathered around in wicker bouquets of stacked chairs all locked to the same chain. The restaurants had all closed and in the distance you could hear the tinny pulse of house music, but then it seemed to drive off in some Polar Bear's Lamborghini.

With the ocean snoozing away on the other side of the grass dunes I knew this would be the perfect night of sleep. Far away there were people having *after*-after-parties and negotiating small sales of local drugs and discussing its relative virtues with strangers they would never see again. I would not.

I went back to my room, completely exhausted, and packed up my record bag and suitcase, carefully laying in my new headphones and needles. The spoils of Winter Music. In the bathroom I splashed some water on my face and idly checked out the unused soaps and shower caps. I got dressed in another outfit and set my alarm for fifteen minutes. That's all I would have time for on this day.

The alarm went off at pretty much the same time I picked up the girls for the airport that same day. I started that day at Beauty Bar, played two shows in Miami, and now every single thing we'd worked for would happen all at once.

LOS
ANGELES

Pedal to the floor, thinkin' of the roar, gotta get us to the show

The obnoxious sunshine gleamed off of stark white airplanes and airport windows. Just glass and sky for miles with the puniest palm trees sticking out of the dusty landscape like unplucked hairs. The dancers had the sour look of unrested beauty. On the shuttle to the rental car place I got a message: "Hey, I have some great news for you. The casting director would like to feature you in a new music video filming this Monday. Call us back today for more details."

"That's funny," I said out loud as we all squinted our way through the sandy white parking lot. "The director just called saying that I have been cast in our video."

We laughed about it as if we were just coworkers on a business trip, bitching about other people from work. Those boobs! I imagined them as a bunch of listless actors, slumming it as casting directors and texting their friends.

That day the dancers pulled rank. To keep the video under budget the Pro Tools had sent us out here early to avoid any more hotel fees or airline costs of sending us all the way home for two days and then back out to LA. But between the show and the video the dancers called their manager. They were tired of being treated the way they were. They were professionals. They had rehearsed. They were willing to fly directly to LA from WMC to defray costs. But they were not going to wait it out in Gaga's empty bachelorette pad while everyone else schmoozed around Miami.

By crowning myself the ad hoc tour manager, I now had the great task of making sure the dancers got settled at the Grafton Hotel on Sunset. But there would be no room for me. I wanted to be there for Stef the whole way, even if they didn't technically need me for the video. They could probably pay some LA scenester to stand behind the turntables in the video, but I wanted it to be me.

Sheryl and Katie went into the rental car place and I called the casting director back. "So we'd really love it if you could show up camera-ready. We want everyone to dress themselves, very Lower East Side, hipster, heroin chic." I heard the penultimate word as *heroine*, so my tired brain wondered if I were supposed to dress like Wonder Woman or Amelia Earhart. Then I realized a casting director from Los Angeles was going to tell this Lower East Side badass how to dress *hip*. Something I'd never get over was the way people from outside your scene talked about it. They always jumbled words and mangled their cadence for no reason. (There's probably no un-obnoxious way to say this: They throw that meaningless word— "hip"—around so much. It's one of those words like "amazing" or "douche bag." And I've always believed that "douche bag" is in the eye of the beholder. That would be like the original test pilots in the space program going, "Gee, I like this jumpsuit. Let me see what the other astronauts think." Or Johnny Rotten going to a show and exclaiming out loud, "Lucky for me I've worn my punk pants to the club!")

"Okay, but I'm not one of the extras. I'm the DJ."

"Oh."

"I mean, I'm here to be in the video. I'll dress like I did on stage. But I just thought I'd let you know. In case you need to get more extras."

"Okay. Either way. Same deal."

I quoted her delightful phrasing and assumed she meant we should dress like the in-color version of those black-and-white Partnership for-a-Drug-Free-America ads.

Just then the girls pulled up in a black Mustang.

THE GRAFTON ON SUNSET WAS the visiting New Yorker's dream. It had just enough restaurants and shops for you to walk to from your room. And the room itself had enough hilarious LA things to keep your allegiance up. Aside from the health-spa minibar in the fridge, the bathroom had a separate minibar of personal beauty projects for you to try. Everything was part avocado. That or the carrot-ginger hair treatment or dried-cucumber exfoliating soap. I was hungry and still hadn't eaten since Miami and wondered if the new diet in California was to just put food on your face.

Fifteen dollars would get you a sex kit with three condoms, cherry-flavored lube, a personal massager, and a vibrating cock ring. Out of my unending curiosity I slipped the package open and noticed that some other enterprising visitor had found a way to get one of the condoms out of the package without getting charged for the whole sex kit. Bravo. To make it more confusing, the hotel had arranged a basket of various bottles as if you were going on a picnic with moisturizers and dried-blueberry foot scrub. Tucked in among it all was a pink mask with a can attached to it—a sixteen-dollar bottle of "personal oxygen."

While the girls lay out by the pool, I sat down at their desk and tried to get some work done. Finishing the adaptation of *Mercutio* would prove difficult. Everyone knew how he died. I wanted the ending to be dynamite. Academics theorize on how he gets cut down in the middle of the story. I sat down to think on this for a second. It can be done. But only I can do it. Who else could better know the psyche of the long-winded drunk more that me?

I stared at the keyboard until it changed alphabets. No help. I couldn't concentrate. Who had seen our show? When could I see photos?

THAT'S WHEN I GOT MY second very strange phone call. This time from Leah.

"I just wanted to let you know that we aren't going to have you play the DJ in the video."

"Are they cutting the DJ part? That makes sense. Well. I still want to be there for her."

"We said the same thing," Leah assured me. "We still want you and your look in there. But we are going to go with someone else as the DJ."

"Okay." I really was okay with this. I am a real DJ—I don't just play one on a music channel no one watches anymore. "Who?"

"Space Cowboy is going to do it."

"The guy from that Christmas song?" Weird choice. Gaga and he had worked on a holiday jingle. Only they did it in the off-season.

This video was supposed to be a microcosm of my life. I DJ at the end of a cool party and after it dies this pop star shows up and makes everything incredible. I knew I had a tendency to take pop matters too seriously. On a good day that meant I played "Billie Jean" all the way through 'til the end (the kid *is* his son!). On a bad day this meant I refused to play a show because the flyer didn't have the year on the date (what are we doing here if we're not making music history, people?). And this was one of the bad days. Won't it seem weird to people that she skipped a party where her own DJ was playing? Didn't make any sense.

"Yeah, but we still want you in the video. And if you can have any of your friends send us their info we could use some more people."

Ain't gonna do you wrong while you're gone

Suddenly I got overtaken with the idea that the video would suck. What if the casting company just sent over a unit of twenty-two twenty-two-year-olds in drugstore reading glasses and clean American Apparel clothes with the tags still on? Ohmygod. Then what would we do if it worked? What if kids watch this video like we did and try and reenact different scenes? What if they started dressing like this?

We needed something to make it real and fun. This had to go down like the Beauty Bar party with all the chaos and flare feeding into it like a party furnace. I called around to Beauty Bar LA and asked them to send over some kids. But that wouldn't help enough.

I needed a miracle. I texted Justin from Semi Precious Weapons. "Gaga and I just left Miami. We're in LA shooting the video on Monday. Is there any chance you're around?"

After that I took a six-dollar shower with things like papaya seeds, ground kale, and raw pistachios. I put things on my body that

I usually put on a salad. Afterwards I felt like I'd made a healthy choice and still felt hungry. Luckily they didn't charge for towels.

Justin texted, "You're filming your video on MONDAY IN LA? You know we fly in Sunday for our show, don't you?"

"We need extras. Can you guys be in it? It's an all-day shoot but it's a paying gig."

"Of course!"

I emailed Gaga the great news. She wrote back with such a joy. But maybe not enough. "Sorry. I've had a rough day."

WE HAD SO MANY DISTRACTIONS at home. Not enough here. Home had a buzz, a feed, a constant drip of expectations, drama, and excitement. Something was missing. I checked the clock. It would be almost midnight at home, about the time Leigh usually got out of work.

When she answered the phone I heard the cheers of people and loud, inexpertly mixed music. "Hello?"

"Hi," she said, like she was waiting for the other person to speak.

"Can you hear me? It's me."

"Yeah. It's just . . . I'm out with some friends."

"That's good—fine. Normal." I'm not one of those guys who got jealous at things like this.

"I can't really hear you."

"Step outside?"

"Fine." It got slightly less noisy. Although the honking clutter of street noise made me homesick. "Look, it's still really cold here."

"Okay." Did my phone have a bad connection? Did we? "Hi."

"Look, I was expecting to hear from you when you got done in Miami."

"This is it. I just got to LA." I could feel the distance. "I just wanted to talk."

"Do you know when you're getting home?"

"Not yet. But the video is tomorrow. Hopefully it's just one day."

"Look. I gotta go. And we'll talk when you get home. If you ever do."

Uh oh.

We can't rewind, we've gone too far

Shuttered truck bays creaked open in the chill of early morning to deliver lights while curious neighbors peeped through their blinds in tightly clutched bathrobes at the video shoot. The video would take place at a house party, so we rented a house. Across the street from the location house on 4304 Enoro Drive, the production company had rented out another house just to feed us. They filled the driveway with tents and tables and a buffet from a parked food truck. Not two days before, I walked myself to one of our gigs and set up my own equipment, and now we were on a video shoot that had to cost more than the entire record.

We didn't have the money to put me up at the Grafton, so that weekend I slept on an air mattress in a friend's kitchen. He had a rented studio in Echo Park, where I was able to foil the air mattress's devilish wish to deflate at some point in the night by pumping it up in the tiny kitchen. The now inaccessible stove and refrigerator acted as a headboard and footer. In the dark kitchen, I slept like an inflatable god. He dropped me off early on his way to work.

As the first one to the shoot that early morning, I had the

experience of wandering around a foreign city as it woke up for the day. A support van made deliveries nearby. The crew made every effort to have this area run like a single office building complete with security staff, parking shuttle, staff bathrooms, an employee lounge, and a cafeteria.

I got there before the other on-camera people and learned how shoots like these went.

The director runs the show but the assistant director does all the bossing around. The pecking order at mealtimes enforced a bit of law into a land that could have become Diva Central. First the crew eats. The gaffers and lighting hands, the technical producers and the guys running wires. They have a long day ahead, yelling at each other or getting yelled at en masse by a higher up. Their meal status makes up for their pay status, judging by the cheap prepaid phones they kept checking on breaks. Then the managing crew eats, although they do it with an I-don't-have-time-for-this-shit vigor. They stand while eating and bully younger employees into proclaiming that they are both eating the best fucking ham sandwiches on the planet. After them the lowest of all get to eat. A gaffer takes over for a security guard over by a tent where everyone has hidden their backpacks of headshots and alternate costumes so the security staff can have a bite. Only then can the lowest of the low get in line and pick away at the buffet: the actors.

This production has no actual acting involved in it, so the hired faces become known as "background." Because of my new position as a character in this ensemble, I have become an extra in my own music video. I am background. I jump when the AD shouts, "Okay, background! Let's eat and get back in there at five!" He splits us into two groups and learns names—of me and my fellow backgroundlings—and then promptly forgets them just in case he wants to change the groups up.

The background had all fielded the same phone call I got this week and they all arrived in pitch-perfect LES uniforms. Just up the hill from Crenshaw Boulevard and Martin Luther King Drive a group of tired, messy-haired kids in tight jeans and thrift-store jackets wandered around the sunny, suburban, black middle-class neighborhood.

THE DANCERS SHOWED UP AS I finished the best fucking huevos rancheros of my life. (I take back everything I've ever said in regards to East Coast vs. West Coast.) They had a later call time than the rest and would orbit the crew somewhere as Background First Class, their matching outfits telling all the other camera-ready actors dressed in their own clothes how much they outranked them.

"Did you visit your mom?"

"*Yes*," Sheryl said, "and she was so surprised!"

We discussed what else we had all done since Friday (sleeping, mostly) and looked around the set. We were three coworkers having a coffee on a Monday morning and talking about our weekends.

I WANDERED AROUND THE SET the way you would explore a music festival while you waited for your favorite bands to start. The back of the makeup trailer had two trailer toilets, which never once got dirty the entire day. On the other side of that trailer, a pair of nonplussed makeup artists dealt with the un-camera-ready makeup needs of the various background divas. Many background actors who could not accept that they would be out of focus throughout the entire shoot grimaced into the makeup mirrors, forcing the makeup artists to believe them that they were getting a zit.

In an office trailer—also parked at the hilarious hilltop angle of our cafeteria—I heard of a problem. Casting had gone—shall we say—*too* well. Everyone had a vision of what the, y'know . . . those kids . . .

with their . . . *haircuts* . . . and their *outfits*. Every person in the office had a different word for them. Some went by neighborhood: Silver Lake, Wicker Park, some place called "William's Bourge." But they tackled the subject with that fantastic Left Coast alacrity. "Didn't you say these were supposed to be *Brooklyn* kids?" "Can any of *Akon's* people make it?" I knew the problem right away. They were filming a video in the 'hood for a hip-hop label and it was supposed to take place in Brooklyn. Where were the damn black people?

I pulled the AD aside and told him that I had a friend in the neighborhood who Gaga knew and who could be in the video. Here's how to say that in Californese: "Somebody told me you want to improve the diversity of the cast?"

Within half an hour I had Sandy, the girl who beat eight thugs off of me with her purse at St. Jerome's only a few months before, at the shoot in heels and a dress. We had the team together. All we needed was Semi Precious Weapons.

WHEN I FINALLY SAW GAGA, she looked right at home at the top of the hill. The talent hung around on the other side of the house in a private area. Lots of favors had gotten called in to get some Interscope brass to crowd together on the couches. Gaga had on a normal outfit for her: a disco-ball bra and a torn white undershirt and heels. Because we had to do all the shooting in one day, we spent all day doing the inside shots with all the windows blacked out so that we could get the night shots in all at once at the end. This meant that the intro and the establishing shots outside would get taken when it got dark. The background all hung around in their own clothes and so did the star.

"You look great," she said to me. I had worn the same outfit for a week: black jeans, black leather jacket, and white sunglasses. But the AD wanted me to go talk to wardrobe, so I switched into a pair of vintage white Nikes, pink fingerless gloves, and, for no reason, a sparkly cummerbund. I would never wear something like this at home, but when I saw it I said, "This is what we look like to them."

When no one was looking she plopped down next to me and let out a deep breath.

"Everything okay yesterday?"

"Huh?"

"Said you had a rough day."

She looked down at the driveway as people carried props around and carried the man's hilarious furniture out. "Yeah. I wanted to tell you—"

"BACKGROUND!" The AD came in and abducted six of us for our first scene.

I turned back to Gaga as I got pulled into the video's orbit. "I'll stick around this week and we can catch up."

Her big eyes looked up at me, lost at first, and her mouth hung open. She reminded me of that little girl I'd met only a year before, hungry for the scene. She'd wanted everything and now she had it. She took a breath and morphed back into the star, nodding her head at me as I went away.

We walked into an unbelievable relic, a house from the seventies that must have spent the last thirty years under glass, pinned perfectly in place like a butterfly in a museum. Shag carpet like you wouldn't believe, only you would believe it perfectly once you saw the harvest gold couches, three of them in a row, trimmed in gold rope. Floral polyester masterpieces. A short hallway with one bookshelf separated the sitting room from the living room. Both had unbelievable details. No wonder they had to move so much furniture into the driveway. This man was addicted to couches. I counted eight total, plus the plush armchairs outside.

Gaga walked into the sitting room and found me helping the people in there with their costumes like we we're getting ready for a Motherfucker party. She smiled at the production. "You guys look like my friends," she said wistfully, as if by staging this production in LA she had conjured the people she missed all winter. I smiled over to her. She looked at me. "Well, you're my friend. But they look like our friends."

"ACTION!" THEY PLAYED THE SONG about halfway in so that our totally professional dance motions would sync up. We all looked around, hoping for the first time that the camera would show us out of focus. Some girls tromped on the couch with their heels on. I grabbed a bottle of André champagne. It was warm and still had the sticker on it from Ralph's.

Dancing in place during a make-believe party felt unbelievably moronic. We looked like go-go dancers stationed on couches. I wished Starlight were here.

Instead I stood around with a half dozen American Apparel employees and pretended to have a good time. It's like a party in Williamsburg.

A big part of this production involved nothing getting mic'd. This helped because none of us had studied being music-video extras at Julliard. When the music played we all tried to look happy and drunk while we interpreted it together. This wasn't a hip-hop video, where we could look taut and sexy in slo-mo.

"BACKGROUND—MOVE AROUND! YOU EVER GO TO A PARTY WHERE EVERYONE JUST STANDS STILL IN PLACE?!" The AD stirred us up from just behind the camera.

We tromped around the room, trudging over furniture and spilling three-dollar champagne on the ottoman we just kicked over.

Gaga stood in front of the sitting room while a production assistant guarded the front door to make sure no one messed up the espionage lighting we had going. The idea was to make a motion-picture version of the photos that came out of downtown parties like Misshapes, Motherfucker, and our own nights at St. Jerome's. Very washed out, no-time-to-get-it-perfect. The idea worked.

After that the actual director walked in. She had finesse where the AD had force. She could tell you just with her gaze where you needed to stand to keep up your part of the video's unified vision. After styling the party room she told us she wanted us to come through the beaded curtain one by one. Gaga would stand on the other side of it singing a verse and we had to walk past her like we would anybody else at the party.

On Gaga's side of the curtain you had the lights, camera crew, audio playback, and the director.

On our side you had the goddamn AD screaming, "BACK-GROUND, MOVE AROUND! C'MON! KEEP WALKING AROUND. NOW COME THROUGH ONE AT A TIME."

Because of the front lighting, you could see Gaga where she stood and sang a verse while everyone passed. The first girl through walked by as if Gaga were the bitch who wouldn't get out of the way in the slippery hallway where everyone dropped a splash of vodka cranberry as they negotiated down three steps in heels. Gaga remained unscathed from the interaction as if she were playing in a club where the way to the bathroom is just a few feet from the stage. The next guy just marched straight through like a nervous extra in a music video who just wanted to get his part over with already. Everyone looped back around the living room and past the front door to come back to the sitting room when they finished, as if they were having a good time, and then went to the kitchen to refuel.

The next guy to go through kind of offended me. Wardrobe put him in a leather jacket and a pair of nerdy glasses. My schtick. He strolled through the gold-beaded curtain and looked Gaga up and down. I stopped doing my fake dance when I saw him. He paused and threw Gaga against the bookcase and tried to make out with her. I could just imagine how much Guy would want to kill this guy. After that, the Asian girl in the dress walked by in her heels as if she could not possibly care. We did a couple of takes. Mostly on loop. Because of my incurable need for authenticity, I went for my launch and when I came to Gaga at the bookcase I slapped her on the back of the shoulder like I would if I ran into her downtown. "*Gaga*? What are *you* doing here?"

"CUT! CUT!" Music stopped. Production halted and the front opened like a drawbridge, bringing in propmasters with the relief of a constipated doorway. Some nervous lads had hidden in the garage for the entire take, trying to keep an ice sculpture from melting in the California sun.

The AD ran in the room. "OK, BACKGROUND! I like what I'm seeing but I want more. More movement, more interaction. If you have a bottle in your hand you should be offering it to everyone around you. This is a party. Move around. Leave the room. There's no reason that everyone would leave a room at a party individually. Run around. Have some fun. Maybe two of you have to go to the bathroom at the same time. Maybe you took a picture you want to show someone in another room." He spoke with that lumbered, old-man cadence that tried to respect his inadvertent need to make fun of the young. We get it, pal, say the backgroundlings. We'll be more obnoxious and self-involved.

Just then the director parted the curtains and walked out, all smiles. "That was *great*, you guys! I love the interactions and the way it looks like a party!" She can't be any older than I am. "I want more. More interactions. Don't ignore Gaga just because the camera is on her. Move around. Interact. You"—she pointed at me—"I like that moment when you walked up and tried to grab her and press her against the wall. Do it again? Only this time, y'know, like *move in* for it, okay? Like you're gonna *kiss*."

My face nodded and smiled. My soul cried out, *One time. They're going to torture me for kissing someone one time.*

"Brendan," the director said, "you'll be fourth through the curtain."

Great. Now when the video comes out Guy can go find Nikki and say, "See? We weren't crazy. They couldn't even keep their hands off of each other at the shoot!" And then add, "You wanna go back to my place?"

The director had more advice for the other background kids but I couldn't pay attention. The director of the music video—my music video?—has just asked me to put the moves on my friend's girlfriend.

I found myself taking a big swig of the warm bottle of André in my hand. It fizzled on top of the huevos rancheros in my nervous stomach.

The director turned around and caught me taking a swig and smiled. "Good!" she said, after giving everyone else their notes. "It's a party in here! Let's have some fun!"

ASIAN GIRL TROMPED THROUGH. NERDY boy in leather did my schtick this time for some reason—*Gaga? What are you doing here?* A real-life drink spill made the next girl in heels clutch both walls and step over her as Gaga wriggled on the floor. Then someone pushed a hand into my back and sent me in. It's just theater, right? Everyone back home will barely see it.

I hopped off the couch and rushed through the curtain like a drunk scenester looking for the bathroom. The curtains parted and I walked through like someone coming into the live room at Pianos between songs: *Sorry, is this where the party's at?* I grabbed Gaga on my way through and she turned to me like a girl who thought she'd spotted her boyfriend by the touch. Her eyes followed the black leather jacket up to me and when she found my eyes we locked gaze.

Only we were not two Hollywood actors.

We were not two kids in a high school play who had to pretend to be lovers.

Every single thing about this moment felt wrong.

Gaga looked up at me.

Our eyes met.

I felt like the drunk guy at the party should feel when everyone looks at him in pity. Only it's 9:45 in the morning on principle photography of a music video. And I've just grabbed my friend's girlfriend for a love scene. Instead of leaning in for the kiss I ran off and found myself wishing wardrobe could have stitched a tail between my legs.

"CUT!"

I sat back on the arm of the couch as the other backgroundlings discussed whether they might have time for a smoke. Everyone went back to the conversation they abandoned only minutes before. ("My cousin is a PA on that show but he said they already hired a full cast through a separate agency." "I only go there on Mondays . . .") I felt terrible. I felt like Guy had threatened me the month before because he didn't want this exact moment to happen. If the damn guy had shown up to the video we wouldn't have this problem. And where were the boys from Semi Precious Weapons?

An older man walked over to me with a stern face. I wondered for a moment if I was getting fired. Can anyone flunk out of the world of music video extras? "Hey, uhm . . . "

"Yeah?" I said, facing the music. "What?"

He turned out to be the owner of Alexander Residence. The proprietor of couches. He elected to stay on location and watch a bunch of Hollywood extras jump on his furniture and pour dirt-cheap champagne on the shag carpet. Now that the cameras had stopped rolling he had something to say. "Don't sit on the arm of the sofa. It's not good for it."

This guy and his fucking couches. I guess he would know best how to keep a couch from the seventies going.

Soon we got a flood of cameos. Colby O'Donis did his verse. The one I was singing three days ago. We had exactly as much interaction as I ever expected and I never once met him again. Akon and I had a scene on the couch where we rocked out and spilled champagne among our tacky plastic party cups. He passed the bottle around like a playboy in Saint-Tropez. I told him that where we came from, rock stars knew how to pour a drink.

BUT THE MOMENT I WILL keep with me for the rest of my life happened just a minute after. Over by the edge of the living room—the antithesis of action—I found Gaga standing by the wrapped cord and lighting rigs. It occured to me that if Guy and the Weapons had made it to the shoot, she might have had to entertain them for the day. It was the scenester's curse that you might invite all of your friends to see you play and then ignore them the entire time you have on stage. But instead I found her over by the VTR, where they watched the playback of the video they'd just shot.

She stood there with her arms folded in front of her chest, her right hand gripping an elbow and her left hand by her mouth with a manicured fingernail pressed to her teeth. By all laws of diva-ism and music videodom, she could have sat in her trailer. The girl had a boyfriend to Skype and a business to run. She really shouldn't have to worry about what the local kids looked like when they pretended to look like out-of-focus Lower East Side scenesters. But to Gaga right then, there was nothing more important than every single frame that came through that camera. Editing didn't matter. Fine adjustments didn't matter. Gaga didn't even have a record out yet, but I could see the way she wanted to fine-tune the details right from the start. But she knew the rules:

A record is only as good as the tracks.

The tracks are only as good as the mix.

The secret to a good mix is good recording.

In my mind I've started to see things clearer

At the next break outside I looked up and realized that I was standing in front of Space Cowboy, the guy who would play the DJ in the video. He sat next to my nerdy stunt double in the leather jacket. He stood out from the thrift-store crowd in a smartly tailored Savile Road suit from London. He held a black-and-red Blackjack phone, checking with it occasionally as if it were his secretary on a slow day at work: *Any calls?* For no apparent reason he has taken my small, anonymous part in a music video for the day.

There is a reason for every single thing in the world, Brendan. However, that reason is rarely evident.

He looked a bit like he'd only got invited to the party so he could DJ and never made any attempt to talk to anyone. Neither on screen or off. Even here he stood tribeless among the music video world. The Pro Tools don't consider him one of theirs and the AD wouldn't even know what to tell him he's doing all wrong. He didn't eat with the crew or mix in with the other people from Interscope. It felt for a second as if I were watching them dress someone to play me on camera, especially the way he was in the thick of the video and still removed from the party, alone.

Then I remembered the last time someone who looked like me took over my role.

This is probably unhealthy to entertain, but I will go ahead and say it: The guy who replaced me in this music video looked like the guys who girlfriends replace me with right after we break up. He's just another *James*. We looked identical in every way the camera would see. Shaggy brown hair, weekly shaven stubble, and the lazy-eyed look in our pronounced lower eyelids that came from working hours like these. If you put a pair of sunglasses on him we might look far too identical. When Nikki left me for that waiter, our mutual friends all referred to him as the "less handsome version" of me. That's supposed to make me feel better. But it begs the question: What is so goddamn wrong with me that you would run to the shorter, dumber, or "less handsome version" of me the second we break up? Especially since no one has ever listed "wish you were just a little bit less handsome" when breaking up with me. What do these other guys have going on that they can afford to lose a couple of inches or have a crooked nose and still beat me out? Obviously he must snuggle better, pick her up from work five minutes before I would, and remember all of her sisters' names and birthdays or something. It's probably all written down in that phone he clutched.

He looked up at me and that's when I realized I was staring.

"Space Cowboy?" He followed my voice hopefully, wondering if he might be needed on set. "The gangster of love himself." I apparently don't know any jokes—I just say things out loud like a joke. I suck at life.

"Hey."

"Hey."

Have you ever had a good strong magnet that you can barely peel of the fridge? Like the kind that feels heavier than regular magnets and will stick to anything—except another magnet? If you placed one on top of the other on a flat surface the one at rest would politely shove the uninvited magnet away.

We introduced ourselves.

"How's LA treating you?"

"Good."

"Good."

"Hey, I like that Christmas song you and Gaga did."

"Oh," he said, as embarrassed as he could possibly be about a song that he probably recorded in a day and never thought about again.

Earlier he seemed preoccupied for want of distraction. He was busy looking for something to keep him busy and—although he had almost certainly ruled it out as a possibility—he checked his phone once again.

Out in the driveway of the location house, a few of the PAs put the finishing touches on a pair of turntables, which they had custom inlaid to an old sewing desk. They did a real great job of it too, carving out a hole just wide enough to bury the heavy turntables into the desk and to make them flush with the surface. If I lived in LA I probably would have asked them if I could keep it at the end of the shoot. They even painted the desk when they finished.

"Sweet setup." I motioned toward the turntables.

"I usually don't do vinyl. Just CDs."

"Oh."

Two PAs came out at a brisk pace, their janitor rings of keys clanging from the clips on their jeans. They each took one side and repo'd the turntable desk, hauling it inside.

"You think you're going to stay in LA long?" (I think *he* asked that, not me.) Not sure, actually. I can't tell us apart.

"Uhm, not sure. I don't have a return ticket. Hopefully we can get a few shows and I'll just stay."

He paused at this, then looked up. "That's right. You're a DJ."

"You think you're going to stay in LA long? Are you going to move here?"

"Looks like it. It's really a matter of getting a studio space all set up, " I—no, okay, that definitely must have been him. I must've been the one asking about the moving.

The AD barged through the door briskly—film production workers, I'd discovered, were the only people on the West Coast who moved at this pace. The afternoon sunlight temporarily blinded him. He squinted with one hand, making a visor over his face. "Where's Gaga's DJ?!"

"Right here," we said, in such perfect unison that it may have gotten misheard as production-perfect reverb. The emptiness between us made it possible. Space Cowboy and I then took mirrored steps forward and looked at each other. I laughed. He laughed too. Stupid East Coast boy doesn't know what's real and what's pretend on a location shoot in LA.

Gaga stepped out into the bright light of the doorway. She froze when she saw us both together. Her sunglasses fell from her forehead and onto her snout, covering her eyes.

I stepped aside, embarrassed. "Right. For the *video*."

"Right . . ." He tried to echo me on this one but he couldn't force it out. He repeated my words, but they didn't sounds like they meant the same thing when he said them. "For the video."

"JUST IMAGINE YOU'RE ALL AT a party at a friend's house." This is the director herself talking to us. Melina Matsoukas had worked for Black Dog for a couple years, making simple videos with stark visuals like Snoop Dogg's "Sensual Seduction" and "Upgrade U" for Beyoncé. She had a good-cop tone in her voice in comparison to the iron-fisted AD. "It's late and far away from home. Maybe you guys all came back from a show and somebody's parents are out of town. You've been out. You're tired. You can't party anymore and you pass out. Right there on the shag carpet." She let out a little laugh as if to acknowledge that, yeah, we had found the most heinous location to shoot in for the day. "You sleep in your clothes because you didn't bring anything else here. And it's like a dream you would have when you were a little kid and you woke up to find Michael Jackson at your birthday party."

I'd made friends with an extra named Keith, who chuckled, "I'd be pissed if Michael Jackson woke me up."

The director was unscathed. "Good," she smiled. "Use that. If the camera's on you and we shine the light in your face, act like you just got woken up by a cop with a flashlight. Turn away. Be natural."

The AD butted in, yelling as always, "But that's your thing. Everybody has a thing. But you can't all do the same thing."

We fanned out all over the house to pass out. It actually evened out just like it would at a sleepover. The diva girl headed straight for the longest couch and lay down. Stoner dude just took a slouch in a chair. Sandy went and sat in the Archie Bunker and put her feet up on the ottoman. I found the prettiest girl in the room and lay down next to her on the floor. That's *my* thing.

The AD searched the room. He did that thumbs-and-forefingers movie frame. He looked down at me and the girl. "You. Over here." He liked that we were lying on the floor. But he would like us to lie on the floor over there. Then he styled our arms and legs because we had not passed out on the floor to his exacting standards. When he finished, my character had a new girlfriend. They were getting pretty serious about each other.

"Hi, I'm Brendan," I said to my party girlfriend.

"Hi," she giggled from the excitement. "Did you get this gig through your agency? Mine sent me over. I don't know why. But I guess it's good exposure. Do I know you from somewhere? I feel like we've been background together before."

Gaga walked into the room in a flamingo-pink coat with embellished shoulder pads. She took off her sunglasses for a moment and looked around.

For the next five seconds we were just Stef and Brendan, hanging out and getting ready before a show.

"You look great," I told her. "I love those sunglasses."

"Thanks. Don't you love them? They're from a collector. We had to sign a paper saying we wouldn't steal them. But I really want to. I'd buy them anyway."

"They're great. You look great." I leaned up on my elbows. "Hey, if we get done in time, let's try and see Semi Precious Weapons later."

"Yesyesyes!" She didn't seem to notice that the boys couldn't make it to the shoot. The girl had plenty on her mind.

"I already talked to one of the extras about it. He said he'd drive."

"Cool. Yay!"

"He's super cool. He wants me to DJ at his party on Wednesday."

"Awesome. We should go anyway just to get out. Look, uhm—"

"Stop," I said. "What did I tell you at rehearsal that made Laurieann so happy? I'm a real DJ. I didn't come here to be seen. I came her to be there for you."

She smiled.

The director entered and Gaga turned back into her character on set. We both put our sunglasses on. She is the star of her music video and I'm the guy passed out on the floor of the dining room.

One of the extras looked up. "What's the name of the band?"

"Lady Gaga."

"Oh." He took in the name. His face registered what a lot of people had said either *sotto voce* or aloud that year. That's a clunky name for a pop star.

A girl turned to Gaga, seeking some kind of clarification or backstory. "Is Gaga your real name?"

"Yes," Gaga replied. And she meant it.

The AD walked in. "MUSIC."

ON THE WAY TO CRAFT services I heard a booming voice from behind me. "There he is!" Joe, Gaga's father, marched over to me and greeted me like we were in one of those Olive Garden commercials. He wore his trademark "Bada Bing!" hat. Gaga's mom looked around. She'd been told to expect a big production, but not this big. "Is all this for Stefani? There must be one hundred people on this street. Are they filming another project here too?"

"How you getting along out West, huh?" He slapped me on the shoulder. "You an actor too now? Wanna give me your headshot?"

I smiled. "I heard you're a big-time producer now."

"You're gonna be a star, kid."

We joked around until the director came over for me.

"Mr. Bigshot!" Joe called out after me. "Hey! Which one is your trailer? I'll answer your fan mail until you get back." I chuckled all the way to my big scene.

The set dressers had planted a flock of lawn flamingos out behind the kiddie pool. They wanted me to ride a flamingo (what?) and then fall to the ground. It's hard to say what's worse: that I agreed to do it or that it took me like three takes to get it right.

"BACKGROUND! BOTH TEAMS, I WANT EVERYBODY IN THE LIVING ROOM." The AD rounded everyone up, jogging the team into the living room. "THIS IS THE BIG PARTY SCENE. I WANT EVERYBODY IN HERE—EVERYBODY." The finale came together in the living room with the whole cast together. Lipstick-on-the-mirror girl touched up her color. Tattoo boy put on his shades. American Apparel clerk straightened his unbuttoned shirt. Pocahontas came in with her headdress. The dancers waited offstage, Akon and Colby O'Donis had left, and Space Cowboy went home for a spot of tea or something.

This scene was just us kids in the twelfth hour of this shoot. The sun went down on the mysterious western coast just outside while we all hid in the blacked-out location house. Now the fun began.

We had the living room to ourselves—no props or lip-syncing to do. Just dance. They cranked up the music and we had our fun, passing Gaga around like the hostess of a party. Everything we did the director loved. "*Yes. Interact* with her," she said when one girl pulled Gaga's shirt off. "Let's have some fun here."

One scene—with Gaga behind a keyboard and us all dancing to the beat—channeled the sort of parties we'd thrown before. I stood behind her for that scene and had my own lost moment. There comes a time when you're out and find whatever it is you're searching for in nightlife—in crowds of strangers, in the dark. You find that you've gotten lost. And then you feel like for once you are right where you need to be. It's a wonderful feeling.

Gaga picked up the disco ball and we started passing the heavy thing around the room as a team. Just us extras. Games at the company picnic for our whole department. We needed matching T-shirts that had our company logo on the front, and on the back, where our names would go, they'd all just say "Background."

We abandoned any pretense of acting or being in character or even being ourselves. Gaga ended one scene with a backbend that planted her face square in my crotch. I had become so lost in the scene that it didn't occur to me until later how pissed Guy would get when he saw that on film.

Just then the lights went out and the music stopped. Gaga sat up. "Did I hit someone?" She looked up and saw the cameraman checking his lip for blood and inspecting his camera for damage. "Ohmygod, are you okay?" Gaga had thrown a disco ball off camera. Only it hit him in the face.

Keith put a hand on the cameraman's shoulder. "You need a stunt double."

BY SOME SMALL MIRACLE WE finished in time to see Semi Precious Weapons play in Hollywood. I took Keith, my new best friend, with me to see the show. This had nothing to do with him having a car. He was actually trying to sleep with Sandy.

Justin put us all on the guest list and we strutted in the door to the sleepy club like we were the stars of a Lady Gaga video.

Keith asked me to stick around for Wednesday so I could DJ with him at a cavernous Hollywood club called Boardner's, and I said yes in the name of raising up plane fare.

Semi Precious Weapons took the stage in their usual epic roundup. I needed to get back to New York because I didn't have enough money to idle around LA. Justin took the stage and helped me out a little bit. "We're Semi Precious Weapons from New York City." If I were alone and broken in the world I was at least in a kindling pile of lone and broke people. "*I can't pay my rent,*" he screamed, "*but I'm fucking gorgeous!*"

Seeing my favorite New York band broke the spell of Los Angeles for me.

I was homesick.

There's no other word for it.

I missed Leigh.

I want to tell you something you've known all along

In the morning, I woke up on the floor in Sandy's mother's studio apartment in East LA. I took a walk to a strip-mall coffee shop on the other side of the highway with the cool, damp whitenoise of LA traffic. I didn't see another person on foot and it made me feel like Manhattan was not an island but a ship drifting out to sea. I needed to go home.

My phone rang—actually rang—and it surprised me at first. Even the most industrious New Yorker would have only just woken up.

It was Gaga. "I just want to thank you for coming out to the shoot."

"It was so much fun! I made some new friends with the extras, and one of them is going to have me DJ at Boardner's with him on Wednesday."

"That's great," Gaga's dry, early-morning voice said. I could tell she had been crying. "It was really great to have you there. You were good at getting the right spirit for the party. I really needed you there. So thank you."

"It's what I do."

Gaga sounded distant. I felt closer to her on our transcontinental all-night yak sessions. Now we had so much to talk about and nothing to say. "I'm sorry I'm going to be so busy this week," she began. When we hatched this trip on our phone calls months earlier, she had wanted me to come to LA early and just spend time with her. When you move to a new city you find yourself eating at places you want to share with people and going to bookstores you know just the friend to take to. I'd forgotten all about the hypothetical rental car we'd imagined on our first trip out here together.

"You know what I've always said. It's your thing. You do your thing. No worries or judgments from me. Ever."

"I just thought you should know. . . . We broke up the morning of the shoot." Her voice had that beautiful husk to it.

"Ohmygod. Really? Oh, wow."

"That's it. We live in two different worlds."

"Well good for you. Good for you for knowing it's for real, right?"

"Take care of him for me when you get back to New York."

"Okay. I'm not leaving for a while."

"But when you do, keep an eye on him. I really wanted it to work out."

"Now you can write about it." I felt kind of corny saying that. "What was it you said before when you guys broke up in December? You didn't want to write about it because it would be like sealing the envelope."

"Yeah . . ." Things felt very unsettled.

"I think it's more like what you told me in November," I said. "Remember what you said to me that day? When I was all stressed out? You wrote it on the pages I brought to your house. Do you remember what you said?"

"No. What did I say?"

"I found it the other day when I was packing. You wrote: 'No story should ever end in resolution.'"

NEW YORK

They'll hurt me bad, but I won't mind

A week later I gathered up all the sunshine from Miami and California and brought it back to New York. It was spring, an early spring that sneaked up on everyone one delightful morning in early April.

I went straight to see Leigh from the airport.

She stood at the door to her apartment with her arms crossed over her chest. "Nice of you to visit."

"I'm back!" I smiled.

"Not for long." She told me that a friend of hers had asked if she could score her a pair of tickets to the Lady Gaga show the next night in San Francisco. "Then I look it up and there's a whole West Coast tour. Were you going to even tell me that you—"

"Hey." I had more to say, but I didn't know about the tour. "I'm not going back. I want to be here. With you."

"I know you. It's always the same. Always running off to the next adventure."

"Hey." I stepped in and looked into her eyes. Our arms hadn't felt so free together in too long. "I've been thinking about it a lot. This is the next adventure."

* * *

I GOT A NEW FULL-TIME job and paid off every one of my bills. I stayed away from my beloved downtown and worked twelve and fourteen hours slinging drinks in midtown at a new rooftop bar. On my first day there I made more than I ever made behind the bar at St. J's. Total. When I knew I could afford to breath again I took Leigh out to dinner. We started talking about the future: where we would go, what *we* would do. Not what we would do that night, or quickly together before work, but in life. Together.

SOMEWHERE AROUND MY TWENTY-SIXTH BIRTHDAY in May, I got a call from Sheryl, the tough-talking backup dancer from tour. "How's tricks?" I said.

"Ehh," she said in her husky voice. "They decided to go with a new look so we got canned."

"Who are the skinny bitches they hired?"

"I don't know. But the good news is they're keeping me on to choreograph Gaga's first TV performance. So it's like one door closes, one door opens."

"That sounds like fun. Gaga has been planning her first TV appearance for years."

"Do you wanna be in it?"

"Uhm . . ." I couldn't take any time off. She said the taping would be in the afternoon on my day off. Whatever. "Do I need to bring turntables or anything?"

"I actually need you as a dancer."

"Oh," said the guy who never thought of himself as a dancer. "I mean, I—"

"I actually thought about it in rehearsals on Valentine's Day. I wish I had thought to work more with you. You're very expressive and you have good timing, which is all you need to be a dancer."

"Okay . . . I mean—"

"I'll train you. Come meet me early. There are no dancers your age with your look. You'll be great."

"Uhm . . ." I hadn't said yes to something so adventuresome in a long time. I used to say yes to everything. I used to like that about me. Fuck it. "All right. I'm in."

"TRL studios tomorrow."

THAT SAME DAY THE VIDEO came out. It looked great and very professional. Watching it was like meeting up with your friends after a lost weekend and exchanging stories over a late breakfast on Sunday. There was the American Apparel kid bonking his head on the coffee table and Gaga stepping over me to get to the dining room in the beginning ("There's my leg!"). Leigh and I watched it together, squealing with laughter every time I danced on camera. The first time Gaga sings *"Just dance"* all you can see is me, pogoing around the anonymous living room like I'm having the greatest time in the world at a party where I wasn't invited. The images flashed around the screen like you would page through the photos in your camera in the cab on the way home. I loved it. They kept in every golden moment. When Gaga tossed a disco ball and accidentally wailed the camera, you saw it. An extra peeled off her T-shirt, exposing her disco bra. At the end of one take, she reached down to fix her bra and the editors synced it up with the music. Gaga came across as the perfect debut star. *No one is going to know who I am. But they are going to want to know who I am.* Keith roamed around in the background in his drum-major jacket, talking to girls and saying hi to people. Sandy had a scene where she sneaked behind a chair and came up, jolted and sniffing her nostrils. The timid girl who lay on the floor with me, checking her lipstick, seemed to hide in the bathroom for half the party. I got not one but *two* flamingo-riding scenes and plus a shot of me, on camera, sitting on the arm of that location house's precious, precious sofa. All the jokes and details came through. You can see the *Best of Blondie* records next to New Kids on the Block. When you see the girl on my lap you can tell that I am nervous about getting caught. For the most part, though, I just danced along to the Gaga song in the background with my good friend and maybe she's the only one I knew at the party. And that's not a bad way to be remembered.

Georgie called me twice the day the video came out. "Loved it! Just had a meeting with Gaga. I want to book you guys. Do the whole thing. You DJ, performance by her. Go-go dancers. Let's make it happen."

"Great!" When I hung up I decided to just let him find out on his own that it wasn't going to happen.

THIS WAS PART OF THE plan we'd dreamed out on the floor of her bare apartment months earlier over pint glasses of cheap red wine. *I'm going to come out on stage at an awards show where no one has every heard of me. I'm going to blow away the entire crowd and all everyone is going to say is, "Who is that girl?" And I'm going to come out on stage and sing the song for the first time in front of everyone. And I'm going to be in my underwear just to let everybody know that I don't give a ffffuck what anybody else thinks.*

I smiled. Everyone has hopes and goals. Most of us just dream. But Gaga had a way of holding onto her dreams until they became a reality. For her these goals never had an end. She planned a lifelong career in music for herself and she saw this as a way of gaining street cred, of building up a resume for that day when she would be a producer and bring in new talent and become the grandmother of pop she had always talked about.

This day would begin the battle that would make that career possible. The people she was up against would fail slowly because they would see it as a contest. They would want to be adored or to have a hit song or sell a platinum record. Gaga wanted to do all those things on her way to somewhere else. This puts great and even pressure on every step. A lesser star might focus so hard on making a record go platinum that she either fails or can't produce anything after that. Another star might micromanage an awards show performance. Gaga nailed that record in order for it to go platinum so that she could nail an awards show on her way to promoting the next single.

Laurieann Gibson had told us that anyone could be a dancer if they could count to eight. Gaga just knew the right steps that made up the dance.

TRL STUDIOS SAT IN THAT mythic New York where you would think all transactions took place if you only knew about New York from watching MTV. You went into a door right off Times Square at the MTV building on 1515 Broadway and went up the escalator to a series of semi-manned desks.

My occupation was listed as "Backup Dancer." They pulled us into a multi-use rehearsal space for our 2:45 call time. That's when I met the crew. I was the only straight white guy in the room. The rest of them acted exactly like the rehearsal-space mean kids in one of those teen dance movies. Everyone wore sleeveless layers, fingerless gloves, sweat bands. I felt like I was going to get jumped by the crew in the subway station in the beginning of the video for "Bad." Most of them taught at the same dance studio and I was the only unfamiliar face.

They yelled at each other, counting off for people who miscounted. I could just imagine what they'd do to me when I went up.

Sheryl marched right up to me when she saw me and brought me in for my dance tutorial.

"So did you do any of the shows that I saw listed?" I asked. Lady

Gaga had played a half dozen shows on the West Coast between the video shoot and this TV appearance.

"No. Just this for now."

"Huh," I said. And then I just had to ask. "Who's, uhm . . . who's the DJ?"

"I think Space Cowboy has been doing that." It amazes me how I can always be the last one to know about these things. It was so obvious that I should have just suggested it.

A group of the male dancers had challenged each other to a break-dancing competition. Some of the other dancers got in an argument about how to count off in break dancing. "Five, six, seven, eight!"

Sheryl pulled the group together. The shoot was very simple but we needed to be on point. Had everyone seen the video? Okay, good. Just like that we're going to stay completely still. Everybody's passed out on tables and on the stage. The music will start but don't go until fourteen. It's got to be *crisp*.

I pulled Sheryl aside. "What's fourteen? Fourteen of what?"

"Y'know. Fourteen. Of eight."

"To be a backup dancer you only have to count to eight?" I did the math and realized that we had to start two-thirds through a particular verse.

She nodded. I smiled. That's all there is to DJ'ing too.

We did a few run-throughs, everybody in their movement clothes and wifebeaters. They needed the whole ensemble to do the dance scenes from the video in one take. We looked funny, lying out on the floor and getting ready to turn into dancers, but this time the video wouldn't get pieced together. All of us—including Gaga—had to do the whole thing in one shot. We rehearsed it several times with a boom box.

You're probably saying to yourself, "Now how did they get along without a masterful DJ pressing play?" I'd answer that, but right when we did the blocking for the camera Space Cowboy showed up with his gray PC laptop. My life had always been so awkward that I felt like it might be awkward not to speak to him. "Hey, champ."

"Oh, hey," he responded. Hey. There's that fellow I replaced.

"Excited for the show?"

"Yeah. Definitely."

"Good."

"How long are you in New York?"

"Looks like it will be a couple of days."

"You should have me show you around. We can get lunch and I'll show you around the vintage clothing stores and record shops."

He looked up with a smile that clocked in at about one degree centigrade. "Wonderful." He took a seat on a folding chair and opened his laptop. He mapped out the show in a music software program with all of the songs on one track. During the show he would stand behind a pair of unplugged CD players and act the part of the DJ, with the principal job getting handled backstage by a sound tech.

Sheryl and the other dancers marched over then. One of them said, "So you're the DJ?"

"He is Space Cowboy," Sheryl said. "You know? Remember that song? 'My Egyptian Lover'?"

Space Cowboy had some minor dance hits here and in London. "My Egyptian Lover" came out the year before and made a minor splash, but it would also go on his album the next year.

"I don't know that one," the dancer said.

"You know it. You've gotta know it." Then Sheryl did the best thing you can do in a situation like that. She sang the incessant chorus. "*My Egyptian lover (there is no other). My Egyptian lover (there is no other)."* The other dancers, activated by boredom, counted off and sang along, dancing, their shoes squeaking out the beat. Just having a gay old time.

Space Cowboy stood up while they all sang along, slammed his laptop shut, and quietly exited the room. They danced him to the door, giggling.

SUDDENLY THE MANAGEMENT COMPANY PEOPLE came in to tell us we were about to hear from Lady Gaga herself. She strutted in at a regal pace, wearing what can only be described as couture business, never removing her sunglasses. She spoke with a Buckingham realness and sat down in a chair, and everyone waiting for her to speak. "I know you all are capable of many things, and you haven't been waiting your whole lives just to be on TV for an eighteen count, but that's what I need from everybody today. This is my first time on television and everyone has to be ready, perfect in position on fourteen, or it just won't work. Everybody got it?"

This was the first time I saw Gaga like this. This was a girl who was dancing for dollars (alone) just a few months earlier.

She danced in two shows and now she's a choreographer. She filmed one music video and taught herself how to be the star and producer.

I couldn't help thinking she was born for it.

We went into the studio for another run-through. It took no time and we were out and ready. On the day of the show I saw Justin from Semi Precious Weapons walking up the stairs of TRL studios in heels and makeup. They had been nominated for the same category and had come to do the taped television version of the red carpet. They actually won the award for a "Brink of Fame" song. But Gaga would perform. No one could create such a perfect vision as that girl.

* * *

"You're back!" Justin said to me with his usual candy-necklace smirk.

"I'm back for good, actually."

"Then let's get into trouble this summer."

THE NEXT DAY WE WENT back to do it for real. This time the studio provided us with props inspired by the Lady Gaga video—plastic tiaras, toy necklaces, a cheap Indian headdress someone found. They kept us in a conference room on the twentieth floor, where everyone discussed dance technique.

I tried to listen as much as I could. Hearing someone else discuss the nuance of a profession always interested me. Everyone has their little tricks. One thing that universally bothers all small groups of people is when a movie comes out that's supposed to tell the story of their profession. I wished Katie were here because this time many of the dancers made fun of the genre-atrocity *Step Up 2: The Streets*, which Katie had danced in. Like many "montage-in-the-life-of—" movies, it glossed over too many details. It left out the important moments. Things always seem too easy and Hollywood also adds a bit of story or a touch of CGI to take something real and cram it into two hours. Nothing is pure joy, but if you want to tell it right you have to get right to the heart of it.

Just then Leah walked into the room while we waited to get called. I hadn't spoken with her since she called to tell me I'd been replaced as DJ in the video. She wanted to make sure everyone got paid in cash before the show. We lined up and she checked off our names.

"Didn't think I'd see you here," she said.

"Glad I could make it in. Very proud of our girl. This is going to be great."

"Yes."

* * *

Leah paid me for the day of rehearsal and the show. She also honored my cab receipts from Miami (she had ignored an earlier email from me about them), and she asked me if I had change. I gave her a ten and she gave me a hundred. Keep the change. And with that I never worked for her ever again.

BEFORE THE SHOW, GAGA LEFT her dressing room in TRL and took the elevator up to see us. She needed to prepare for the show, and this was how she prepared. Like a hostess who didn't want to spend all day getting ready for a party if no one was going to show up. She entered the conference room and the other dancers fawned over her outfit. Instead of coming out in her underwear (like we planned to last year over pint glasses of red wine) she wore an enigma. The black lacquered catsuit had pronounced shoulder pads, a black hijab headdress, and leather gloves. She had on the good old Gaga chain belt.

The dancers all quieted down with her in the room. She got them to act natural by complimenting their outfits. "You look great. You guys all look great. This is going to be great." Her infectious positivity spread through the room. The slouched dancers started to grow taller. They had seen her march into the room, and slowly they stood up. They were here for her. Gaga walked into a room and everyone gravitated toward her, ready to dance. They in fact inadvertently ended up reenacting the video for "Just Dance."

When Gaga came to me she took off her sunglasses for the first time and turned her back on the room. She didn't look like a pop star about to make her television debut. She looked like the curious girl I'd met while killing time at a bar over a year ago.

"How are you?"

"Good," I said, which was true.

"I missed your birthday."

"It's okay. I had fun."

"Still dating the same girl?"

"Yeah, uhm . . . I got a new job."

"Oh? Where?"

"Just in a bar, uptown. A rooftop bar. It's good. Steady."

"Good." She nodded and swallowed.

I caught the look in her eye. It's the same look that exes give when they run into each other years down the line. It looks like the guilt of broken promises. But if you look deep inside it looks more like the comradely look of someone you'd gone through hell with before. I was supposed to be here with you, it says.

But that promise didn't matter as much as the one she'd kept to me.

I looked her square in the eye and reminded her what I had made her promise so long ago, after we'd already cried as much as we ever could about people who didn't get us. *There is going to come a time when you are going to have to leave me behind. And when you think you've gotten to that point, I want you to do it.*

And making it to that moment was just as good as getting there in the first place.

TELEVISION TAPING ROOMS WERE NOTORIOUSLY frigid. Some say it's to keep the lights from overheating, some say it's to keep the audience attentive. This awards show had a small audience at makeshift cocktail tables. The dancers and I spread out on the stage and among the crowd. I went to put my foot up on a table and pass out on another and this knocked over a drink. "Fuckin' freezing!" someone shrieked as he stood up, away from the spill. A PA came by to refill the martini glasses with Vitaminwater. "Can we have a break to warm up? It's freezing in here."

The PA turned his headset microphone aside and brushed them off. "This is the last act. We're done in five."

Lights. Camera. Action.

Michelle Williams—who was another third of Destiny's Child alongside a young Beyoncé—strutted through the icy room. "Just when you thought the show was over, think again boys and girls. That's right. The NewNowNext awards are not over, until the Gaga lady sings," she said, reading the teleprompter. The shivering bodies in the room hung on her words. The dancers froze in place. The audience was just frozen. Even then, with the crew pushing overtime, she stopped. And then broke away. She looked around the crowd and paused again. The AD of this shoot craned his neck around the VTR screen, trying to see what the holdup was. A PA double-checked the teleprompter, but she went off script: "Get ready for an amazing performance of a song that I swear you won't be able to get out of your head. Nominated for the online award Brink of Fame song and performing for the first time on television. It's a pleasure for me to present her. I love this young lady. She's gonna do big things. Give it up, y'all! Get on your mothereffin' feet!" She turned to the teleprompter, lost when Gaga entered the room. "Give it up for Lady Gaga!" The frigid crowd warmed to the moment. The lights followed her to the stage. The applause died down. The music started. We counted to fourteen. And nothing was ever the same again.

Epilogue

My debts at the time were just silly little promises I'd made to myself. Tomorrow you'll have enough money for these things. Tomorrow you won't have to worry about them. Tomorrow you won't have to wait until tomorrow. That summer I put poor *Mercutio* away for good and I picked up shifts instead. I wore a uniform again, slinging drinks for tourists. Every night the entire staff went out. And I went home. After three weeks I'd paid off my electric bill, then the gas. Then every credit card and every debt I ever owed.

It was on this rooftop one muggy night in the shadow of the Empire State Building that I first heard a DJ who wasn't me play a Lady Gaga song. The crowd had squeezed onto the roof to watch the Fourth of July fireworks over the greatest city lights in the world. I ran from my station, through the narrow service area where dozens of bartenders coursed between their customers and the registers behind them. Everyone had seen the video in the office one day, laughing at Brendan the service bartender in his tight pants that he now wore as workpants. This time everyone on the clock stopped and grabbed for me, happy for their coworker. I ran downstairs through the kitchen and the chef looked up, smiling over the sound coming through the door. I came to the DJ booth and hugged the very confused man I found in there. It was on, it was real. And no one could ever take that away.

Afterwards I came down to St. J's to celebrate. I saw Guy when he walked out. He strutted out the door in full summer regalia, a little bit too drunk in a pair of girls' jeans, cowboy boots, feathered hair, and a leather vest.

When he saw me in front of him he threw a shoulder into me like a high school bully and ran to the nearest cab. It was then that I began to pity him.

I came back to work the next day and the next day after that. And I didn't stop even when I'd finally made good on all my debts. Gaga's first record was what you called a "slow burn," which I loved because I knew that was how you build up heat. She caught on over time, like the Killers had. First the single came out, then the video; the record followed almost six months later. Then the second single started to pick up. It didn't even hit its peak in the first year, but it didn't take long for her to have the number-one record in the country. She broke all-time records with her debut and followed it up again and again.

AN ASTOUNDING CAST OF PERSONALITIES turned up to Don Hill's funeral service at Saint Patrick's Basilica on Mulberry Street. No one saw it coming—not his staff, not his new business partners, not even the cab driver who brought him to the hospital where he died of heart failure.

Everyone was civil to each other as if we had shared the same recently deceased grandfather (and as if we each thought we were the favorite). Michael T. was in the church with generations and generations of scenesters. I saw him and Georgie make up. Rows upon rows. Grown up club kids. Go-go dancers, waitresses, bassists, DJs, drag queens, bartenders, sound techs, performers, artists. We don't all get along and we don't really need to. But if Don was so good to us, you'd think we could afford to be good to each other.

We went back to Don Hill's after the funeral. We didn't know it at the time but the club wouldn't stay open another month and I'm glad Don didn't have to see it close.

Gaga and I played our worst gig ever at Don Hill's. We made no money, we drank too much, and Gaga couldn't remember where she put what clothes when she went from the go-go stage back to dance in the booth with me. It was in that booth where we shared a mistake together and never told anyone. Where we rode out a terrible night for both of us. Where we had to believe in ourselves because we didn't have anything else. And that's the night that became "Just Dance."

I still think of Don Hill's every time I hear that song. I hear "Boys Boys Boys" in my head whenever I walk into Motor City. "Vanity" whenever I walk into Pianos. "Lovegame" sounds like Le Royale. "Money Honey" when I'm in LA. I think of bare apartments and red wine in pint glasses when I hear "Papparazzi." Sneaking around while Guy was at work sounds like "Again Again." And I hear Gaga bluffing with him when I hear "Poker Face." Great songs have always reminded me of great times and great people in my life and I'll always have this.

The kicker of living in New York is that everything you love about the city changes, and you have to learn to love even that. A lot of the places we used to go to have gone. Even my beloved Chelsea Hotel isn't the same any more. But the thing about the city is that it's constant and you don't watch the places disappear, you watch as they become something else. It is the same with people in your life.

Georgie told me about his new three-story venue downtown and I wanted to show my support when they had their friends-and-family-only opening. It sounded wild. Room for live music, a restaurant, even a roof deck. It was the most ambitious space downtown and I couldn't wait to see what it would look like. I'd already heard that they were pulling talent from St. Jerome's, so I knew I would feel at home.

"I can't believe you're here," Georgie said when he saw me walk in.

"It's been a while." I figured he'd meant that I hadn't been around. Which was true. I'd left our tiny scene for a new life on the road, DJ'ing in big clubs every night. No hassles with management. Just pure, raw music. And wherever I went I found myself inadvertently counting to eight like the dancers taught me. My foot tapped it out whether I wanted it to or not. I really loved music and soon I found myself working with young bands.

"No, I mean. You know who's managing, right?"

That's when I looked up and saw Guy. He and Georgie had opened this place together, which would have been good to know three minutes earlier when I'd opened a tab at the very crowded bar. Before I lost my nerve I went right up to him. Right in front of everyone. He wasn't ready for this. Four years had past.

I said, "I wanted to tell you that you were in my dream the other night."

"Of course I was." He smirked and looked away.

But I didn't flinch. "I don't remember anything about it. But I do remember that you and me were cool with each other and it wasn't a big deal. And it wasn't that hard. And I was happy about that."

"Really?"

"Well," I said with a smile, "a guy can dream."

A month into the opening, the community board found out he was operating the top two floors without a liquor license and shut them down. He left the bar business entirely.

* * *

I DON'T SEE MUCH OF that crowd anymore. Conrad married the girl whose shift I was covering the night I got jumped. DJ AM never worked with Gaga and he died of a drug overdose. Space Cowboy did a promo tour with Gaga and then with LMFAO, who broke up shortly after. Leah left the management company. I put Dino in rehab. Laurieann choreographed the next few Gaga videos and then they parted ways. Sheryl and Katie moved to LA. Nikki did a lingerie line for Urban Outfitters. Gaga executive-produced the next Semi Precious Weapons record with Interscope. The boys later moved to Epic Records. Nothing lasts forever, and that's what I remember most about the scene. Every night was different and it had to be and always would. Once upon a time I loved nothing more than staying out all night, and now I loved coming home to Leigh.

Remembering these things now feels like hanging out with old friends again. It's like we had a fun weekend out and all met up on Sunday for breakfast to piece together the chaos. Memories of those days come back to me now and they are always happy ones. I have to be reminded that it was stressful and hard. One day it all came back to me when I rode through Central Park and tunneled from east to west through a city of possibilities, looking for which one was mine.

You have moments like this, moments where everything afterward will change forever. But wherever you go for the rest of your life, you will go there with this moment tucked into your back pocket, reminding you that things happen. And being there while they happen matters more than whatever happens.

You have moments like this. And you have them to keep for as long as you live.

MY NAME IS BRENDAN AND this is what I did with the prime of my life.

Acknowledgments

When I talk about what makes a record great, I am invariably referring to its "third thing," which is often a single chord. When I was younger, I did not do well in school or make friends because I didn't know what my third thing was. And then one year I had a teacher. Only one. He's retired now, running the night shift at a liquor store back home. All the extra hours after school, all the grammar lessons, and all the patient hours he put in will never be enough to put into words how much that meant to the shy little kid in the back of the class. Mr. Provost, your third thing is not listening when the other teachers say a student is hopeless.

Before he came along, the closest thing I had to a role model was the late Raymond "Raybeez" Barbieri. From Raybeez my interest in music became a passion for the scene, which was a gift we were to care for before passing it on to another generation. This book is my humble attempt to fulfill the promise I made to him when I was fourteen, just because he died. It is because of Raybeez that I can stand back and see any crowd with the same starry eyes as the man who first spotted the northern lights. You'd say, "It may be different but in our hearts it's all the same." I'd give everything in this story just to hear your accent say the word "hearts" one more time.

Everything else I know about writing as a vocation I learned from columnists Susan Campbell and Jim Shea, as the animatronic presses roared beneath our desks at the *Hartford Courant*. From them I learned that when you're a reporter people get upset with you for getting things wrong, but when you're a journalist they get upset with you for getting things right. Later I had patient guidance from the American poet Janet McAdams and the Australian poet John Kinsella, who both employed me in college when I was broke and still woefully undereducated. Also to the patience and generosity of Harold Bloom. Thanks also to the writers David Lynn, Lewis Hyde, and Alan Shapiro. The rest was supplied by the late Barry Unsworth, a first-rate novelist whose soul is with me, on loan from the rolling vineyards of the Italian countryside, where it can still be heard quoting Homer in hexameter and opening another bottle of wine. Every visual image in this book is just a mirage of that great master's technique.

When I set out to find my story, I had the fortune of learning from DJ World in Chicago, who showed me how nightlife becomes culture. Shouts to A-Trak, ?uestlove, Mixmaster Mike, Omri S. Quire, Alex English, and Grandmaster Flash. Learning with you was like taking woodshop from Jesus. Also to the late Don Hill, who did not make it out of this story alive. Through Don I learned that we can either turn all of New York City into a playground for wealthy people or we can take people's thirst for life and use it to feed the hungry furnace that burns inside of every musician.

God's gift to writers is Meg Thompson at Einstein Thompson Agency. Those who toil in the void without her in their lives may consider themselves cursed. Meg's third thing is her grace, which springs from within and which I have tried for two years to exhaust.

Meg was with me for every move, only she had to do it backwards and in heels. I can bring flowers to your office and thank you at readings, but the most honest thing I can say here is that I am so proud of you, Meg Thompson. Every day in New York City I feel like I am an extra in the movie of your life. Proud of that, too.

At its center this is a book about a girl who learned to believe in herself at a time when her industry did not. The project itself went through an equally frustrating gestation, and I'd take twice as many setbacks if it meant that I'd end up with Mark Chait as my editor. Mark Chait's third thing is his integrity, and I look forward to watching him pass that along to his young son. It was Mark, not me, who figured out this project's third thing, and when he discovered it every paragraph and comma that did not perfectly embody it seemed to melt away. At the beginning of this story I am a restaurant employee two blocks down from the HarperCollins office. I used to dream that someday I'd write a book and get to meet with a publisher, and never, for all my wild dreaming, could I ever have imagined meeting with such a brilliant crew. That's due to Cal Morgan, publisher and patron saint of hopeless writers. Thanks also to Carrie Kania, Jonathan Stein, Denise Oswald, and the great Kevin Callahan.

And Gaga. Thanks for the adventure of a lifetime. What makes you great is not the quality of your voice or talent, but your soul. It has a density twice that of a diamond, and the way you share it with the world is inspiring. I want you to promise that you will always take care of it for me. It's your third thing.